Soulmates

*Following Inner Guidance
to the Relationship of Your Dreams*

Carolyn Godschild Miller, Ph.D.

HJ KRAMER

NEW WORLD LIBRARY

Copyright © 2000 by Carolyn Miller

AN H J KRAMER BOOK
published in a joint venture with
NEW WORLD LIBRARY

Editorial office:
H J Kramer
P. O. Box 1082
Tiburon, CA 94920

Administrative office:
New World Library
14 Pamaron Way
Novato, CA 94949

Editor: Nancy Grimley Carleton
Editorial Assistant: Claudette Charbonneau
Cover Design: Jim Marin/Marin Graphic Services
Composition: Classic Typography
Permissions: Please see p. viii.

All rights reserved. No part of this book may be reproduced
or utilized in any form or by any means, electronic or
mechanical, including photocopying, recording, or by
any information storage and retrieval system, without
permission in writing from the publisher.

Library of Congress Cataloging-in-Publication Data

Miller, Carolyn Godschild, 1946–
    Soulmates : following inner guidance to the relationship of your
dreams / Carolyn Miller.
        p. cm.
    ISBN 0-915811-86-3
    1. Man-woman relationships. 2. Mate selection. 3. Intimacy
(Psychology) 4. Soulmates. I. Title.

IIQ801.M567 2000
646.7'7—dc21
                                                        99-047400

First printing, April 2000
Manufactured in Canada
Distributed to the trade by Publishers Group West

10 9 8 7 6 5 4 3 2 1

Contents

CONTENTS

Preface

If you long to create an unconditionally loving soulmate relationship, wouldn't it make good sense to follow in the footsteps of those who have succeeded in doing this themselves? People who've actually achieved "a love that was meant to be" understand very well that this is not a matter of luck or destiny, but rather the logical outcome of certain critical choices. There are realizations would-be soulmates come to, and specific steps they take, so that a truly satisfying intimate relationship can manifest in their lives.

This book is my gift to all who are suffering from the lack of love as I once was. I offer it in gratitude for my own soulmate marriage, and in the happy knowledge that a fulfilling relationship is within the reach of anyone who desires it enough to take the necessary steps. Together we will explore the extraordinary romantic experiences of ordinary people who achieved "a match made in heaven," and find out exactly how they did it. As you'll see, many were coached through the process by a wise inner voice that some thought of as an inner guide and others regarded as intuition. Whatever you choose to call it, the fact remains that a great many soulmates are convinced they would never have gotten a relationship to work without it!

It's my belief that the human longing for a deeply satisfying intimate relationship is divinely inspired, and that the universe itself stands ready to support us in fulfilling it. I'm convinced that Love answers the prayer of our heart for a soulmate by sending each of us a fully awakened teacher to help us connect with an ideal life partner, and create a relationship that will delight us, body and soul. However, this invisible mentor seldom offers unsolicited advice, so if we want guidance, we have to ask for it. As long as we prefer to implement our own plan for our romantic happiness, the teacher heaven sent to show us the way can only wait and watch in respectful silence. We won't even know she or he is there!

Will following the examples of successful soulmates help you find an ideal partner and create the kind of relationship you've always wanted? The only way to find out is to try it, and see what happens. All I can tell you is that it worked for my husband and me, and for a great many other happily mated individuals, and there's every reason to believe it will work for you. Why waste any more time waiting and hoping for true love when you could be striding down the path that leads to it?

Acknowledgments

I'd like to express my deepest gratitude to all of the couples and individuals who contributed their inspiring personal stories to this book. Their wit and insight enliven every chapter, and they have greatly enhanced my understanding of the soulmate phenomenon. Certain names and identifying circumstances have been changed in order to protect the privacy of those involved, but except in these nonessentials, I've tried to give an accurate account of the experiences they shared with me.

I'd also like to thank my publishers, Hal and Linda Kramer; my editor, Nancy Carleton; and all of the people who helped in the preparation of the manuscript by critiquing drafts, sharing personal stories, or helping me connect with others whose stories I've used. Regretfully omitting the names of those who prefer to remain anonymous, I deeply thank: Madeline Covert Appelbaum, Richard Blons, Anne Bunney, Connell and Gloria, Carmela Corallo, Robin Davis, Marcia Emery, Geri-Ann Galanti, Mary Gallagher, Ellen Heuer, Mary K. Jackson, Ilene Krems, Peter MacDonald, Jessica Parfrey, Jan Phillips, Gary Pinder, Karen Proft, Craig Ng, Hayden Schwartz, Nancy Siegel, Paul and Susan Tuttle, and Michael Zannella.

And special thanks to my soulmate, Arnie Weiss. I can safely say that without him, this book would never have been written!

Permissions

Grateful acknowledgment is made for permission to reprint:

Portions from *A Course in Miracles,* copyright © 1975, 1999, reprinted by permission of the Foundation for *A Course in Miracles,* 1275 Tennanah Lake Road, Roscoe, NY 12776-5905. The ideas represented herein are the personal interpretation and understanding of the author and are not necessarily endorsed by the copyright holder of *A Course in Miracles.*®

Excerpts from *Conversations with God,* Book 1, by Neale Donald Walsch, copyright © 1997 by Neale Donald Walsch, used by permission of Putnam Berkley, a division of Penguin Putnam Inc.

Excerpts from *Conversations with God,* Books 2 and 3, published by arrangement with Hampton Roads Publishing Company, Inc., Charlottesville, VA 22902.

Quotes from Raj, courtesy of the Northwest Foundation for *A Course in Miracles,* Kingston, WA 98346-1490.

Excerpts from *Only Love Is Real* by Brian Weiss, copyright © 1996 by Brian L. Weiss, M.D., by permission of Warner Books Inc.

Excerpts from *Guideposts* magazine reprinted and adapted with permission from *Guideposts* magazine, copyright © 1990 by Guideposts, Carmel, New York 10512.

Excerpt from *Grace and Grit* by Ken Wilber, copyright © 1991, reprinted by arrangement with Shambhala Publications.

1

Going about Things All Wrong

The whole conviction of my life
now rests upon the belief that loneliness,
far from being a rare and curious phenomenon,
peculiar to myself and a few other solitary men,
is the central and inevitable fact of human existence

—Thomas Wolfe

Like a lot of people who grew up in dysfunctional families, I had always found intimate relationships complicated and frustrating. By my early forties I had worked my way through a long succession of painful love affairs without ever finding the soulmate for whom I longed. Each relationship began with such high hopes, only to end in disillusionment and heartbreak. The men I loved, didn't love me—or at least, not enough. The men who loved me, I didn't love—or again, not enough.

Nor was there any indication that my luck was about to change. My relationship with my then-sweetheart Brent was turning out much the same. I'd been seeing this fascinating man for the better part of a year. We got along wonderfully well together, and he said he loved me. But despite the magical moments we shared, Brent's time was largely taken up with his business, and we weren't getting together as often as I would have liked. As the months wore on and the situation did not improve, I had to face the fact that I was not the chief priority in Brent's life.

My reaction was to obsess about the relationship constantly, trying to figure out how to make Brent see how perfect we would be for each other. It seemed absurd that this highly accomplished, sensitive, and spiritual man couldn't recognize the mistake he was making in placing so much more importance on his career than on our relationship. Why didn't he understand that life is about sharing love, not making money?

The possibility that I might not be everything Brent was looking for in a woman was one I was frankly unprepared to consider. No, this was definitely about Brent's misplaced values, not about me! Everything would be perfect as soon as I got him straightened out. Nonetheless, I was not about to approach the problem of changing my lover's mind head-on. At some level I was aware that if I asked Brent about his reservations, he just might tell me.

I figured that my best strategy was to make Brent feel he needed me, while at the same time convincing him that he would be bad and wrong if he hesitated to commit. On the one hand he would see what a great time we had when we were together, and what an ideal, utterly undemanding wife I would make. On the other, I would find subtle ways to show him how hurt I was by his neglect. There would be plenty of time to ask Brent what *he* thought once I was sure that he would say what I wanted to hear. In the meantime, I'd just continue to give the impression that I couldn't care less whether the relationship ever went anywhere.

Reaching for Guidance

My obsession with getting Brent to commit began to occupy just about all of the time and attention I could spare from my career as a psychologist and university faculty member. At the time, I was studying meditation with a spiritual teacher and counselor named Carmela Corallo, and was also deeply involved in study-

ing the spiritual text *A Course in Miracles.** Both encouraged me
to believe that through meditation, I could learn to access the
advice of an inner guide who would help me realize my highest
possibilities. Prepared to accept help from any quarter, I began to
set aside time each morning to reach within for guidance about
my relationship.

I would still my thoughts, invite my inner teacher to speak
to me, and then fall silent to listen for a response. And sure
enough, it wasn't long before answers started coming. I was soon
holding daily dialogues with an inner voice which purported to
be that of a fully enlightened male guide. This inner presence
welcomed my questions, and his responses were consistently insightful. The only problem was that his perspective on my relationship wasn't very much to my liking.

I guess I had been assuming that if I had a guide, he or she
would be solidly on my side. Where my love life was concerned,
I figured my companion spirit would commiserate with me over
my romantic misfortunes, alert me to the faults and hidden mo-
tivations of the men I dated, and generally show me how to get
my relationships to turn out the way I wanted.

Unfortunately, the guide I actually got seemed to have a very
different conception of his role. He was anything but sympathetic
when I poured out my pain and anger over the ways the men in
my life had let me down, it wasn't possible to engage him on the
subject of Brent's faults, and when it came to finding strategies
to make the guy commit, my guide was no help at all. It quickly
became apparent that my companion spirit wasn't the least bit
interested in the ways the men in my life had mistreated me. All
he ever wanted to talk about was how badly I mistreated *them!*

Scarcely a meditative session went by without some comment from my guide about the way I was trying to impose my
will on Brent. I deeply resented his implication that I was some
sort of designing woman. Besides, what was I *supposed* to do?

---

* Published in Mill Valley, CA: Foundation for Inner Peace.

Give Brent complete freedom to make up his own mind about our relationship without reference to my needs and desires? What if I gave him his choice and he left?

Nevertheless, my guide was relentless in pointing out the negative effects of my high-pressure tactics. I had been aware that my boyfriend's mother and ex-wife had often controlled him through guilt, and my inner voice now showed me that, as a result, there was a part of Brent that deeply believed he was a destructive person who always hurt the women he loved. According to my guide, Brent was convinced that love relationships necessarily involved suffering and sacrifice. He could either give up the things he wanted to please a woman, or else do what was best for himself at the cost of hurting her. There was no way for both to win.

My guide claimed that a large part of Brent's reluctance to commit to our relationship was due to his fear of disappointing me, and having to feel even guiltier than he already did. And here I was, playing upon his bad feelings about himself, and calling it *love*. What had Brent ever done to me, my guide gently inquired, that he deserved to be treated with such a gross lack of consideration and respect?

I once heard meditation described as "one long series of humiliations," and during this period, that characterization struck me as apt. My guide devoted a number of our morning discussions to pointing out the ways I had used my feminine wiles to ensnare men and bend them to my will. I remember one session when I was feeling especially sorry for myself. "Why do I always have to get mixed up with such incredibly stubborn, inflexible men?" I moaned.

I thought it should have been obvious that the question was rhetorical, but my guide wasn't about to miss this opportunity. "Because you would have pulverized anyone less tough," he had the nerve to reply.

"Well, thanks a lot!" I snarled. "You seem to think I'm a real bitch!"

4

"Not a bitch," came the response. "But don't kid yourself. You have all of the power of any child of God, and when you focus it to dominate the mind of someone else, you are a very formidable opponent. If you hadn't recognized that fact at some level, and had the good sportsmanship to pick men who were strong enough to stand up to you, you'd have done even more damage.

"Actually," he continued, "you deserve a certain amount of credit for not taking unfair advantage of guys who wouldn't have stood a chance against you. As it is, I've had to search the four corners of the globe to find you partners who are accomplished psychic warriors themselves. You throw the whole power of your mind against theirs, and then wonder why things aren't working out amicably."

"But I don't *mean* to hurt anyone," I protested.

"Of course you don't," he responded. "You are just trying to get the men in your life to do what you think will be best for both of you. But don't you see how arrogant it is for you to insist on being the one who *knows* what is best? God gave your partners free will too. They get to have their own point of view, and to decide for themselves what is best for them."

"But if everyone is just going to go their own way, doing their own thing, how do people ever get together?" I demanded.

"They get together if, and when, they both want the same things. People properly commit to each other when they both believe that doing so serves their own individual purposes. And they properly stay together just as long as that continues to be true.

"It doesn't look as though Brent sees a future with you as the thing that will make him happy. You may think he's making a bad decision—and you may even be right. But the point is that it's *his* decision to make. It's perfectly all right to try to persuade him of your point of view, but it isn't fair to try to put him under some sort of sexual spell, or coerce him with guilt. He shouldn't be tricked, or made to feel like a bad person for not wanting the same things you do."

Little by little I began to face the fact that I was trying to make Brent do something he did not think was in his own best interests, just because *I* had decided that it *would* be best for both of us. Put like that, it really didn't sound like a very nice thing to do. I certainly wouldn't have wanted anyone to do that to me.

Gradually I came to see that behind my mask of innocence and fragility, I had been shockingly manipulative. This was not love, my guide pointed out, but naked violence. I was using my sexuality like a rope, and my talent for inspiring guilt like a gun, in an effort to dominate and control a man whose only offense had been to care for me. The fact that my intentions had been good counted for very little in light of my ruthless behavior.

Still, it didn't seem all that fair that I was being asked to accept responsibility for such unattractive motives when I had been completely unaware that this was what I had been doing. My guide was quick to point out, however, that it had been my choice to keep these machinations out of consciousness. That way I could rationalize that I was an innocent victim of the men in my life, while feeling free to do them psychic violence whenever it suited my purposes. I could control *them* while they were busy feeling guilty about allegedly controlling *me!*

Worse yet, my guide began to insist that it wasn't enough to simply acknowledge my destructive behavior to him in my meditations. He said I ought to tell Brent exactly what I'd been doing to him, and then release him to come or go as he thought best. We spent weeks arguing about this, but my guide is a much better debater than I am. He made a very compelling argument for releasing Brent and moving on to look for someone who wanted the same things I did out of life. Listening to him, I would find it obvious that there was really nothing else to do.

But then I'd come out of meditation and slip off into romantic fantasies about how wonderful everything was going to be when Brent came to see things my way! These idyllic reflections alternated with images of the tragically lonely life I would have if the relationship didn't work out. If I lost Brent, maybe I would never find anyone to love and marry. I would be alone forever. I couldn't bear to think about it. But then, why should I think about it, when I was so close to inducing Brent to come around? So what if it did involve a little friendly persuasion? He would thank me in the end!

But in the end, I was the one who came around. I reluctantly surrendered to my guide's point of view. "All right," I said grimly. "What do you want me to do?"

My inner voice indicated that I should call Brent up, ask him to come over, and then acknowledge to him all the ways I had been trying to manipulate him through sex and guilt. I should reveal every dark recess of my thoughts about him, and then assure him that in reality, he had been a great blessing in my life and that I had only gained through knowing him. Then I was supposed to release him to find a new partner with my gratitude and blessings.

Well, I did it, although the conversation was one of the most excruciating experiences I've ever had. It was unbelievably embarrassing saying out loud all of the sneaky, mean-spirited things I had done to make Brent feel bad about himself.

"Remember that time in the restaurant when you said, 'x' and I said, 'y'? And you wound up feeling so awful? Well, I just did it to make you think you'd said something really insensitive that hurt me a lot."

Brent seemed riveted as he listened to my confession. I couldn't read what he was thinking on his face, possibly because I was having so much trouble looking him in the eye. But what was there for him to think, except that I was an incredibly conniving bitch?

"I guess that's all I wanted to tell you Brent," I finished weakly. "Thanks for giving me a chance to say it. Thanks for everything. You've been a wonderful blessing in my life and I'll never forget you, or regret anything that has happened between us. You're a terrific guy, and I've gained so much through knowing you. I really do apologize for all of the ways I haven't been much of a friend to you. I hope life brings you love, and success, and everything else you're looking for."

I was not at all prepared for Brent's response. "You really are the most amazing woman!" he exclaimed, a huge grin splitting his face. He crossed to my chair, scooped me up in his arms, and carried me into the bedroom, where we laughed and cried and made love. A shadow had been lifted from our relationship. I had never felt so close to him, or so aware of his love for me.

The new clarity in our relationship spurred both of us to face the fact that, despite the love we shared, we were not right for each other. At this particular stage of his life, Brent's aspirations were focused on his career, and the amount of time and attention he was prepared to devote to a relationship was necessarily limited. We parted a few weeks later as the best of friends. I knew that it was right, and so did he.

In releasing Brent I felt that something had shifted within me, but I can't honestly say that the change felt very positive. On the one hand, I was determined never again to allow myself to behave so destructively toward the men in my life. On the other, the realization that I was no longer going to be able to manipulate them with sex and guilt left me feeling more hopeless about relationships than I'd ever been. It was as if I were in a rowboat and my oars had been taken away. Now I was adrift on an unfriendly sea with no way to maneuver at all.

Here I was, entering middle age with no special beauty, wealth, success, or any other big attraction. And of course all of this was happening at a time when the media were so obsessed with that statistic that claimed a single woman my age had a better chance of being killed in a terrorist attack than of finding a husband. If I was no longer going to ensnare men with sex and guilt, what hope was there for me?

I guess at some level I just gave up. For the first time in my life, I faced the likelihood that I would never find the soulmate I'd always wanted. I had reached forty without any outstanding success in that department. Maybe I was destined to be single for the rest of my life.

As I came to terms with the possibility that this was so, I felt my priorities shift. After all, if this was the way things were going to turn out, I had better make the best of it. It didn't mean I couldn't have a decent life in other respects. I still had interesting work and wonderful friends. I realized with surprise that the vast majority of the most precious moments of my life had had nothing to do with romance.

I decided to quit trying to control everything and leave it to my guide to figure out what to do about my love life. When I faced how totally I had been messing up my relationships all these years, it suddenly didn't seem so scary to let someone else take charge. I stopped living for the day I'd meet Mr. Right, and began to focus instead on making the most of whatever was going on at the moment. And as it happened—perhaps as it always happens—facing up to the unpalatable truth led not to defeat, but to unanticipated good. No sooner had I chosen to make the best of the single life than I met my soulmate, Arnie!

It's clear to me in retrospect that I would not have found my husband when I did if I had failed to learn the painful lessons of my relationship with Brent. Until my guide helped me recognize my mistakes and correct them, I wasn't capable of a genuinely loving relationship with *anyone*. I can't help wondering about how much sooner I might have found the love I was seeking if I'd been prepared to heed my guide in my teens, or twenties. As it happened, it took a long succession of failures and disappointments to convince me to pay attention to what my inner teacher was trying to tell me. As long as I remained committed to the dysfunctional strategies I'd been pursuing, a partner who was truly available for the kind of unconditionally loving relationship I wanted would have been wasted on me.

Couldn't a good psychotherapist have given me the same kind of help my guide did? Maybe. But probably not. I'm a psychotherapist myself, and I have great respect for what therapy can do. But we therapists mostly work on the basis of what clients tell us, and I couldn't have told anyone what I was doing to

Brent, because I wasn't aware of it myself. My defenses were so sophisticated that everyone I talked with came away with the same impression I had myself—that I was once again being let down by a man who was unable to overcome his own pathological fear of commitment.

I can hardly wait to tell you how my inner teacher finally helped me find the love relationship I'd always wanted. But before I share more of my personal story, or the experiences of other soulmate couples who believe they wouldn't have found each other without some sort of inner guidance, it might be a good idea to pause and take a closer look at the whole concept of soulmate love. What makes someone your soulmate? Who are our guides? And why does it seem to be so darned hard for some of us to find the kinds of loving relationships we so badly want?

Guidelines for Actualizing a Soulmate Relationship

1. Stop focusing on your partner's faults, and start asking that your own be revealed to you.
2. Learn to listen for the voice of your guide in meditation.
3. Be willing to face the truth, even if it seems terribly embarrassing or disappointing.
4. Gracefully release relationships that are no longer fulfilling.
5. Face your mistakes with compassion and take the necessary steps to correct them.

2

What's Keeping You from Finding Your Soulmate?

Tolerance for pain may be high, but it is not without limit. Eventually everyone begins to recognize, however dimly, that there must be a better way.

—*A Course in Miracles*

It will, of course, be love at first sight. You'll glimpse your one and only for the first time across a crowded room, and as your eyes meet, a thrill of recognition will pass between you like an electric current. There'll be no need to speak. You'll move to-gether as if drawn by some irresistible inner magnetism, and as your hands touch, violin music will seem to swell around you. Everyone else will simply disappear!

That's the way true love is, isn't it? Immediate. Irresistible. Lavishly orchestrated.

Well . . . no. The stories of soulmate relationships we're going to be discussing in this book are going to make it very clear that *this is nothing like the way true love works* for most people who have the good fortune to find it. You might be surprised to learn that while a small minority of meant-to-be lovers are instantly smitten, the initial reactions of many range from disinterest to active dislike. For example, when former President John Adams first met his soulmate, Abigail Smith, at a party, he went home and filled his diary with a catalogue of her shortcomings. As he loftily pointed out, men were simply not attracted to girls of her type!

In truth, many soulmates have to meet *repeatedly* before any romantic attraction develops. And if true love is seldom heralded by a racing pulse or hallucinations of symphonic music, the converse is true as well. People who make us swoon seldom pan out. Far from being an unerring indicator of goodness-of-fit, that swept-off-your-feet feeling is usually reserved for lovers who can be counted upon to break your heart. When it comes to telling whether someone you meet is your soulmate, chemistry misses the mark by a mile.

This is not to deny that your soul may resonate within when you first glimpse your beloved. There probably will be some instantaneous feeling of familiarity and comfort in his or her presence. But these internal stirrings are relatively subtle, and can be drowned out very effectively by racing thoughts about all of the good reasons why this person is not for you. Strangely enough, our soulmates seldom appeal to our personality—our *ego*. That's why they are called *soul*mates, rather than *ego*mates.

I believe that all of us who long for love have ideal partners we are destined to meet in this life. But sadly, many of us will never bother to woo and win the ones who would have suited us best. It's entirely possible that you've already met your soulmate—perhaps more than once. But, if you've been letting the more limited aspect of your mind direct your romantic affairs, you were probably too busy falling madly in love with all the wrong people to spare him or her much attention. Chances are you won't recognize your meant-to-be love next time you meet either, because—chances are—he or she isn't even your type.

How can you change your prospects and wind up with "a match made in heaven"? Well, if you've had your fill of "lookin' for love in all the wrong places," it might be worth considering an entirely new approach to romance—one that utilizes the guidance of a higher power.

An Aside to the Skeptical

But perhaps you don't believe in a higher power. No problem. It isn't my intention to promote a spiritual belief system—just to share a strategy for finding love that has worked well for me and many others. Whether it will work for you is an empirical question that requires an empirical answer. In the final analysis, the only way to find out is through personal experimentation.

The couples and individuals who shared their stories of meant-to-be love with me came from a wide variety of religious and nonreligious backgrounds, including Christians, Jews, Muslims, Buddhists, Hindus, and proponents of New Age thinking, as well as agnostics and atheists. While their personal beliefs influenced the way each of them *interpreted* incidents involving inner guidance, neither religious faith nor its absence affected the actual *occurrence* of such incidents. It's clear that we needn't have a belief system that supports the existence of an inner guide in order to hear from one.

Indeed, if you're like most people, you've probably had some sort of personal experience of your own with inner guidance. Perhaps you received an "intuitive" insight, heard a wise inner voice, or had a wild hunch that paid off. Maybe your guidance came in the form of a "coincidence" so profoundly meaningful that it almost seemed to have been orchestrated by an unseen hand. Have you ever reacted to some personal disaster by muttering, "Something told me this wasn't going to work"? If so, it's likely that you've experienced what I am calling *guidance,* although you may not have recognized it as such.

Who or what is this "something" that "tells" us when we're on the right or the wrong track? Who offers us glimpses of a possible future, and arranges odd coincidences to make a point? Opinions vary. Some folks feel they receive direction from a guardian angel, patron saint, power animal, nature spirit, or ancestor. Others believe they are hearing from their own higher self, or God, or the Holy Spirit. Individuals who prefer a more conventionally scientific view of the universe often attribute this mysterious sense of knowing something they have no way of knowing to a little-understood faculty of the brain such as a "sixth sense," "extrasensory perception," or "intuition," while the psychologically oriented are more likely to say that they are tuning in to their own unconscious or superconscious mind.

My personal belief is that we are guided by enlightened beings who lovingly mentor us in much the same way older siblings watch over younger brothers and sisters. And while I'm convinced that these invisible helpers work with our minds at unconscious levels throughout our lives, I think we can make much more effective use of the help they have to offer by learning to communicate with them consciously.

Guidance is real, but the things I'll be saying about it are only my own best efforts to understand and articulate a phenomenon that is mysterious, subtle, and complex. If you operate within a very different conceptual framework, I hope you'll feel free to reframe the things I say in language that makes better sense to you. What I call *guidance,* many other people prefer to call *intuition.* What I call *meditation,* others think of as concentration, contemplation, or reflection. You needn't agree with my personal perspective to find these true stories of soulmate love fascinating, inspiring, and highly educational.

What Are Soulmates?

Let's begin our investigation of soulmate love by defining some important terms. What makes someone your *soulmate?* What is a *soul?* Why is it sometimes so difficult to recognize the partner who would suit you best?

The totality of your being is what I will be calling your *self,* and this self has certain capacities. It has a capacity to *feel,* which I'll call your *soul;* a capacity for recognizing truth—*knowing*—which I'll call your *spirit;* and a capacity to *think,* which I'll call your *mind.*

Now I've said that your soul is your capacity for feeling, but as such, it is also *your capacity for experiencing love.* Souls also experience *desires,* but these desires are always for opportunities to *give,* and therefore *experience, love.* Thus, a *soulmate* is someone your soul desires to be with because that particular association offers enormous scope for the expression of love.

Spirit is your capacity for *knowing.* When your mind is in conscious contact with spirit, you experience *revelation* of the truth. At such times, everything suddenly makes sense, and the fundamental goodness and perfection of all creation becomes evident, rendering fear impossible. When our mind communes with our soul, we resonate lovingly to particular individuals, but when we focus on our spirit, we love everyone equally.

The self's third capacity is for *thought,* including both conscious and unconscious awareness. When we direct awareness to our soul, we experience its joy in sharing love. When we direct awareness to our spirit, we think in realistic ways, and consciously experience the ultimate all-rightness of everything. When mind, soul, and spirit are all in communion with one another, we are said to be *at one* with our*selves.*

However, while it is *natural* for our mind to commune with our soul and spirit, it is *possible* for it to become divorced from our inner being. When this occurs, our thoughts cease to be grounded in reality, and drift off into a realm of imagined possibilities. This process is inevitably frightening, since it involves setting aside our understanding of what things actually mean, in order to speculate about what they *might* mean if their true relationships to other events were ignored. By fragmenting our perception in this manner, we generate the experience of a disjointed world where nothing we see ultimately means anything. The aspect of our mind charged with the responsibility for conjuring up plausible ways to misinterpret reality is what I will be calling the *ego.*

Please note that I will be using the term *ego* in a manner more consistent with common usage than with Freudian theory. The virtues many psychologists attribute to a strong, flexible ego,

I attribute to the influence of soul and spirit. I regard psycho-pathology as the result of intense ego identification, and mental health and mystical awareness as progressive levels of ego transcendence. In my view, the less ego identified ("egotistical") a person is, the more loving, wise, and realistic he or she will be.

How Our Ego Generates Illusions

It's clear that the human mind is adept at playing with ideas. We can imagine all sorts of things that don't really exist—the infidelity of a faithful lover, for example—and when we invest thoughts about unreal things with belief, they seem real to us. Once we shift our mental focus away from our soul and spirit, it is as if our mind goes off to play in a dream world where each event can be seen from many different points of view, and we feel free to *choose* what to believe about it, unconstrained by knowledge of what it actually is. We take enormous pride in our ability to see things in our own individual way, and we like to think that our personal perspective makes us unique and interesting.

Indeed, by the time we're adults, most of us have come to equate our personal perspective with our individuality. For example, if someone wants to know *who you are,* you'll very likely respond by explaining *where you stand* on various important issues: "I'm the sort of person who . . . never shirks a difficult task . . . hates math . . . can't bear cruelty to animals." What you've done is to essentially reinvent yourself as someone who sees things *this way* rather than *that way.* But of course your unique point of view actually says nothing at all about who you really are. If you'd grown up in a different family or society, you'd see things from a very different perspective, but it would still be *you* doing the seeing.

Again, the self you imagine yourself to be on the basis of the beliefs and attitudes you've adopted, is what I will be calling your *ego* or *personality.* The problem is that once you identify with this false sense of self, everything you do is designed to further *its* interests, rather than your own. When you strongly identify with the role you happen to be playing in this life, you see everything as that character would see it. You find it natural to do the things he or she would do, and to seek out the kinds of experiences such an individual would value. And if these activities don't happen to be meaningful to your true self, you'll feel empty and unfulfilled without knowing why.

Why Is It So Hard to Recognize Our Soulmates?

The fundamental obstacle to finding a soulmate is that when we are identifying with the ego we've invented to represent us, our romantic choices are strongly influenced by whatever preferences, aversions, and prejudices our upbringing has taught us. Each ego develops a list of specifications for the kind of mate it wants, involving the particular physical characteristics it has been conditioned to find attractive, as well as the manners, temperament, social standing, beliefs, and attitudes it associates with an ideal life partner. Psychologists call this our *love map*. When we encounter someone who closely corresponds to our ego's concept of an ideal partner, our false self is thrilled and fancies itself in love. If we are identifying with our ego while this is occurring, we will be just as enchanted as it is, and feel quite sure that this person is our soulmate!

However, our ego is not our *self,* but merely our *self-image*— a made-up character looking for fellow actors it can recruit to play complementary roles. When we allow our false self to run our love life, the partners *it* chooses are not likely to be ones that will make *us* happy. Our ego is only interested in the dramatic possibilities of relationships, not their potential as opportunities for sharing love.

Our soul seeks partners with whom deeply meaningful, mutually fulfilling relationships are possible—individuals who function at our own level of consciousness, share our life's purpose, and challenge us to grow beyond limiting self-concepts. In some cases, our true self may select these soulmates before we are even born, making appointments to meet them at the appropriate periods of our respective lives. But if we are caught up in identification with our ego, we are going to have a hard time recognizing these ideal mates when they come along.

Our Romantic Dilemma

So here is the human romantic dilemma in a nutshell: Individuals who attract our ego are seldom the ones our soul deeply desires to be with, and our soulmates are often people who look all wrong to our ego. As long as we continue identifying with a false sense of self, we are doomed to pursue one partner after another who fascinates our ego, but has little to offer us at the level of our soul.

Unfortunately, most of us are so caught up in ego identification that we have very little awareness of our soul and its desires. We can see that we always seem to fall in love with people who wind up disappointing us, but we have no idea what we'd need to do differently in order to create better outcomes. And many of us commit the disastrous error of assuming that we'll be able to recognize our soulmate by the degree of enthusiasm our ego has for the match!

The Solution

Fortunately, help is available, and it comes in the form of inner guidance. *We* may have lost sight of our life's purpose and our soul's desires, but each of us can learn to contact an *inner guide* who remembers our true will for us. It doesn't really matter whether we think of guidance in spiritual or psychological terms. Whenever we tune in to the most loving thoughts available in consciousness, we achieve a degree of wisdom and insight we wouldn't otherwise have had.

How does this method for finding a soulmate differ from others? Most romantic self-help programs offer the tools to connect with an eligible partner, and establish a viable relationship. They teach things such as communication skills, self-presentation, effective courtship behavior, conflict resolution, and so forth. The problem as I see it is that *tools* can take us just so far. What good are tools if you have no idea what kind of relationship to build, or who to try to enlist as a partner in building it?

You might think of your soul as the *architect* of the soulmate relationship you truly want to create, and of your guide as the *general contractor.* In the absence of the blueprint your soul has lovingly designed to meet your real needs and desires—and of your guide's assistance in mobilizing resources and directing the construction effort—it isn't going to matter how many tools you have, or how skillfully you use them. You'll still be like a child trying to build a palace by hammering boards together at random.

If you hope to accomplish something, it makes sense to follow the advice of others who've succeeded in doing what you want to do. As the stories of meant-to-be love we're going to be considering show, there is a process people go through on the way to achieving the relationship of their dreams. There are inner changes that must take place before romantic fulfillment will be possible, and there is an inner voice that talks us through these changes and helps us recognize our soulmate.

Here's the bottom line: Each of us has two inner advisors: (1) an ego (personality) we ourselves cobbled together out of the information and misinformation we acquired in the course of our upbringing, and (2) a wise and loving guide who is dedicated to helping us achieve our highest potential. Both offer to help us find true love, but only one of them can actually deliver on this promise.

If you've been having a hard time finding a soulmate, it may be that you have simply not yet reached the period of your life when the two of you are to meet. But it is also possible that you *have* met your soulmate—perhaps repeatedly—and rejected him or her. As long as you continue listening to the wrong inner voice—that of your ego—your future romantic choices aren't likely to turn out any better than the ones in your past.

Who Am I to Advise You About Romance?

What makes me such an expert on finding soulmates? Well, as a clinical psychologist, I've been professionally trained to help people with their relationships, and my work as a psychotherapist has certainly provided a wealth of opportunities to study the romantic successes and failures of others. Then, too, I've either read about or interviewed quite a number of couples who appear to be enjoying matches "made in heaven," and I've gained some valuable insights through studying their experiences.

But frankly, my most relevant qualification lies in the fact that I eventually succeeded in following the advice of my inner guide to a wonderful soulmate marriage of my own. And having made every imaginable mistake along the way to that happy outcome, I not only know what works—I've also got a pretty good idea of what *doesn't* work!

There *is* a better way to look for love. If you aren't fully satisfied with the method you've been using, I invite you to consider changing your tactics. As the Monty Python crew used to say, "And now for something completely different!"

GUIDELINES FOR ACTUALIZING A SOULMATE RELATIONSHIP

1. Consider the possibility that there is a source of wisdom within you that knows better than you do which partner will be most likely to make you happy.
2. Don't be discouraged just because your attempts to find true love have not worked in the past. A new approach may produce results beyond your wildest expectations!
3. Stop listening to your ego, and start listening to your soul and your guide.

3

A Match Made in Heaven

*Committed relationship is
the crucible of Awakening.*

—Raj

I'd like to preface this account of my first meeting with my soulmate by recounting an incident that foreshadowed it. Many years before I met Arnie, at a time when I was still living in San Diego, I had been talking with my spiritual teacher, Dr. Carmela Corallo,* about the problems I was having with an earlier boyfriend I'll call Craig. Consulting her own inner guidance, Carmela said that she did not see things working out for me with this man.

"He does love you," she acknowledged, "and it looks as if there is still a chance he might decide to marry you. But even if he does, I'd have to advise you against accepting his proposal.

"You've had many lives where your husband had to be away much of the time, and you've always hated those separations. If you marry Craig, it will be the same thing all over again. He has something he came here to do that he is just getting started on, and it's going to be something he has to do alone in lonely places. I don't see you being happy with a married life that involves long separations.

---

* Dr. Corallo continues to offer spiritual counseling and enlightenment training in the San Diego area. She can be contacted through the Infinite Winds Center in Encinitas, California.

"If you let Craig go and wait, you'll someday meet another man who will be the kind of husband you really need—someone who wants to share *all* his time with you. As much as you and Craig love each other, you'd be miserable married to him."

This was a very depressing pronouncement, especially since it was so obviously insightful. Craig's work was already taking him away for months at a time, and there was no plan for this to change. Our separations were agonizing for me, and I knew that Craig felt guilty about making me unhappy. I hated to give up the hope that we would somehow make a good life together in spite of this, but I had a lot of respect for Carmela's clairvoyance and I knew she was probably right. Craig wasn't going to change, and I would never be happy with a part-time husband.

"If Craig and I don't marry," I asked Carmela, "when will I meet this other man?"

"I'm seeing that you'll probably marry him in your early forties," she replied after consulting her guidance.

"But that's ten years from now!" I protested. "How am I supposed to wait ten years for someone to love?"

"I'm sorry," she replied sympathetically, "but that's what I'm seeing."

"Well, who is this guy I'm supposed to marry once I'm too old to care anymore?" I grumbled.

Carmela turned within and continued. "I'm being shown images of drafting tools and the symbol for atomic energy. One makes me think of an engineer, and the other of a physicist. I'm not sure which he is. He's tall, and he seems to be a bit older than you—oh, not so much as to make a big difference, but definitely older. You'll meet him somewhere up the coast from here . . . not as far up as San Francisco . . . it looks more like L.A. or Santa Barbara. I see you being very happy together! I keep getting images of the two of you snuggling in bed, laughing and talking far into the night."

"And he's some kind of engineer or physicist?" I pursued, without much enthusiasm.

"It isn't exactly clear. He seems to be semiretired actually. I see you going out to work while he works at home. It looks like he's writing something. I see him sitting at a long table, poring over books and papers."

"Great!" I snorted. "So I'm supposed to wait ten years to meet some broken-down nerd who'll keep me up all night telling jokes. I can hardly wait!"

Carmela's prediction was long forgotten by the time I moved from San Diego to Los Angeles and met Arnie eight years later. I wouldn't have associated it with him anyway, since he had retired from his work as a physicist/engineer in the aerospace industry eight years earlier in the wake of a serious illness. Following his recovery, he'd gone back to school for a doctorate in psychology. By the time we met, he was a clinical psychologist, just like me!

Arnie and Me

A few weeks after my breakup with Brent, I received a call from a stranger with an accent that was straight out of the South Bronx. To a former New Yorker like myself, it had a warmly familiar ring.

The caller identified himself as Dr. Arnie Weiss and said he'd been given my number by a former student of mine who thought we should meet since we were both psychologists who were students of *A Course in Miracles*. Arnie explained that he had been thinking about doing some workshops and seminars on the *Course,* and felt that it would be a good idea to find a like-minded female therapist to co-lead them. We arranged a breakfast meeting at a local coffee shop to explore the possibilities.

Arnie turned out to be a tall, attractive man some years my senior. I was struck by his obvious intelligence, playful sense of humor, and encyclopedic knowledge of the *Course,* which is not easy reading. He was open, friendly, and easy to talk to. It seemed to both of us that we might work well together.

I liked Arnie at that first meeting, but frankly it never occurred to me to think of him as anything more than a professional associate. For one thing, I had only recently broken up with Brent and was enjoying the novel sensation of not needing a boyfriend in order to be happy. For the first time since puberty, I wasn't evaluating every guy I met as a potential mate!

Then, too, Arnie wasn't my type. I tended to go for adventurous, flamboyant, outdoorsy guys, and Arnie, with his background in science and business, seemed too conservative and intellectual to be of any romantic interest. The twelve-year difference in our ages completed the picture of a man who might well become a valued friend and colleague, but nothing more than that.

Arnie felt much the same way about me. He had a firm policy of not dating women under forty, and it wasn't clear that I was within his target range. Besides, his concept of feminine beauty ran toward petite brunettes. As a 5' 10" blonde, I didn't ring his chimes any more than he rang mine. Which was just fine, as far as he was concerned, since whatever professional relationship we might develop would only be complicated by sexual attraction.

Nevertheless, Arnie tells me that one unusual thing did capture his attention at that first meeting. As we were getting ready to leave the booth where we had been breakfasting, he remembers that he reached across the table, placed his hand over mine, looked deeply into my eyes, and said, "I'm really glad to have met you!"

All perfectly innocent and appropriate behavior, but what was strange was that Arnie didn't know where it had come from. He wasn't in the habit of touching women he'd just met, or of gazing into their eyes and assuring them of his regard quite so enthusiastically. He says that it was as if his hand had reached out to touch mine, and his mouth had uttered those words, all on their own. I don't recall the incident, and he remembers it only because the warmth of his own behavior took him by surprise.

Encouraged by this first meeting, we arranged to get together again a few days later to consider some specific directions our work together might take. We met for dinner and spent most of the meal getting to know each other better. By the time we returned to my apartment to talk about work, neither of us had a very clear idea of where to begin.

"What do you think we ought to focus on first?" Arnie asked.

"I really don't know," I replied. "Maybe we should think about the content of a workshop we'd like to put on. Or maybe we ought to start with an ongoing class or a psychotherapy group of some sort. What do you think?"

At that point Arnie picked up the copy of *A Course in Miracles* from my coffee table. "Maybe we should ask for guidance," he proposed. To that end, he opened the volume at random, plunked his forefinger down in the middle of a page, and began reading aloud the passage he had struck. It was the following:

> *You must ask what God's Will is in everything,*
> *because it is yours. You do not know what it is,*
> *but the Holy Spirit remembers it for you.*
> *Ask Him, therefore, what God's Will is for you,*
> *and He will tell you yours.*
> *It cannot be too often repeated that you do not know it.*
> —*A Course in Miracles*

"Well, that's right on the money!" I laughed. "It sounds like we're supposed to go into meditation and ask what we should do. Let's take a few minutes to meditate right now." I closed my eyes and visualized myself walking up to my guide with Arnie in tow.

"Hi," I said. "This is my new friend, Arnie. Well, I guess you probably know him already, don't you? Anyway, we were wondering what you think we ought to do together. We've been talking about classes and workshops and stuff, but we just aren't sure where it would be best for us to begin. What do you think we ought to do?"

"You should start by establishing a holy relationship," my guide replied without hesitation.

That shut me up in a hurry!

For the benefit of those unfamiliar with *A Course in Miracles*, let me say that it offers a path to spiritual awakening through the medium of a holy relationship—one characterized by unconditional love. As an enthusiastic student of the Course, I had been eager to find a partner with whom to attempt such a relationship for a long time. But the idea that this stranger sitting on the other end of my sofa might be the one with whom I would do so was both shocking and embarrassing. As I've said, I wasn't even attracted to Arnie, and I had no idea whether I ever could be!

Further, what was he going to think if I went back to the room and said, "Oh, by the way, my guide says we ought to form a holy relationship"? He'd think I was propositioning him—and doing it in a particularly transparent and pathetic manner! And what if he got the wrong idea and started coming on to me then and there?

"Come on, now," I protested. "You can't seriously expect me to go back to that room and tell a total stranger I want to have a holy relationship with him." But my guide just remained silent, gazing at me with a patient, somewhat expectant expression. I hung around a while longer, hoping to be let off the hook, but he had nothing further to add, and I finally realized I'd better just go back and get it over with.

Opening my eyes I saw that Arnie had already emerged from meditation himself. As a delaying tactic I brightly inquired about the results of his reflections, but he replied that he hadn't gotten in touch with any guidance and asked whether I had. I was on the spot. Short of lying, it didn't seem like I was going to be able to worm my way out of this.

"Well, actually I did get something, but I feel really uncomfortable saying it. So I guess I should just say it and get it over with. But I don't want you to take it the wrong way.

"Anyway, I imagined the two of us going up to my guide and asking him what we should do—you know, workshops or whatever—and, well, he said we should form a holy relationship."

I watched the subtle play of expression on Arnie's face rigidify into a carefully composed look of polite inquiry as he took in my meaning. As I had feared, my new friend was looking a little shell-shocked. "Yeah, this was a great idea!" I silently hissed at my unapologetic guide before hurrying on to see if there was anything I could say to reassure Arnie that I wasn't certifiable.

"Not that that necessarily means anything," I mumbled, backpedaling furiously. "I mean, I probably got the message completely wrong. Or it may not mean . . . that is. . . . Well, I don't want you to think that I'm suggesting. . . . Boy, is this ever awkward!"

As I temporized, Arnie gradually emerged from his state of suspended animation. To my relief, he was looking serious and thoughtful rather than offended.

"Well," he said carefully, "I have to admit that I've wanted a holy relationship for a long time. I've tried to persuade several former girlfriends to work on one with me, but they weren't *Course* students, and they kept telling me it just wasn't their 'thing.' I really hadn't been thinking. . . ." He broke off in confusion, and we sat together in silence for a minute, digesting the situation, before he slowly resumed.

"Well, I can't say I expected anything like this. I don't suppose you did either. But I guess what it comes down to is—if someone offers to work on a holy relationship with you, it's really an offer you can't refuse. So, if you're willing to try, I'll try too. I don't exactly know what all of this is going to mean, or what we're supposed to do next, but I can't very well say no to the possibility of a holy relationship when that's what I've been asking for from God for so long."

"I haven't a clue what we're supposed to do either," I replied. I was relieved by his response, but on the other hand it now opened up a whole new realm of problems. "I guess we'll just have to play it by ear . . . you know . . . get to know each other a bit better and see what develops."

Arnie seemed to think that this was a reasonable approach. We were both anxious for the evening to end so that we could have a chance to think over this bizarre development. We parted with an awkward hug after agreeing to get together again soon. As I closed the door behind him, I was wondering what the hell I had gotten myself into. He was wondering the same thing.

As it turned out, what I had gotten myself into was an amazing relationship with a very remarkable man. Over the course of the next year, we came to be the best of friends and the best of lovers. It was strange at first, pursuing a relationship "in cold blood." There was none of that intoxicating swept-off-your-feet feeling I'd always found so addictive in other affairs. Since neither of us was infatuated, the whole thing was carried out in an honest, friendly, mutually respectful manner that nourished my soul as much as it frustrated my ego.

A year later, my inner teacher began pointing out that it would soon be time for Arnie and me to decide whether we wanted to marry. He urged me to broach the subject of commitment with my new partner, but I was very reluctant to do so. Part of it was a sense that it was the man's place to make the first move. However, my guide pointed out that Arnie was quite comfortable with the situation as it was, and saw no need for change. I was the one who wanted to experience a wonderful marriage, so I would have to be the one to ask for it.

Then, too, I wasn't sure I *wanted* to marry Arnie. "How do I know he's really right for me?" I asked.

"You get along well, you are dedicated to a common purpose, and you both want someone to love, and be loved by. Why not decide to be that for each other?"

"I don't understand," I objected. "Are you telling me that Arnie and I are *supposed* to marry?"

"I'm saying you could marry if you both want to. Whether it works out would depend upon what you both do. You could be good partners for each other if you decide to be."

"But what if he doesn't want to marry *me*?" I went on.

"If Arnie decides he doesn't want to marry you after he's had a few months to think about it, then it will be time for you to move on to someone else who is ready for a deeper commitment. After a year together, you know each other about as well as you ever will unless you decide to commit more deeply. The information is sufficient. It's just a matter of deciding whether to take a chance on each other."

"But it sounds so desperate for a woman to tell a man she wants to marry him," I objected.

"Why should you be embarrassed about wanting to marry?" my guide asked. "Isn't that what most people want? Isn't that what most people *do*? What is so shameful about wanting what everyone else wants?

"Besides, you will really just be telling Arnie that you have made up your mind to have the experience of creating a wonderful marriage. You are doing him the honor of inviting him to join you in that adventure. If he doesn't want to move forward into a wonderful marriage with you, that's fine. Someone else will. But to continue this relationship indefinitely if it is not going to deepen into the kind of marriage you want is not appropriate for you. Give him six months or so to think things over, and if he still can't decide to move forward, you'll need to go on alone and look for another partner."

I began to share the content of these meditations with Arnie, who was understandably upset at what seemed to him to be pressure to marry me. At my guide's direction I emphasized that I was not trying to make him do anything he didn't want to do, and that I was not pressing him for a quick decision. Still, if after reflection he did not feel that he wanted to make a future with me, it would be sensible for us to part and find new partners who wanted the same things we wanted out of life.

I explained that I longed to experience a deeply committed, holy relationship and to learn the lessons that went along with that. Arnie had already had a marriage and raised two children, so I could understand if he didn't care to remarry, or if he didn't feel that I was the one with whom he wanted to embark on that adventure. But we would not continue to be happy together if I longed for a commitment he didn't care to make. That would leave me feeling rejected, and I would eventually come to believe that staying with him had cost me the kind of life I wanted. It would be better to part as friends while we still loved and respected each other than to descend into bickering and resentment. I asked Arnie to promise me that he would keep me informed about where I stood. If he became sure that he *didn't* want to marry me, it was important that he tell me, so that we could both get on with finding more appropriate partners.

Arnie asked what would happen if he couldn't decide either way. When I put the question to my inner teacher, he said that if Arnie's inability to decide went on too long, it would amount to a decision not to marry me, and that he would advise me to move on at that point.

All of this was very upsetting and not at all the way I had imagined a soulmate relationship. Having to ask a man to marry me was about as far from fairy-tale romance as you could get! "Why couldn't God have found me a man who would be crazy about me?" I asked my guide.

"Because God honored you with a sensible one instead," he replied blandly. "Sensible men don't make life-changing decisions without a lot of careful thought. And sensible women don't give up on good men just because their egos aren't being flattered."

"But I feel so helpless!" I protested.

"You *are* helpless," he responded. "It takes two people to make a relationship work. If Arnie doesn't want the marriage as much as you do, there's nothing you can do about it except respect his decision and look for a new partner. You've done what you can. Now the ball is in his court, and you have to wait patiently and see what he'll decide."

Arnie and I discussed the subject of marriage repeatedly over the next couple of months, and I later found out that he was discussing it with his children, his mother, and his close friends as well. He had been divorced for eleven years at that point, and although he'd vaguely hoped to remarry, he didn't like to feel pressured into a decision. I just kept explaining that while I understood his desire to have things go on as they were, the arrangement would not continue to meet my needs indefinitely. I said that I wasn't sure if he was right for me either, but that I was willing to take a chance on him if he wanted to take a chance on me.

About three months after our marriage discussions began, I talked the problem over with Carmela. She wisely pointed out that no sensible person is *ever* 100 percent sure they are making the right choice at this stage of a relationship. That, she said, is what engagements are for. Engagement gives a couple the opportunity to move into a more committed relationship gradually. They make the decision to marry, and alert their social circle to the fact that this is the direction they've chosen. But they only carry out their decision if their feelings do not change over the period of the engagement. If the feelings of either do change, he or she can call things off with nothing worse than a little embarrassment.

When I repeated Carmela's suggestion to Arnie, he saw immediately that this was the middle course he'd been wishing for— a way for us to move forward into deeper commitment without plunging in over our heads.

"Okay," he said. "Let's get engaged. We can plan to marry in a year if all goes well." This solution to our dilemma seemed so simple and right that we were both giddy with relief. We merrily set off to buy a ring, and we married a year later as planned.

Now that Arnie and I have been together for eleven years and happily married for nine, our life together is very much the way Carmela described it so long ago. Arnie, who is semiretired, sees a few clients on behalf of our foundation, but he is usually to be found poring over his books and papers—which, I'm sorry to say, are themselves usually to be found all over our dining room table! At the moment, he is putting in twelve to fifteen hour days working on his plan to fundamentally revise the statistical techniques used in the social sciences.

As Carmela foreshadowed, Arnie and I fall asleep most nights giggling together in the dark. What do we find so amusing? That's hard to say, although we do spend a lot of time laughing about what idiots we both were for being so hesitant about marrying each other. He claims that as soon as he completes his current projects he's going to begin serious research into having me cloned. That way he'll always have one of me handy when the other needs to be out of the house. Now that I see how much Arnie and I miss each other after a separation of even a few hours, I can't believe I ever considered marrying a man who wasn't planning to be in the same state half the time!

GUIDELINES FOR ACTUALIZING A SOULMATE RELATIONSHIP

1. Don't be afraid to ask for what you really want.
2. Don't hold out for perfect certainty before being willing to move forward with your relationship.
3. Focus on one relationship at a time, giving your partner every opportunity to respond as you hope she or he will.
4. Look elsewhere if your present partner doesn't want to share the kind of relationship you have in mind.

4

Your Two Inner Voices

Those who follow that part of themselves
which is great are great men;
those who follow that part
which is little are little men.

—Meng-tse, Confucian Philosopher

I've said that we have two internal advisors competing for our attention, yet we all seem to have *many* voices chattering away in our head, all of which we think of as our own thoughts. Only one of them is that of the advisor who knows how to help us find our heart's desire. The others are the various voices of our ego, and they will only lead us astray. Assuming that you want to try following guidance to the love of your life, how are you supposed to figure out *which* inner voice to listen to?

Sorting Out Your Inner Voices

The subject of inner voices can seem extremely mysterious, and even a bit frightening, until you grasp how very ordinary it is. We all spend much of our time carrying on silent discussions with aspects of our own mind that speak on behalf of different points of view. All but one of these inner voices represent what I will be calling our *subpersonalities.* Collectively, these subpersonalities make up what I am calling our *personality,* or *ego.*

Your subpersonalities might be thought of as different points of view you've learned to adopt, mostly through contact with the people who raised you. For example, if your mother was big on cleanliness, you probably have at least one subpersonality that is very judgmental about matters of hygiene. If your older brother bullied you, there's a good chance you've developed an inner voice that knows how to intimidate others—as well as one adept at placating an aggressor.

It is not at all uncommon for one subpersonality to represent a point of view that conflicts with the way other aspects of our egos see things. You may, for example, have a set of attitudes that is patterned after your mother at her most nurturing. When you are upset about some failure, this internal voice quickly pipes up with words of comfort, as she once did: "But you couldn't have known that that was going to happen. You meant well—that's what's important."

Yet even as this maternal subpersonality tries to console you, another fragment of your ego—possibly patterned after a father who was not quite so forgiving—may articulate a contradictory point of view: "You damn well *should have* known what would happen! The road to hell is paved with good intentions."

Rapid shifts from one train of thought (subpersonality) to another lead to the sensation many people describe of carrying an argumentative committee around in their heads. The thing to remember is that your ego is composed of the many understandings and misunderstandings you've absorbed through contact with your environment. As such, *it knows nothing you don't already know,* and can only replay attitudes you've seen others adopt in similar situations.

Now, if you grew up with parents who felt good about themselves, adored each other, and were crazy about their children, you've undoubtedly had a great many opportunities to see love in action. Constant participation in affectionate family exchanges would have strengthened your awareness of your soul, since that is the only aspect of your being that is capable of experiencing love. And since souls are perceptive, spontaneous, and insightful, this would lead to social behavior that is flexible, and appropriate to each situation.

As an adult, you would not be limited by your ego's reper-toire of conditioned responses, you'd respond to others authen-tically, "from your heart." You'd have a realistic outlook, a sense of purpose, and be good at reading the feelings and intentions of the people around you. In short, you'd have most of the skills you'd need to identify an appropriate life partner and create a ful-filling relationship.

Those of us who weren't so fortunate, however, tend to be oblivious to our inner being, and this leaves us to make relation-ship decisions on the basis of our ego's *thoughts* rather than our soul's *feelings*. And since our ego derives its ideas about love through observation of the models in our environment, we usu-ally wind up making the same mistakes we watched our unhappy parents make.

Of course, even our ego can often recognize that it would be foolish to repeat our parents' most glaring errors, but its only solution is to try to do the *opposite* of what our parents did. For example, a woman whose father was a dour, emotionally with-drawn teetotaler might try to change her luck by looking for a husband who is everything her dad was not. As a result, she may wind up married to an alcoholic or a womanizer who quickly becomes just as emotionally unavailable, albeit for different rea-sons. Unfortunately, the extreme opposite of a defective pattern of behavior tends to be defective in its own right.

Adaptive responses are characterized by appropriateness and flexibility, but egos only feel safe when adhering to established formulas grounded in habit, tradition, prejudice, and superstition. And since they tend to switch formulas without warning, the be-havior they inspire is often contradictory and self-defeating. The subpersonality that was enchanted by a new acquaintance last night in the bar may not be the same one that wakes up in bed with him or her the next morning!

Our Ego Knows Nothing About Soulmates

Your soulmates are not selected in consultation with your ego. Your false self knows nothing whatever about how to recognize an ideal mate. This is probably a very good thing, since, as we shall see, your ego is actually dead set against your ever finding true love. If it were capable of identifying your soulmate, it would be even more ruthlessly efficient at messing up your love life than it is at present!

There is simply no way to make good romantic choices unless we are either in touch with our true self, or following the advice of the guide who speaks on its behalf. As long as your false self is running things, you can expect to walk by ideal partners without the least suspicion of all they have to offer. However, if you think you may have made just such a mistake already, don't despair. Our guides do their best to arrange repeated opportunities to connect with soulmates who made no impression on our ego-identified minds the first time around.

Second Chances

When I was single, I used to agonize over the possibility that I had already met my soulmate — and permanently blown my chances with him! What if he once bumped my grocery cart in the supermarket, but instead of striking up a witty conversation about the price of cantaloupe as I was meant to do, I'd unburdened myself on the subject of clumsy oafs who don't watch where they're going? Do people get second chances for meant-to-be love, I wondered? Third?

Happily, the answer is *yes*. The interference of our ego can be counted upon to make the recognition of our soulmates difficult, but I've found many instances where people's souls and guides brought them together with their intended partners over and over again. Of course, identifying your ideal mate is a whole lot easier if, like Yasmeen and Mohammed in the following account, you're paying attention to the inner voice that speaks on behalf of your soul.

Yasmeen and Mohammed

While working on her master's degree in Library Science at Wayne State University in Detroit, Yasmeen, an African-American woman, left her Baptist roots behind and converted to Islam. Although Yasmeen did not adopt the Muslim custom of full purdah, she did begin "covering" — modestly concealing her hair and neck beneath a shawl when out in public.

As she was walking across campus one day, a man with a lilting foreign accent came up behind Yasmeen and asked, "Are you a Muslim?"

"I guess I must have been feeling a little exasperated by all of the ignorant comments people had been making about the way I was dressed," Yasmeen told me, smiling guiltily at the memory. "I wheeled around and snapped, 'Now, why *else* would I be wearing this?' The guy backed off without another word and walked away, but as I watched him go, a little voice in my head said, 'That's the man you're going to marry!'"

"What did you think when you heard that voice?" I asked Yasmeen.

"I didn't really know *what* to think." She shrugged. "But after that first meeting it seemed as though this stranger and I were being thrown together constantly. I started running into him everywhere I went. I found out that his name was Mohammed, and that he was an engineering student from Pakistan who was himself a Muslim. And suddenly it seemed like I couldn't leave the house without bumping into him."

"I was also having some strange experiences," Mohammed added. "I would wake up in the middle of the night seeing Yasmeen's image, and being told that I was to marry this woman. It happened three different times, so I knew practically from the start that she must be the partner Allah had in mind for me. We fell in love in no time at all and were married within two months of that first meeting."

"Had you been hoping to find someone to marry?" I inquired of Yasmeen, curious about the events that had led up to this meeting.

"Oh, I'd been praying for the right man to come along for quite a while—and my mother had been praying right along with me. We'd both told God *exactly* the kind of husband I wanted . . . only somehow it didn't occur to either one of us to add that he should be of my own race and culture. I guess we just assumed that that went without saying. Well, take my word for it—*it doesn't!*

"Mohammed was everything I was looking for in a man," Yasmeen continued with an affectionate glance at her husband, "but I never expected to have to deal with the kind of issues you get with an interracial, intercultural marriage like this one. The thirty years we've been together have been quite an education. A situation like this is where you *really* learn the meaning of culture!"

"It's a funny thing, though," Mohammed added. "All the time I was growing up in Pakistan, I never really felt as though I fit in. Other people used to comment on it. I just didn't think the way the people around me did, and I always seemed a little out of place. I guess that's why, as soon as I got my undergraduate degree, I was so eager to come to America.

"Yasmeen says that she had a similar feeling of not fitting into her culture. So in a way, as hard as it has been, maybe coping with our differences hasn't been as difficult for us as it might have been for another couple. Neither of us was ever strongly committed to doing things in traditional ways."

"That's true," Yasmeen agreed. "And knowing that we were brought together by God really helped smooth our path, too. I guess there are times in any marriage when you look at this other person who seems so strange, and hard to get along with, and wonder if you made the right choice. But in spite of all the additional problems we've had to face because of our differences, at least we've never doubted that we really were meant to be together."

Despite the number of times their guides managed to throw these two together, ego-based preconceptions about the kind of person they ought to marry could easily have prevented Mohammed and Yasmeen from recognizing how right they were for each other. Fortunately, because both were paying attention to their guidance, any misgivings they might have had about the suitability of this match were quickly laid to rest.

If we are to recognize the true worth of another, we must learn to look past our ego's conditioned preferences and aversions to that person's soul. Radiant spirits come in all kinds of packages. Our soul and our guide try to direct us to individuals who share our purpose in life, complement our strengths, and supplement our weaknesses. But there is no guarantee that these ideal mates are going to look the way we expect, or be of our own background. That's only one of the reasons why they are so easy to miss if we are not listening for guidance.

Instant Attraction

This is not to say that there is no such thing as love at first sight, but the issue is more complicated than it initially appears. First of all, egos are very prone to instant infatuation with anyone who is especially powerful, good-looking, and glamorous. People fall in love at first sight with folks like Brad Pitt and Michelle Pfeiffer every day, but that doesn't mean that they are these movie stars' soulmates—or even that they really love them.

Soulmates who fall in love at first sight seem to be more the exception than the rule. And even when the attraction looks instantaneous, it would appear that the "instant" must be the right one for both. What seems to be love at first sight is sometimes preceded by a long series of encounters in which meant-to-be lovers pass each other by without any sign of recognition.

Norman and Carrie

The first time Norman remembers seeing Carrie was at a campus political meeting, and it was definitely love at first sight as far as he was concerned. The third-year law student had come to the gathering with a lesbian friend named Sandra, and the minute he caught sight of the striking brunette who had walked in the door after them, he was a goner!

"See that girl over there?" Norman told Sandra. "I'm going to marry her!"

"Oh no you're not!" his friend quickly countered, following his gaze. *"I am!"*

But it was Norman whose prediction came true. When he went over and introduced himself to Carrie, he certainly met with no resistance. As it turned out, the young woman he found so attractive had been mooning around the student center for weeks hoping to find an excuse to talk to *him!*

But before we get too carried away with the love-at-first-sightness of it all, it's only fair to point out that this was almost certainly *not* the first time Norman and Carrie had seen each other. For one thing, they subsequently discovered a wealth of interconnections between their families, some of which may have brought them together as children. For example, Carrie's grandmother had been Norm's brother's teacher, and Norman's mother had worked at a camp that was founded by Carrie's grandfather.

More significantly, although they met while attending law school in Buffalo, it turned out that both earned their undergraduate degrees at the State University of New York in Albany. Norman had been a junior when Carrie entered as a freshman, but their tenure there had overlapped by two years. Further, Norman had worked during that period as a waiter in Carrie's favorite campus hangout! It's hard to imagine that these two were *never* in the same place at the same time, although neither remembers seeing the other there.

There seem to be many cases where soulmates discover that their paths have crossed repeatedly prior to the magical moment when they supposedly fell in love at first sight. I don't know whether these anonymous encounters are truly missed opportunities, or if the time is simply not yet right for the two to really connect. But I can well believe that when a couple's ability to tune in to guidance is not as well developed as that of Yasmeen and Mohammed, it may take a lot longer for them to notice each other.

While Norman and Carrie *probably* saw each other repeatedly before they fell in love at first sight, Herman and Roma remember having had a number of such encounters. Their companion spirits apparently had to arrange one meeting after another before they finally got together!*

Herman and Roma

Herman saw his soulmate for the first time through the barbed wire fence of a Nazi work camp in Schließen, although the eight-year-old Roma was certainly not of any romantic interest to the sixteen-year-old Jewish inmate. As far as he was concerned, she was just another gentile who lived near his prison—one who would soon enough grow up to despise Jews like him. But he desperately needed help, and there was no one else to ask. On the chance that this little girl hadn't yet fully absorbed the fascist lessons of fear and hatred, Herman called out to her, imploring her to bring him some food. Amazingly, she said she would.

Little Roma returned to the fence the next day with an apple, a piece of bread, and some water—a feast to the famished inmate. She assured him she'd return every day with more, but still he could hardly believe his good fortune when she fulfilled her promise. Day after day, the child faithfully kept their assignation

---

* The following story is based on an article called "A Miraculous Love Story," by Leslie Russell, in *Beshert,* Summer 1996/5756, The Beshert Publishing, LLC, Beverly Hills, CA.

at the barbed wire frontier that separated their worlds. And every day she brought the handful of extra food that made his continued survival possible.

Strangely enough, although Roma fed Herman daily for many months, they never became any better acquainted. Their encounters were necessarily as brief and impersonal as possible. Roma would approach the fence and silently throw the food through to Herman, who would grab it and quickly run away. They didn't even exchange names, since both knew that Roma would have been in trouble if she'd been seen talking to a prisoner. But although Herman was concerned about her safety, only she knew how great a risk she was really taking!

Roma was not the gentile child Herman assumed her to be, but rather a Polish Jew like himself. Thanks to the help of a sympathetic Catholic priest who had supplied fake identification papers, she and her family spent the Second World War hiding in Germany, pretending to be Christians. At eight, even little Roma understood the vital importance of behaving exactly like the Germans around her. Yet she never seriously considered abandoning the starving Jewish boy who depended upon her for his very survival.

Herman and all of his relatives had been rounded up and sent to the camps in 1939. He was one of only four family members to live through the experience. There can be no doubt that Roma's supplemental rations had made a critical contribution to his ultimate survival.

Seven months after Roma had begun her secret deliveries, their relationship ended as abruptly and impersonally as it had begun. Herman called out to her one day that she should not come anymore. He said that he was being transferred to the concentration camp at Therensienstadt in Czechoslovakia. Herman watched Roma's eyes fill with tears at the thought of never seeing him again. He was moved to tears himself, although he ruefully admits that his own grief was more related to the prospect of starving to death without Roma's help than to any idea of missing the little girl herself!

Like many Jewish survivors of the Holocaust, Roma and Herman both emigrated to Israel at the end of the war. Strangely enough, they met there repeatedly, but did not recognize each other. He was a soldier in Israel's 1948 War of Independence, and she was a nurse. They were distantly acquainted as members of a group of Polish young people, but had no special interest in each other and did not discover their earlier connection.

Some nine years later, both had moved to New York City, where mutual friends arranged a blind date for them. Herman and Roma recognized each other from their meetings in Israel, and this time they clicked! Herman had been engaged three times by then, but had always broken things off because of doubts about whether the girl was really right for him. When he met Roma in New York, everything felt "right" from the very start.

Naturally enough, the two expatriates fell into a discussion about their experiences in World War II. Roma disclosed that her family had survived the war by passing as Christians in Germany. She talked about the many dangers and hardships they had endured, and mentioned that during one period of her childhood, she had made secret food deliveries to a starving Jewish boy in the Schließen work camp.

Electrified, Herman began questioning her about the details: What had the boy looked like? What food did she bring him? How long had she continued the food deliveries? What finally happened to the prisoner?

We can only imagine what Herman must have felt as Roma reeled off all the correct answers. Here before him was the little "Christian" girl to whom he owed his life—not a Christian at all but a Jew like himself, who had risked her life and her own family's safety to help him. It must have been a very profound moment indeed, because despite the fact that this was only their first date, Herman proposed marriage on the spot! Now happily married for over forty years, their union blessed with children and grandchildren, Herman is convinced that he and Roma were brought together by angels.

As far as Herman and Roma are concerned, it was angels who arranged their marriage. Still, one wonders how much sooner these two might have found their happiness if they'd been paying more attention to these "angels" nine years earlier back in Israel. Was it just that the time was not yet right, or did these soulmates miss out on years of joy they might otherwise have shared?

Our guides bring people to us from across the street, and across the world, but it sometimes takes a number of tries in order to effect so much as a simple introduction. Take the case of Stan and Marion.

Stan and Marion

Stan's undergraduate days at Arizona State University had been a very alienating experience for him. Raised in a politically active Jewish family in New York City, it was hard for him to relate to the slower-paced lives, and less socially conscious concerns of his fellow students. Despite the similarity of their ages, he felt much older than his classmates, and seemed to have little in common with them.

The displaced New Yorker used to cope with his loneliness by driving out to a desolate mesa he had discovered towering above the desert floor. He would hike to the top and then sit on a ledge for hours at a time, staring off into space and daydreaming about a happier future when he hoped he would find a wonderful girl to love and marry. Stan drove out to his special retreat several times a month. There seemed to be a kind of spiritual energy about the spot, and he deeply enjoyed the solitude it offered.

The sense that this was his own personal hideaway was enhanced by the fact that Stan never saw another living soul on the mesa. The small dirt parking area where he left his old blue Ford near the base of the trail was always empty—except, that is, for a red Volkswagon Beetle. Sometimes the VW would be there when he arrived, and sometimes he would find it baking in the sun as he returned to his own car. He couldn't help being curious about the mysterious driver who obviously shared his enthusiasm for this magical place, but he was just as happy that he never encountered anyone on his way up or down the trail. He didn't want to share his private retreat with anyone.

Ten years later, sitting over coffee in the San Diego kitchen of a friend's home, Stan was introduced to the woman who would become his wife. Marion was recently divorced, and her good looks and lively sense of humor attracted him instantly. It didn't take them long to figure out that they had both been students at the University of Arizona at the same time, and that neither had much enjoyed the experience. Stan told Marion that he had never felt that he fit in very well with the other students, and that loneliness had been a big problem for him throughout his four-year stay.

"I know just what you mean!" Marion exclaimed. "Everybody seemed so caught up in the most trivial stuff. I guess that's where they get the expression *sophomoric*. I just couldn't get excited about sororities, and frat parties, and sports.

"It was so depressing, wandering around that campus surrounded by all of these kids having a great time together, and not feeling part of it all," Marion went on. "Sometimes when I just couldn't stand it another minute, I used to get in my VW and drive to this mesa way out in the desert where I would sit and meditate. I did a lot of daydreaming there too, I guess," she laughed.

"It was my own private world—nobody ever went out there. Well, *almost* nobody. I used to see this beat-up blue Ford a lot in the parking area, but there was never anybody around it, and no one ever disturbed me up on the mesa. Still, I guess it must have been a special place to somebody besides me."

GUIDELINES FOR ACTUALIZING A SOULMATE RELATIONSHIP

1. Your soulmate won't necessarily share your background, or look the way you expect.
2. Your guide may bring you together with your soulmate repeatedly, but it's up to you to decide whether to accept the introduction and pursue the acquaintance.

5

Put Your Ego Aside, and Let Your Soul Decide

The holiest of all the spots on earth is where
an ancient hatred has become a present love.
—*A Course in Miracles*

If you are not aware of ever having heard the voice of your guide, it is probably because you've never invited him or her to speak, and then silenced the chatter of your various subpersonalities long enough to hear a response. Unlike our ego, our guide seldom intrudes upon our thoughts with unsolicited advice. Our inner teacher respects our free will and is very reluctant to force him or herself on our notice.

But chances are you *have* had moments when you've heard your guide's voice. You just didn't realize who was speaking. The problem is that your companion spirit doesn't pontificate in the booming, Charlton-Heston-as-Moses tones that would be clearly distinguishable from other trains of thought. If you're like most people, your head is so full of babbling subpersonalities that you'll be tempted to dismiss the input of your guide as just more of the same.

In my experience, individuals who learn to listen for guidance generally discover that they have already had many conversations with their companion spirits without realizing it. I've taught this process of inner attunement to a number of people, and I have found that the most common reaction to getting in touch with guidance is not "Wow, that was the most incredible thing that ever happened to me!" but "What, that? You mean *that* voice? Well sure I've heard *that* voice before. You mean *that's* the voice of my guide? You're kidding, right?!"

How You Invite Your Guide to Speak

Now didn't I just get through saying that your guide would not address you unless invited to do so? And here I am telling you that even if you've never invited your guide to speak, you've probably heard from him or her at times all the same. Before you throw up your hands over my lack of consistency, let me clarify what I mean by an *invitation*.

One type of invitation is the *formal* variety you issue your invisible mentor when you ask for guidance and then settle down to listen for an answer in meditation. This is a little like mailing a letter inviting a friend to a dinner party. You explicitly state your desire for the visit and eagerly await a response.

But there are also *informal* ways of inviting someone to communicate with you, more akin to striking up a conversation with a stranger while standing in line at the bank. When you address a remark to another person, you are implicitly inviting a response. Similarly, when you turn to your guide with a question or comment, you will receive an answer, whether or not you realize whom you are addressing.

How does your guide *know* whom you are addressing? By the nature of your inquiry. If you sincerely want to know the truth about something, you turn to your guide. If you are only seeking an interpretation of events that will put your own behavior in the best possible light, your ego is the one you instinctively consult.

Let's say, for example, that a lover accuses you of making a snide comment, and you're looking for a way to justify yourself.

Your ego can be counted upon to come up with any number of convincing arguments in favor of your innocence. In the present instance it might point out that (a) your critical remark was well intended and perfectly valid; (b) your sweetheart badly needed this honest feedback; and (c) he or she has no right to complain, having often leveled mean-spirited comments at you. When it comes to putting a spin on events that justifies hostile, destructive behavior, your ego is the acknowledged expert.

However, if you are willing to see what is *really* going on—even if the truth might turn out to be embarrassing or inconvenient—you are implicitly addressing your guide, and that is who will answer. In truth, this inner counselor is the only one who either *knows,* or *cares,* what is really going on.

Take my question concerning the reason I always got involved with such tough, inflexible guys. If all I had wanted was further reason to regard myself as the innocent victim of unreasonable men, I would have implicitly addressed this question to my ego, and the answer I received would probably have had to do with how unfair life is, how cowardly men are when it comes to admitting mistakes, and so on. But there must have been some part of me that sincerely wanted to know the truth, because my guide was the one who responded. It wasn't at all pleasant being confronted with the ways I had been mistreating the important men in my life, but it was information I badly needed if I were ever to break my romantic losing streak.

Whenever you seek the unvarnished truth, you instinctively turn to your inner teacher for answers. It isn't necessary to be religious or to ask for higher guidance in any formal sense. Simple curiosity about what is really going on authorizes your invisible mentor to supply the knowledge you seek without fuss or fanfare.

This, by the way, explains why people who don't believe in spiritual realities have no more difficulty getting in touch with their guidance than those who do. For example, I suspect that successful scientists cultivate very close working relationships with their guides. However, only a very few realize that this is what they are doing. While a number of the world's most distinguished researchers say that it is as if answers are being fed to them from some higher intelligence, most simply assume that superior intellect and creativity account for their ability to solve problems that baffle their colleagues.

The bottom line is that if you want to experiment with guidance, all you need to do is be curious about the truth, and willing to hear an answer you didn't expect. In the following story we'll see how one woman grew so disenchanted with her ego's self-serving rationalizations that she became utterly committed to ridding herself of illusions. Her dedication to the truth eventually opened up a dialogue with her inner teacher, who, in turn, was instrumental in leading her to the soulmate relationship of her dreams.

Helene and Gideon

Helene was born in Austria in 1930, a time when that nation was still reeling from the devastation of the First World War. Despite widespread poverty and unemployment, Helene's parents were fortunate enough to have jobs as teachers. But when she was five, her father was killed by a motorist while riding his bike home from school, and the family's financial situation worsened dramatically. In the face of low wages and skyrocketing inflation, it was all Helene's mother could do to feed her family. Yet a short distance from their home in Salzburg, the German economy was booming under the vigorous leadership of Adolf Hitler.

The people Helene's family knew all regarded Germany's dynamic führer as a savior sent from heaven. Besides, he was an Austrian himself! There had long been talk of uniting the two German-speaking countries, and the impoverished Austrians could not witness the resurrection of their neighbor's economy without wishing that they too might benefit from Hitler's inspired leadership. So widespread and enthusiastic was pro-Hitler sentiment that the Austrian government outlawed the Nazi party, fearing a violent overthrow. The police were brutally repressive toward anyone suspected of Nazi sympathies.

Still, many Austrians joined the Nazi party in secret. Helene's adolescent brother Hermann was one of them. He proudly flouted the Austrian border patrols, sneaking off to work for good German wages at nearby Berchtesgaden. Like many of his countrymen, he eagerly looked forward to the day when Hitler would deliver his people from their national sufferings, just as he had saved the Germans.

But the police soon noticed Hermann's long absences, and his family's newfound ability to buy meat for their table. They suspected the truth, and when Hermann returned home for his older sister's wedding, they seized him and his younger brother and beat them with rubber hoses for hours in an attempt to make them identify fellow Nazis. Little Helene was very proud that, despite this torture, her brothers betrayed no secrets. She longed for the day when she too might have an opportunity to suffer nobly for their beloved Hitler.

When the Nazis marched triumphantly into Austria in 1938, Helene's whole family went to witness the great event. And just as Hitler had promised, there was soon work for everyone. Helene hated having to wait until she was ten to join the Hitler Youth, but once a member, she learned to understand Austria's defeat in World War I, and its current economic problems, in a whole new way. As writer Elizabeth Sherrill explains:*

It was at these youth meetings that Helene heard the Nazi claim that Austria's past miseries had been due to "the wickedness of the Jews." To Helene especially, this seemed plausible. Hadn't it been a Jew who killed her father? Rage blazed inside her as the leader explained that Jews were rich because they were thieves. That was why

---

* Reprinted and adapted with permission from *Guideposts* magazine. Copyright © 1990 by Guideposts, Carmel, New York 10512.

her father had had only a bicycle to ride, while Jews could go speeding about in cars.

Hatred for these people grew as strong as her love for Hitler. Helene did not know if she had ever actually seen a Jew, but she knew from the Hitler Youth posters what they looked like: fat, with greedy eyes, enormous noses, and thick fingers covered with rings. She cried with relief when told that Hitler would not allow these evil men to hurt her anymore.

When the bombing of Salzburg began, Helene developed a new hatred: Americans. Their wanton destruction of her beautiful city seemed especially contemptible since they were losing the war in any case. Any day now, Hitler assured the Austrians, the American aggressors would be fleeing back across the ocean in terror of Nazi might.

No one could believe it when the American army marched into Salzburg! Like other women fed on Hitler's tales of American barbarism, Helene and her mother fled to the mountains to avoid rape and torture. They foraged for food for months before the winter's cold forced them back into the occupied city. Helene was already deeply disoriented by the realization that her savior Hitler had been lying to everyone about the progress of the war. Now she had the additional shock of discovering that the occupying American soldiers were not the subhuman savages Hitler had portrayed.

The postwar years brought one devastating blow to her thought system after another. In her late teens, Helene became a dental technician and went to work in an American military hospital. There she met doctors who were actual Jews. She was amazed to discover that they looked and acted just like everyone else!

Sickening tales came out about the Nazi extermination camps. Despite the fact that many Austrians insisted these camps had been thrown together for propaganda purposes by the invading

Americans, Helene was by now profoundly tired of lies and self-deception. Wracked with shame and disillusionment, she faced the full horror of what she and her fellow Austrians had countenanced.

Helene's family had never been religious, but in 1974 she was strangely stirred by an evangelist who spoke about Jesus. She longed to be able to believe in Jesus too, but faith did not come easily to one who had been so often deceived. She earnestly accosted the speaker after the lecture:

"Is he real, this savior?" she asked. Once before, she'd put her faith in a savior. "I have to know if he is real."

The speaker smiled. "Ask him," he said.

And so she did, that night, alone in her room. "Jesus," she said, "I never again want to believe what is not true. If you are real, please show me."

She recognized him at once. He was with her in the room—the presence she had known so often on the mountaintop. So real that the rest of her life till that moment seemed only make-believe. So real she knew he would not let her go until he had made her whole.

Helene's nascent spiritual faith was very sustaining to her. Perhaps the sense of well-being it fostered is what eventually stimulated this middle-aged woman to begin wishing for a husband. Her longing for love could no longer be denied.

But for an Austrian woman of Helene's generation, finding a husband was not a simple matter. Most of the men her age had been killed in the war, and virtually all of the ones who had survived were married already. It was hard to see how she would ever find the love she sought, but still she hoped and prayed.

In an idle moment Helene even pulled out a piece of paper and scribbled down some specifications for her future mate. Her ideal husband, she wrote, would have to have beautiful hands, love classical music as she did, and be willing to let her drive the car occasionally. This last she added because she loved driving, and Austrian men always insisted upon taking the wheel. But when she looked back at her list it seemed utterly ridiculous. What absurd things to care about—as if she were in a position to pick and choose! Feeling foolish, she crumpled the paper and threw it away.

As the months passed, however, her desire for a husband grew stronger. A year after writing out her childish list, she was praying one day, when into her mind, as clear as a photograph in her hand, came the vision of a man. *"This is the husband,"* she thought she heard God say, *"whom I am giving you."*

Helene's mouth went dry; her heart pounded. In speechless astonishment she gazed at the picture in her mind. The man had intense dark eyes, beetling black eyebrows, a full head of white hair. The picture, in black and white, was of his head and shoulders only. But what she could see of his clothes told her something more: a jacket in a hideous pattern of crisscross stripes, and the ugliest tie Helene had ever seen.

He was an American. She was as sure of it as she was that God himself was showing this man to her. But Americans had been the enemy! The invaders. Was it possible that God was giving her signs to love a man from the country she'd hated with all her heart?

Or was this always God's answer—where we've hated most, to plant the deepest love?

Helene prayed daily for the American to appear, but years went by with no sign of him. However, in 1979 she accompanied a church group on a tour of Israel, and there, on the Golan Heights, was the man she had been shown!

With no idea what to do, Helene went up to him and mumbled in English, "Excuse me, but it seems to me I've seen you

53

somewhere." They introduced themselves, and Helene did what she could to keep him talking, although he didn't seem very interested in doing so. His name was Gideon, and he was indeed an American, now managing a bookstore in Jerusalem. When she asked how he liked living in Israel he replied, "For us Jews, you know, it's a lifelong dream."

Not only an American, but a Jew! Was she to be spared nothing?

When her tour group got to Jerusalem she located the store where Gideon worked. As she stepped inside, she heard the tones of a Chopin sonata coming from a tape player. "My weakness," Gideon confessed. "I'll go without lunch to buy music."

Not only that, but his hands were beautiful too!

As they talked, Helene learned that, like her, Gideon had grown up in a world warped by hatred. His rage was particularly strong against the Austrians, who had murdered all but a very few of his family. Here was the husband God had promised her, but he detested people like her! How was she ever going to have a chance to win his love?

Suddenly Gideon turned and began rummaging in a drawer.

"I don't know why I'm doing this," Helene heard him mutter. He straightened up. "I've never in my life given anyone a picture of myself," he said, clearly baffled at his own behavior, "but —" and he thrust a photograph at her, "this was taken three years ago."

Helene held it in her hands, as she'd held it so long in her heart. The photograph of a white-haired man with compelling eyes . . . the striped jacket . . . the terrible tie.

Helene made up excuses to see Gideon frequently while she was in Jerusalem, but although he was friendly and polite, he was never anything more than that. She learned that he was divorced and that he had no interest in marrying again.

Back in Austria, Helene wrote Gideon inviting him to visit her. She said that it was important for a Jew like him to meet Austrians and work to bridge the gulf between their peoples. At first he resisted, but after several months he wrote that God was directing him to make the trip. Helene met his plane. As they left the airport she proffered her car keys, but Gideon only stared at them in discomfort.

"I'm sorry, Helene," he said. "Would you mind? You see, I've never learned to drive."

Gideon made several visits in the years that followed. He gave talks to various Austrian groups in an effort to promote greater understanding between them and the Jews, and Helene would drive him around and translate for him. But he continued to seem totally uninterested in her as a woman. Helene had pretty well reached the end of her rope when he told her he wouldn't be seeing her on her birthday, airily saying that as they had no speaking engagements that day, he wouldn't be needing her. She awoke on her special day alone in a strange city with no plans, as depressed as she'd ever been in her life.

She wandered disconsolately into a small bookshop, looking for something to read. There was a rack near the entrance, and in it a solitary birthday card. Why, those were Alpine flowers decorating it! The very ones Helene had picked as a child on the mountains above Salzburg. Suddenly Helene knew that this was her card, her special birthday greeting from God. She opened it to the message: "Blessings on your birthday. What God has promised, that will He also do" (Romans 4:21).

Over the next year and a half Gideon made several more visits to Austria. Despite the fact that he and Helene spent a great deal of time together, they got no closer to any romantic involvement. However, when Helene was suddenly forced to cancel their plans and enter the hospital to have a lump removed from her breast, this man who had seemed completely uninterested in her appeared unexpectedly at her bedside and haltingly proposed marriage!

He had fallen in love with her, he rushed on, that very first week in Jerusalem—and struggled against it every day of the previous three years. "I gave myself all the logical reasons why we could never be close. But Helene . . . it's almost as though our being together had all been settled ahead of time."

"A long, long time ahead," Helene fervently agreed!

The tumor in Helene's breast turned out to be benign, and she and Gideon married that fall. Now the former Nazi and the Jew lead groups of Austrians on missions of repentance to the sites of local concentration camps. As Ms. Sherrill concludes:

The healing ministry they are performing in the world is the work of two people who have undergone their own missions of repentance, who have faced and overcome their deepest fears and prejudices. The old part of Helene has died; the anguish has passed from Gideon's eyes. Drawn together by an irresistible soul connection, the two peacemakers are creating a new beginning not only for themselves but for the wounded born long after the last SS bullet was fired.

Note that Helene identified her inner guide as Jesus, while Gideon, being Jewish, believed that his guidance came directly from God. The personal aspect of God that directs those willing to listen is known as *Shekinah* in Hebrew, although Christians call it the *Holy Spirit,* Hindus think of it as *Atman,* and Buddhists refer to it as their *inner Buddha nature.* It seems clear that the value to be obtained through inner listening does not depend upon who or what you take the source of your guidance to be.

GUIDELINES FOR ACTUALIZING A SOULMATE RELATIONSHIP

1. Don't be unduly discouraged if your soulmate takes a while to appear or to recognize you.
2. If your guide encourages hope, wait patiently to let the true possibilities of a relationship emerge in their own good time.

6

Try It! You'll Like It!

You learn how to be in relationship to everybody
by being in relationship to one other person.

—Raj

Now, I realize that the suggestion that there is some sort of invisible matchmaker out there, just waiting to fit you out with an ideal partner, may be placing a severe strain upon my credibility. However, if you will just try listening for the voice of your guide, I think you're going to be pleasantly surprised by the result. It doesn't take any special talent or spiritual faith to receive this sort of assistance. After all, Helene was not a believer when she asked Jesus to reveal himself to her, but that didn't prevent her from getting a prompt response the first time she sought one.

Note too that her guide's voice was already familiar to her. Helene realized in retrospect that she had felt Jesus' loving presence many times in the past. It had just never occurred to her to associate the peaceful, expansive mental state she'd enjoyed in sunny mountain meadows with *meditation,* or the loving presence she had sensed there with any sort of companion spirit. As far as she knew, she had simply been "communing with nature," and the insightful and uplifting ideas that flowed into her mind at those times were nothing more than her own thoughts.

My guess is that your guide's voice is going to be familiar to you as well. He or she is eager to communicate, and will do so at the least indication that such contact would be welcome. Just look at what happened when Pete decided to do his own personal experiment with guidance.

Pete

A gay man in his midfifties, Pete had had no significant love interest in his life since his tempestuous, live-in relationship with Tom had broken up some fifteen years earlier. Pete had never found anyone he could feel that deeply about since, and he often looked back with regret, wishing he'd tried harder to resolve his conflicts with this man who, he now felt, had been the love of his life. Between his work as an educator, his friendships, and his involvement in the life of his adult son, Pete felt that he had created a reasonably satisfying life for himself. Nevertheless, he couldn't help wondering how things might have turned out if he and Tom had tried a little harder to appreciate each other's points of view when they'd had the chance.

Pete had had a Protestant upbringing and still vaguely believed in some sort of abstract divinity, but he put his real faith in science and rationality. When a friend prevailed upon him to attend a few sessions of my husband Arnie's group based on *A Course in Miracles*, Pete was skeptical but willing to keep an open mind. And when several group members shared provocative personal stories of the seemingly miraculous ways in which an inner voice had guided them to things they'd needed and wanted, he couldn't help being curious.

One gloomy December evening Pete caught himself slipping into loneliness and depression. It was the holiday season, he was on vacation, and his close friends were all out of town or busy with other engagements. This left Pete with nothing to do, and no one to do it with. He realized that he could either sit around wallowing in negativity, or make an effort to go out and try to meet someone. But where should he go?

It occurred to Pete that this might be a good time to try out that guidance stuff everyone in the group was talking about. *A*

Course in Miracles teaches that all of us can receive guidance from a voice in our minds that speaks on behalf of the will our true self shares with God. Well, Pete thought with wry amusement, if that voice was all it was cracked up to be, finding some stimulating companionship for him tonight ought to be a relatively simple matter. It had been claimed that it was easy to get in touch with guidance. If it was all that easy, then he ought to be able to do it right now!

How should he phrase his request to his guide? Of course, what he would like best would be to find another gay man who would turn out to be perfect for him—a soulmate with whom he could begin a loving relationship. Still, all he really needed this evening was someone to talk to. He was quite prepared to settle for the company of anyone who could supply a little intelligent conversation.

Sinking down on his sofa, Pete closed his eyes and turned his attention within, mentally asking, "So? Where should I go to find someone to talk to?" Then he fell silent, listening intently for a response he didn't seriously expect to get.

A single word gradually took shape in his mind: *incognito*. At first Pete was tempted to dismiss it as a meaningless random association, but it didn't seem to be connected with anything he'd been thinking. Then he remembered that he was supposed to be listening for guidance. Just maybe this was his guide's response. But what kind of a response was *incognito?*

Pete could find no message in the word itself, but when he thought about it further, he dimly remembered that there was supposed to be a gay bar of that name somewhere out in the San Fernando Valley. Well, that didn't make a whole lot of sense, did it? A nondrinker, Pete almost never went to bars. Nevertheless, he had asked for guidance about where to go, and the name of a place he could go to had occurred to him. Was it possible that this really was the answer to his request? There was only one way to find out.

Still, Pete hesitated. He had never been to Incognito, but he figured that it must be some twenty miles away from his home in

Los Angeles. It was already late, and Pete wasn't really up for a long drive. Besides, on a weeknight between Christmas and New Year, it wasn't very likely that there would be a whole lot of patrons in a bar way out in the boondocks. All in all, it seemed to him that if he was going to visit a gay bar that night, there were plenty of good ones a lot closer to home. Pete decided to compromise by dropping in at a neighborhood tavern he'd visited once before. He threw on a coat and drove over there, but when he pulled up outside it was closed.

"Well, maybe I should drive out to Incognito after all," Pete thought. The problem now was that he wasn't sure where it was located. However, a solution occurred to him. He could stop in at a store that carried gay periodicals and find an ad for the bar. The address would be there, too. Pete got back in his car and went off to find a paper.

He located the address of Incognito just as he had planned, but as he left the newsstand, a flashing neon sign next door caught his eye. Incognito was a long way off, and here was an open bar right in front of him, and it too appeared to be frequented by gay men. If all he wanted was a little friendly conversation, surely he could find it here without the long trek. He went in, ordered an overpriced glass of water, and sat down at a table.

Soon a young man who introduced himself as Larry drifted over to join him. By way of getting acquainted, the younger man offered to guess Pete's profession, and quickly pegged him as a math teacher. When it was Pete's turn to guess, Larry laughed and said that he had better just tell him what he did for a living, since no one ever guessed his profession correctly.

Larry explained that he was an agent who booked celebrity spots for sports figures, and mentioned some of the famous athletes with whom he'd worked. Almost as an afterthought he added, "Not that I can make a living at it yet. I make ends meet with a part-time job as a bartender at this little place out in the Valley. You've probably never even heard of it—it's called *Incognito*."

Pete was stunned to hear Incognito mentioned again. What was the deal here? Was his guide really trying to get him to schlep out to this other bar? It certainly seemed like it. Intrigued, Pete excused himself, got back in his car, and started the long haul out to the mysterious tavern that, apparently, he was supposed to visit that night.

As he had anticipated, Incognito was virtually deserted. Nevertheless, he took a stool, ordered a Perrier, and began to chat with the bartender. It was late and he wanted to go home, but just maybe he had been led to this out-of-the-way spot for some good reason. He sat tight and waited.

A very interesting development materialized a few minutes later. The door opened, and in walked Tom, the man Pete had loved and lost fifteen years earlier!

Tom was just as surprised and delighted to see Pete as Pete was to see him. As it turned out, Tom was now living some twenty miles away from Incognito in the opposite direction. Like Pete, he had never before been to the bar, although he'd heard of it. He said that around 10:00 PM—just the time Pete had left the other bar—he'd had an "irresistible impulse" to visit it that night, despite the lateness of the hour and the knowledge that it was almost certain to be deserted. What an incredible coincidence to walk in and find Pete here!

The two former lovers wound up talking all night. After closing down the bar, they went over to Tom's to continue their reunion. Both expressed deep regret at the way they had treated each other fifteen years earlier. Tears were shed, laughter followed, and sincere forgiveness was exchanged. Both men felt incredibly grateful to have met again.

I suspect that Pete and Tom had some sort of unfinished business with each other that made a further encounter highly desirable. Maybe exchanging forgiveness was necessary before one or both would be free to move on. Or perhaps this was a chance for them to reestablish their relationship on a new level, although, as things worked out, no lasting bond resulted. For whatever reason, some wise higher consciousness seems to have exploited a brief window of opportunity to reunite these former lovers at a moment when both were genuinely open to healing the breach.

I think Pete's story beautifully illustrates my point that hearing guidance doesn't require decades of meditation training. Like Helene, Pete achieved a few moments of detached receptivity through curiosity alone, and a valuable message got through to him.

Perhaps you can begin to see that there is a limit to what our guides can do for us without our conscious cooperation. Had they ignored their inner teachers' advice, Helene would probably never have connected with Gideon and Pete would probably not have been reunited with Tom. Our companion spirit wants to support us in attaining our heart's desire, but this help generally comes in the form of *specific instructions* which, *if followed,* will lead us to fulfillment. If we aren't paying attention, how are we going to find out what we'd need to do in order to receive the things for which we've been hoping and praying?

Guidelines for Actualizing a Soulmate Relationship

1. Healing prior relationships is often necessary before new opportunities can be given to us.
2. Sometimes guidance seems to make no sense until we try it out and see what happens.

7

Why Your Ego Is Such a Lousy Guide to Relationship

Yet the ego, though encouraging the search for love very actively, makes one proviso; do not find it.
—*A Course in Miracles*

If you are to utilize guidance to find a soulmate, the first thing you need to do is learn to tell the difference between the voice of your inner teacher and that of your ego. This is not really difficult, since your guide and your ego espouse entirely different thought systems. Indeed, cultures throughout the world seem to resonate with the idea that there is a high-minded influence within us that argues in favor of love, humility, and forgiveness, and that it is opposed by another that urges us to be egotistical, selfish, and judgmental. The cartoons of my childhood, for example, depicted what I am calling *ego* as a little red devil whispering malicious advice into a character's left ear, while a winged and haloed angel representing guidance spoke words of generosity and tolerance in the other.

How Your Guide's Thinking Differs from Your Ego's

The simplest way to explain the difference between your guide's perspective and that of your ego is to say that the former believes that love is real and fear is not, while the latter believes that fear is real and love is not. It may surprise you to learn that your ego doesn't believe that love really exists, but it's true. Just think! When you allow your ego to direct your search for love, you are actually asking the only thing in the universe that doesn't know what love is, to find it for you. Talk about letting the inmates run the asylum!

How is it that our false self knows nothing about love? Well, that's the way we designed it. From a metaphysical perspective, the human mind invents an ego for the purpose of making love seem unreal.

And just why would we want to do such a silly thing? A number of spiritual traditions suggest that it is because God is love. They say we wanted to forget about our Creator for a while, so that we could play at being creators ourselves. And since everything that God creates is a perfect reflection of divine love, the only way we could generate an experience that would be uniquely our own was to make up an imperfect world where love's opposite—fear—would appear to rule. Thus, fear is our own original contribution to an otherwise loving universe.

The ego's problem is that any experience of love, however attenuated, threatens to trigger our memory of reality, and spoil the game we came here to play. Its job is to make sure that doesn't happen. Thus, we might compare the ego to the weight belt a scuba diver dons to counteract her natural buoyancy. If a diver took off her weight belt, she would quickly bob back up to the surface. If you and I released identification with our ego, we would quickly bob back up into reality, where it would be apparent that love is everywhere. As long as we prefer to remain immersed in frightening illusions, our ego is necessary to filter every trace of love out of our perceptions—no mean feat in a universe made entirely of love!

The fact is that whenever we genuinely care for anyone, we *do* bob back into reality, although usually only briefly. That's why being in love is so *heavenly!* It's like an all-expenses-paid vacation from fear. Our ego has to be extremely vigilant to nip this sort of thing in the bud. It knows very well that once we start loving, there is no telling where it might end. Today your dog or cat— tomorrow the world!

Why Egos Seek Love

You'd think that if our false self is so intent upon preventing us from experiencing love, it would actively discourage our search for it, but this is not the case. Our ego doesn't just warn us not to trust those who care for us; it also inveighs against the horrors of a lonely old age. Indeed, far from being indifferent to love, our false self often seems almost obsessively concerned with finding it. To hear our ego tell it, no real happiness is possible in life until we unite with that "special someone" who alone can validate our worth, give meaning to our lives, and solve all our earthly problems.

What we need to understand is that our ego knows perfectly well that love is the only thing we really want or need. This leaves it with no alternative but to become embroiled in our search for a soulmate. If it said what it thinks—that love doesn't really exist, and only fear is real—we would very quickly see the absurdity of searching for fulfillment within a loveless illusion. At that point, our ego's whole world of distressing possibilities would be canceled for lack of interest—and our ego along with it!

No, our false self can't induce us to remain in illusion by *ig-noring* our desire for love. None of us is so deluded that we'd put up with that! So instead, it carries out its mission by offering to show us how to find love, *and then making sure that we never do.* Like a carnival scam artist, our ego assures us that there is no reason for us not to win the romantic jackpot on our very next try. But somehow it never seems to work out that way. There is actually no "danger" at all of finding a soulmate as long as we play the game by our ego's rules.

How can our false self guarantee that we will not stumble upon true love despite its interference? It can't. But what it can do is make it very difficult for us to *recognize* what we've found. Egos render love "invisible" in much the same way Siegfried and Roy make tigers disappear on stage in Las Vegas—through the skillful misdirection of attention. First our false self reassigns the name "love" to something that poses no threat to it, and then it keeps us so busy searching for the wrong thing that we wouldn't notice the right one, even if we tripped over it.

I'll say more about the love substitute our ego keeps us searching for in the next chapter, but for now, let me just call it *conditional love* or *infatuation*. When your ego offers to help you find "love," it doesn't mean *real love*—the unconditional kind that fills you, and those around you, with lasting joy and satisfaction. To find *that* kind of love you'd have to abandon your ego and relate only with your soul. No, the kind of love your ego has in mind for you is something quite different. Once you've become deeply embroiled in the search for it, your gaze will pass right over the real thing without a glimmer of recognition.

You see, the human romantic dilemma isn't that true love is so very hard to find, but that it is *too ordinary* to withstand comparison with the exotic illusions our ego offers in its place. In the same way that diamonds seem precious while the pure water we need in order to survive doesn't, we take love for granted and strain after the impossibly beautiful substitute our ego offers in its stead. Infatuation ravishes our senses, and seems to promise gratification beyond our wildest dreams. Unfortunately, when we mistake it for the genuine article, we slowly starve for love even as we seem to gorge ourselves on it.

Real love is actually a pretty pedestrian affair, characterized by simple virtues like patience, forgiveness, tolerance, humor, gentleness, empathy, tact, honesty, discipline, and practical support. It is not heralded by a state of breathless exaltation, but by a sense of peaceful contentment. Chances are you've had many opportunities in your life for "true love" that you passed up without a backward glance.

Take my friend Karen. She was so busy pursuing the glamorous love-substitute her ego touted that she had a hard time recognizing her soulmate even when he had been right there by her side for months!

Karen and Pat

Karen Philipp was definitely one of the "beautiful people." As a singer with the phenomenally successful l960s pop group Brazil '66, she had toured the world and earned several gold records. Her stunning face and figure graced numerous record jackets, and even earned her a spread in *Playboy Magazine*. Tired of life on the road, Karen eventually gave up her musical career and settled down in Los Angeles to work in television. It would appear that she had it all. All except the soulmate for whom she was passionately yearning!

Karen dined at the finest restaurants and attended glittering Hollywood functions on the arms of some of L.A.'s most eligible bachelors. Each was the focus of her hopes and dreams for a brief period, but for all their early promise, none of these liaisons developed into a long-term relationship. Karen was consumed by her desire for love, but all the princely men who romanced her kept turning out to be frogs—and not very nice frogs, at that! Despite fame, fortune, and a social life that would have been the envy of most women, happily-ever-after continued to elude her.

Still, Karen figured, it must be only a matter of time before she found Mr. Right. In an effort to speed up the process, she decided to be more assertive. Instead of waiting for men to make the first move, she adopted the practice of boldly approaching guys who interested her. When she spotted Pat Proft waiting for the light to change at a crosswalk in Century City, she liked his looks enough to hand him her card and say, "Call me!"

Flattered and curious, Pat called, and they arranged a date. But when he came to pick her up, Karen's first reaction was "What was I thinking?"

Somehow Pat seemed a lot less impressive here on her doorstep. At 5' 10" he was barely as tall as she, and his casual dress and low-key, Midwestern style of relating made him a far cry from the glib movers and shakers who usually showed up to wine and dine her. Pat was recently divorced, and eking out a meager living as a stand-up comic while he tried his hand at writing screenplays. In the course of the evening Karen summed him up as, "a nice guy with a great sense of humor, but definitely not my type."

Pat wasn't any more taken with her than she was with him. It was kind of a kick to go out with a glamour girl like Karen, but he could see at a glance that they were far too different to have any basis for a relationship. She was champagne, caviar, and first nights, while he was fruit juice, granola, and TV. He didn't want to hurt her feelings, but he saw no point in pretending that she was the woman of his dreams.

Their date involved dinner and a movie, and no sooner had they settled down in the theater than Pat promptly went to sleep! Karen was more amused than offended to find him dozing peacefully beside her in the dark. Here she'd been so concerned about finding a tactful way to tell him she wasn't interested in a second date, and he was so bored he couldn't remain conscious throughout the first! This was one heart she needn't worry about breaking!

Indeed, the realization that their lack of attraction was mutual seems to have been the very thing that made these two decide to see each other again. Neither would have wanted to lead the other on, but since both understood how preposterously mismatched they were, a certain camaraderie developed. After all, they were in much the same boat, looking for love in a city that idealized shallow, exploitative relationships. They weren't right for each other, but that didn't mean they couldn't be pals.

An unlikely friendship gradually developed. Both Karen and Pat reserved their weekends for their current heartthrobs, but often during the week when neither had anything better to do, they'd get together to share a meal or watch TV. Karen found that she really got a kick out of Pat's screwy sense of humor, and it was great to be able to kid around with someone she didn't have to impress. Her weekends were limousines, exclusive restaurants, and A-List parties. Weeknights were sweatpants and T-shirts on the living room floor, as she and Pat hashed over their current romances, traded witticisms about the inept acting in their favorite sitcoms, and squabbled over the last piece of pizza.

Karen's two worlds collided unexpectedly one Saturday evening when the "Greek god" she was currently nuts about arrived for their date with his collar unbuttoned and his tie askew. "I've had a hell of a week, Karen, and I just can't face that party. Would you mind if we just stayed in this evening? We could order in some Chinese food and watch television or something."

"Of course," Karen replied with instant sympathy. "I love doing that!" But she soon realized she wasn't loving it tonight.

"It was always a laugh a minute watching TV while Pat kept up this hilarious running commentary on every idiotic thing that occurred," Karen told me. "But a quiet evening at home with this guy was just plain dull! As the evening dragged on, I gradually realized that outside the context of expensive restaurant dinners and trendy parties, my date and I had absolutely nothing to say to each other. We *looked fabulous* together, but that was about it! As madly in love as I had been with this guy only a few hours earlier, I found myself longing for the moment he'd go home."

Sitting there in her living room where she had so often sat with Pat, comparisons were inevitable.

"The more I contrasted my date's boring self-importance with Pat's brotherly teasing, insightful comments, and offhand affection, the clearer it became that I'd been barking up the wrong tree.

"And they were all like this, I was stunned to realize. All the rich, handsome, sophisticated guys I dated were exactly the same.

I was ashamed to realize how shallow I had been. My relationships were all about romantic fantasy and looking good in public. Not one of these men was anyone I could confide in. All they wanted was a beautiful woman they could show off, and for all my talk about wanting to find a real soulmate, a handsome accessory was all I had ever expected. They didn't care about me, and I didn't care about them!"

With a little help from a convenient social headache, Karen shooed her date out early. Before the door had even closed behind him, she had made up her mind to find out what Pat would be like as a lover.

"For the first time it occurred to me that it might be interesting to try making love to someone I actually *liked*—someone I knew liked *me*. The whole idea of having sex with a friend seemed kind of weird at first. I mean, Pat was a cute guy and all, but I'd never thought about him 'that way.' And he didn't seem to be any more attracted to me than I was to him. I had no idea if I could even lure him into the sack. But there was only one way to find out.

"So I called him up and told him to get his lazy ass over to my place right away. And when he showed up, I seduced him. Not that he put up much of a struggle!"

Happily, Karen and Pat quickly discovered that mutual affection is not an obstacle to good sex. Six months later, Karen gave up her glamorous single life to marry this struggling unknown who, incidentally, went on to become one of Hollywood's most successful comedy writers, collaborating on such hit movies as *Airplane!* and the *Naked Gun* series. Today her life is one part glittering opening nights to ninety-nine parts Midwestern domesticity. The mix seems about right to her.

Looking back, Karen thinks that she might have recognized Pat's potential much sooner if she'd been paying more attention to the way being with a man *felt* than to her ego's ideas about how an ideal relationship was supposed to *look*.

"The thing that was so different about being with Pat," Karen muses, "was that when we were together, I liked who I was.

When I tried being 'myself' with other guys, I always picked up a kind of subtle disapproval, so I'd go back to trying to be what I thought they wanted. I figured the only way to win the 'prize' of a man's love was to play the game, and do whatever was necessary to make him like me.

"But from the first, Pat liked me just the way I was! He accepted me completely, and that acceptance encouraged me to come out of hiding. The strange thing is, I had no idea how much I actually *was* hiding until I met this nice, funny guy who thought I was delightful company when I was just being *me*. Now that we're approaching our nineteenth wedding anniversary," Karen continued, "I realize that Pat has given me something I never knew I could have. I finally know what it feels like to be cherished."

A Course in Miracles contrasts the *special* relationship—which is based upon infatuation—with the *holy* relationship, which is grounded in real love. Karen's experience illustrates this distinction nicely. Special relationships are all about how love is *supposed to* be. In pursuit of them, we do our best to achieve a union where everything *looks* perfect, regardless of the way it *feels*.

The ego's fantasy of "special love" involves a partner so obviously desirable that he or she reflects glory on us every time we are seen together. A suitably romantic courtship, during which both parties do a flawless portrayal of people in love, culminates in a fairy-tale perfect wedding. Then the lucky couple goes off to live happily ever after in the local equivalent of a palace, producing beautiful, trouble-free, high-achieving children, who reflect well on their parents. It will all be just perfect—as long as everyone does their damndest to keep up appearances.

Unfortunately, concern with the outward appearance of a relationship always comes at the expense of content. It is exhausting to hold a pose for five minutes, much less a lifetime, and however "perfect" special relationships look from the outside, they leave the participants feeling empty and alone. Both know that they are valued only for the act they can put on, and that any attempt to reveal their true selves will be regarded as a breach of contract. As the *Course* points out, the special relationship is a very impressive frame, but the picture it holds is dark and depressing.

Holy relationships (think *wholesome* relationships if you find the religious connotation off-putting) are achieved only when we forget about the frame (the way our union appears to others, all the social and material advantages it does or doesn't offer), and focus instead upon content (the glorious way it *feels* to be with someone we truly enjoy). The holy relationships soulmates work to create don't necessarily look like anything out of the ordinary. Your friends aren't going to drop dead with envy when you walk into a room on the arm of a man or woman whose chief appeal lies is the fact that he or she really understands who you are, shares your enthusiasms, and enjoys hanging out with you. But being with such a person *feels* marvelous! You can finally stop smiling for the camera, let your belt out a notch or two, and be yourself.

Are you beginning to see what I mean about real love being too ordinary to compete with our ego's dreams of achieving glory through the conquest of a very special partner? In interviewing couples for this book, I've been repeatedly struck by the way people seem to reserve hyperbole for individuals who appeal to their egos. When soulmates describe their early impressions of each other, "nice" is the adjective that crops up most frequently. *Nice* feels awfully good, but it is of no use whatsoever to our ego in its quest for glory.

In closing this chapter, I'd like to point out one other interesting feature of soulmate relationships—the way everything else seems to fall into place once we make love our first priority. The Bible says, "Seek ye first the kingdom of heaven, and all else shall be added unto you." The literal truth of this statement is repeatedly demonstrated in soulmate unions where someone gives up "everything" for love, and then winds up getting it all anyway. Karen, for example, thought she needed a man who was rich and successful. By choosing to love and marry her soulmate, despite the fact that he was poor and unsuccessful, that's exactly what she got. Invest in the picture that brings you joy, and the universe may just throw in the frame for free!

Guidelines for Actualizing a Soulmate Relationship

1. Look for the sort of person you'd want as a best friend even if you weren't attracted to her or him sexually.
2. Don't cultivate a relationship with someone "superior" whose love appears to "elevate" you in some way, but with an equal you enjoy.
3. Remember that your soul won't be satisfied with anything less than true love. Accept no substitutes!

8

Love Versus Infatuation

*For the ego cannot love, and in its frantic search for love
it is seeking what it is afraid to find. . . .
Follow its teaching, then, and you will search for love,
but will not recognize it.*

—*A Course in Miracles*

If all of this talk about the ego seems a bit obscure, all you really
need to remember is that *your ego is the part of your mind dedicated
to making sure you never find love.* Egos dissolve on contact with
love. How eager would *you* be to find something that was destined to destroy you?

It's time to take a closer look at the thing the ego offers us
as a substitute for love, which I am going to call *infatuation.* Infatuation is that euphoric state we experience as "falling in love."
Biologically, it is associated with the secretion of liberal amounts
of a brain neurochemical called *phenylethylamine,* a precursor to
the feel-good neurotransmitter *seratonin,* which regulates the activity of two other feel-good neurotransmitters: *norepinephrine* and
dopamine. When supplied with plenty of phenylethylamine, we
experience a glorious sense of well-being similar to that associated with cocaine, amphetamines, and antidepressant medications.

The evolutionary function of this potent chemical cocktail
seems to be to ensure the perpetuation of the species by overrid-
ing our natural caution about engaging in reproductive behavior.

Phenylethylamine induces that giddy, fearless, unreasonably optimistic attitude that makes people "marry in haste, and repent at leisure." When we talk about "chemistry" between two people, we are quite literally talking about changes in their *brain chemistry*.

Most readers will have experienced infatuation at one time or another, and anyone who listens to popular music is familiar with its symptoms: an exhilarating sense of walking on air, heightened awareness of the beauties of nature, an idealized view of our beloved, the conviction that we could never love anyone else, and so forth. It encompasses the whole constellation of physical, mental, and emotional experiences we ordinarily associate with "falling in love" as opposed to simply "loving." This distinction between love and infatuation is what allows us to decode sentences like "I *love* him, but I'm not *in love with* him" and "I *love* her, but I don't *like* her."

To a brain blissfully surfing on a wave of phenylethylamine, all of the realistic impediments to sexual consummation—"But she's married to someone else," "But I might get pregnant," "But I don't want to marry a man who hates children"—seem trivial and nit-picking. Confident that a great love like this must command heaven's blessing, and that both parties will climb mountains and swim oceans as required, an infatuated individual has no hesitation in committing, body and soul. We joyously open up our heart, home, and bank account to anyone who can make us feel this way!

But, although the ego characterizes infatuation as love, in truth the two are very nearly mutually exclusive. Infatuation is an emotion fueled by the tension between hope and fear, while love rests upon a calm sense of trust. Infatuation is intensely exciting, while love is peaceful. Infatuation, being conditional, drives us to make a good impression, while love makes us feel safe enough to relax and be ourselves. Infatuation is "blind," where love heightens our insight into the other. Indeed, the happier and more secure the relationship, the less infatuated the partners are going to be with each other. If it's violin music you want, buy a concert ticket!

Addicted to "Love"

If we are to understand the ego's use of infatuation as a substitute for unconditional love, it is essential to bear in mind that phenylethylamine is a mood-altering substance, and that when we are ego identified, our false self controls our access to it. Infatuation is actually a chemical high. We can become addicted to our own brain chemicals and suffer physical and emotional torment when they are withdrawn. That sense of euphoric invulnerability we experience when we fall madly in love can rapidly collapse into suicidal despair if things don't work out as we had hoped.

But even when the object of our affection loves us back, infatuation eventually fades all the same, and a receding wave of phenylethylamine can leave us beached on a very alien shore. If love has not burgeoned to take the place of infatuation before familiarity has had a chance to breed our ego's contempt, it may be hard to remember what we ever saw in this person. Friends and family members generally find it hard to hide their amusement as the no-longer-infatuated belatedly discover the faults in his or her partner that were perfectly obvious to everyone else all along. Qualities once glossed over as "charming quirks" don't look half so endearing now!

"I love it that his lifestyle is so relaxed and informal" becomes "If that slob leaves his filthy underwear on the bathroom floor one more time, I'm going to burn it!"

"I can't believe I've finally found a woman with such exquisite taste and sensitivity," all too soon deteriorates into "Nothing is ever good enough for her!"

Infatuation and Mate Selection

As a mind-altering substance, phenylethylamine always interferes with the critical judgment necessary to select a compatible partner. That's one reason traditional societies go to such lengths to keep infatuation under wraps with strict rules governing contact between the sexes. Such restrictions are aimed at saving vulnerable men and women needless pain by holding passion at bay until it has been established that the match is a suitable one, and that the intentions of both parties are honorable. It is always dangerous to allow infatuation free rein before good judgment has endorsed a prospective mate's sincerity and eligibility.

Remember, the fact that true love is unconditional doesn't mean that we should not be discriminating in our choice of a life partner. Just as we might love irresponsible friends, and yet have better sense than to enter into business partnerships with them, we can love a great many people with whom it would be foolish for us to become emotionally and sexually involved. Sensible individuals do not indulge an illicit passion for the husband of their best friend, or allow themselves to fall madly in love with an underage girl.

What Turns You On?

As long as you identify with your ego, it controls your access to phenylethylamine and is thus in a position to decide who will make your heart-strings quiver, and who will leave you cold. But your ego makes these decisions on grounds that have nothing whatever to do with *your* best interests. It isn't looking for love, but for someone with whom to play out its favorite romantic fantasies. Then, too, each ego has a deeply personal concept of attractiveness embodied in its thinking about who is, and isn't, its "type." It develops its particular love map out of a mixture of cultural images and early experiences.

From our society we learn what characteristics the people around us regard as sexually desirable. For example, if you are a man who grew up in India, you probably respond to women a lot of American men would consider overweight. Similarly, if you are an American male who went through adolescence in the 1950s, your concept of feminine beauty was probably influenced by the succession of buxom "blonde bombshells" who heated up the Hollywood films of the postwar era.

Cultural influences aside, our ego tends to gravitate toward individuals who unconsciously remind us of our earliest caretakers. Unfortunately, this process works just as powerfully whether the points of resemblance are good qualities or bad ones. Indeed, prospective partners who embody the most frustrating characteristics of our mother and father seem to hold a special fascination for our ego, probably because relationships with such people appear to offer opportunities to obtain compensation for all of the disappointments we experienced at the hands of our earliest caretakers.

This desire to redress old grievances by rewriting the past in the present is the ego's hidden agenda in love relationships—what pop psychology refers to as "emotional baggage." Was your mother narcissistic and uncaring? In that case, your ego may make you swoon over women who are exactly the same way. You enter each new relationship with an unconscious plan to win over a self-centered woman and get her to acknowledge your worth in a way your mother never would. But since your ego selected her in the first place precisely because she was totally self-involved, you aren't really very likely to succeed.

Sadly, even if your new love *does* appreciate and acknowledge you, it probably isn't going to be enough for an ego bent upon obtaining compensation for childhood losses. Since your early life was *so* deprived, your ego argues, it is only fair that your new girlfriend or boyfriend give way to you in *everything*. After all, life owes you a great deal and if you don't get it from your sweetheart, where are you ever going to get it?

The correct answer to that question is, of course, "Nowhere." You aren't going to get it. The kind of selfless care and attention a good-enough parent lavishes upon an infant or a small child is quite different from the cooperative, mutually supportive bond of romantic partners. If your parents were not as loving or attentive as you wanted them to be, that's unfortunate. But it's useless to go through life hoping to find a lover who will take up the job of parenting you where they left off—and this time do it *right!*

I said earlier that our ego is bent upon preventing us from finding love, and perhaps it is now a little clearer how it accomplishes its aim. Under its influence, many of us go through life seeking love from the very people who are least disposed to give it to us, and then destroy any remaining chance for happiness by making extravagant demands our partners couldn't meet if they wanted to. I always think of my friend Patsy in this context.

Patsy

Patsy was as eager to find Mr. Right as I was, and we often went out together to try to meet men. But after a few such experiences I could pick out the guys my friend was going to wind up with on sight. If there was a man present whose blatantly insincere manner advertised an intention to exploit women, he was sure to be a magnet for Patsy.

Our whole circle of friends used to shake their heads over Patsy's fascination with guys who were guaranteed to use her and dump her. And Patsy too was aware that her choices always turned out badly—she just couldn't see what she could do differently.

"What about Mark?" we'd say. "Mark is a terrific guy, and he seems to be crazy about you. Why don't you give him a chance?"

"He just isn't my type," Patsy would protest. "He's a nice enough guy, but I'm not attracted to him. Besides, don't you think he's kind of boring?"

For the ego, *boring* is a code word meaning "not likely to betray, frustrate, or neglect me as I once thought my parents did." Still, Patsy saw no alternative to following her ego's bizarre guidance. "You can't control your heart, can you?" she would sigh.

But, of course, the problem wasn't with her heart, but with her misplaced allegiance to her ego. When we *identify* with our ego's point of view, we think it is *ours*. We imagine that in pursuing the partners who attract *it,* we are doing what *we* want. Yet there was nothing Patsy truly wanted less than to keep on winding up with men who abused her trust, and then cruelly dumped her for someone "better."

Having said that I could pick out the impossible men Patsy would find irresistible, it's only fair to add that she could undoubtedly have done the same for me. My preferred brand of unwinnable men was a little different from hers, but my behavior was every bit as self-defeating, and I had no more insight into the reasons my relationships kept failing than she did. For all my talk about what a great guy Mark was, I wouldn't have dated him either!

As long as we are content to be passion's plaything, it will be impossible to make sensible relationship decisions. Bathed in a rosy glow of infatuation, the most hopelessly inappropriate partners seem absolutely ideal. And while this sort of miscalculation is easy enough to detect in others, it is terribly hard to recognize in oneself.

We watch a male friend rhapsodize over a succession of shallow, materialistic women, and we can't help shaking our head over his inability to see the obvious. And then we turn around and do exactly the same thing ourselves, except that whenever *we* fall in love, it is with someone "extraordinarily kind," "wonderfully insightful," and "devastatingly witty." No one is more surprised than we when our infatuation recedes and this glorious prince or princess turns out to be yet another humble amphibian!

Perpetual Infatuation as Heaven on Earth

Just as infatuation is the ego's substitute for love, a permanent state of infatuation is the thing it offers us as a substitute for heaven. When we are happily "in love," we feel expansive, fearless, worthwhile, and invulnerable. If we could only manage to feel that way all the time, the ego argues, we would have achieved eternal bliss. It is easy to believe that the whole point of life is to find some magical individual who can keep us in a perpetual infatuated glow.

But unfortunately, by its very nature, infatuation can never *be* permanent. It always fades as we get to know the object of our affection. That's because the delicious excitement we feel when falling in love is made up of both our ego's *hope* that it has finally found someone who will compensate it for every disappointment of the past and its *fear* that this person won't. Infatuation is always a function of *uncertainty,* and when the uncertainty fades, so does the magic.

That's why infatuation is always most potent early in a relationship. It is also why movie stars, sports figures, and other distant, unapproachable sex symbols are such ideal objects for infatuation. To the extent that a prospective partner is an unknown quantity, our ego is free to project its fantasies onto him or her, and render this person irresistible through the judicious administration of phenylethylamine.

But the extravagant hopes our ego encourages us to entertain can never be sustained for long once they come into contact with reality. Daily interaction with the object of our affection soon wears away any illusions we were harboring. Even when a partner is right for us in every way, what we can realistically expect of our soulmate will always fall far short of our ego's fantasies of unlimited gratification. Our meant-to-be loves may become the dearest friends we have ever known, but they cannot be expected to make us perpetually happy, compensate us for childhood disappointments, or redeem lives we perceive as meaningless.

Egos Play by "The Rules"

Since infatuation thrives on uncertainty, egos always reserve their most intense passion for those whose hearts remain unconquered. They enjoy the thrill of the chase but quickly lose interest in people who love us back. Ironically, the minute a prospective partner displays the characteristics of a loyal and caring spouse, our false self urges us to start shopping around for a replacement.

You might almost say that egos universally subscribe to Groucho Marx's famous epigram, "I would never dream of joining any club that would have someone like *me* as a member!" After all, what better evidence could our ego have of a partner's lack of worth and discernment than the fact that he or she admires the self the ego disdains? But let that same "boring" partner show signs of defecting and the chase is on again.

Rick and Lorraine

Lorraine broke up with Rick soon after he began therapy with me. In the ensuing months, both of them found that their infatuation with each other faded only gradually. Once they separated, both egos were at liberty to generate tantalizing fantasies about "what might have been." As a result, there were several occasions during the first year after their breakup when they flirted with the idea of getting back together. Yet every time they tried, actual contact with the other person soon reminded them why they had decided to part in the first place.

During what would turn out to be their final go-round, Rick realized he was no longer at all interested in working things out with Lorraine. Since he had long been making noises like someone who *did* want to get back together, he arranged to meet her at a restaurant to break it to her that he had changed his mind. Unfortunately, before he got around to "letting her down easy," Lorraine mentioned that she was going off to visit a man she'd recently met who lived in another city.

"A minute before she told me about the trip, I was sitting there trying to imagine what I'd ever seen in her," Rick told me at our next session. "Then she let it slip that she was going to Portland later in the week, and when I started asking questions, I realized it wasn't just business—she was really going to see this other guy.

"Suddenly I was so jealous I could barely control myself! I laid this whole guilt trip on her about how she'd said she wanted to work things out with me and now here she was making plans to see someone else. When I couldn't persuade her not to visit this guy, I made her promise to have dinner with me as soon as she got back. Am I losing my mind? I don't even *like* this woman!"

In their bestseller *The Rules,* authors Sherrie Schneider and Ellen Fein teach women how to induce their suitors to propose by playing hard to get. The authors' thesis is that the surest way to get a man to the altar is to feign indifference and cultivate an air of mystery. Now that we have some understanding of the ego's use of infatuation as a substitute for love, we are in a position to see why romantic game-playing of this sort so often works—at least in the short run. Women who play by these "rules" are creating precisely the conditions under which infatuation flourishes!

The ego's tendency to respond to rejection by jacking up the infatuation means that a manipulative pretense of indifference can seem to be an effective short-term solution to romantic difficulties. A "Rules Girl" like Scarlet O'Hara often does discover that the less interested she appears, the more obsessed certain men will become with winning her. Unfortunately, infatuation induced by intimacy-avoiding strategies is no basis for marriage. When the ceremony is over, so is the uncertainty that made one's partner seem so irresistible. Once Rhett Butler got a chance to see Scarlet O'Hara up close and personal, "Frankly my dear, I don't give a damn!" was only a matter of time.

Keeping Love Alive

For all their apparent passion, egomates seldom manage to sustain a satisfying sexual relationship for long. The bliss that characterizes the early phases of these affairs deteriorates quickly once it becomes clear that neither party is going to live up to the other's extravagant expectations. Eventually resentment sets in, and we don't desire those we resent, no matter how attractive we may once have thought them.

But egomates don't just stop desiring *each other* when the honeymoon is over; they frequently lose all sense of being desirable themselves. Constantly confronted with their inability to interest or satisfy their partners, they begin to feel unattractive and inadequate. No wonder they so often feel compelled to boost their egos with extramarital flirtations and flings.

Of course, some infatuated married couples try to sustain what they think of as their *love* by finding ways to keep each other off balance. For example, one much-married Hollywood beauty of a certain age recommends that women nurture their husbands' passions by never undressing in front of them, never allowing themselves to be seen without makeup, and always insisting upon separate bedrooms. In this way, she assures us, the magic will last forever—although if the strategy truly works, it is difficult to see why she has been divorced quite so many times!

The truth is that distancing strategies and separate bedrooms do not a loving relationship make. "My partner doesn't understand me!" is the rallying cry of unfaithful spouses and angry litigants, not a state of affairs for which soulmate wannabes should be encouraged to strive. Besides, while jealousy and insecurity may increase our infatuation during courtship, they only lead to resentment once we feel our devotion has earned us the right to real love.

Guidelines for Actualizing a Soulmate Relationship

1. The people who make you swoon may be precisely the ones you would do best to avoid.
2. It's wise to proceed cautiously when you are blinded by infatuation.
3. True love is never blind.

9

Recognizing
Your Soulmate

*The ego is certain that love is dangerous,
and this is always its central teaching.*
—*A Course in Miracles*

No matter how attractive your soulmate turns out to be, she or he is still going to seem like chopped liver to an ego that has something very different in mind. Exactly what *does* your ego have in mind? While it's true that each false self is unique, a great many of them seem to specialize in infatuations with people who can be counted upon to torment and reject us. When it comes to romance, your ego is, quite literally, looking for trouble.

We've seen the way infatuation thrives on the threat of rejection. What this means in practice is that the more difficult it is to please a lover—the less we can count upon him or her to be considerate, faithful, and honest—the more over the moon our ego is likely to be. Our false self quickly loses interest in suitors who don't continually jerk us around with mind games.

The upshot is that many of us go through life unconsciously believing that the love that is hardest to win must be the kind that is most worth having. The worse we are treated, the more we try to please. In the grip of this kind of insanity, individuals who would make wonderful life partners don't even register on our romantic radar. Take Ann for example. Her ego took an instant dislike to her soulmate Andrew precisely because it dimly suspected that he would turn out to be the loving, faithful husband for whom she'd been praying.

Andrew and Ann

Andrew began volunteering at a local mental hospital when the wife of a friend was admitted there with severe depression, but he enjoyed the work and continued his visits after she had been released. He would play the piano for the patients, socialize with them, and sit in on group therapy sessions. In the course of these activities he became acquainted with Dr. Santini, a psychiatrist who had patients on the ward and who also saw clients for outpatient psychotherapy in his private practice. The two men became friends.

Andrew was a devout Christian Scientist who had spent the last three years coming to terms with the failure of his first marriage. Until recently, he had been so consumed with confusion and regret that he had had no interest in other women. But now with his divorce behind him, he felt that he was finally ready to start dating again.

His new friend thought he saw a way to help things along. Dr. Santini told Andrew that there was a young woman he was seeing in his private practice who might be just perfect for him. He urged the volunteer to come to the Tuesday evening group therapy session at his office so that he could meet Ann.

Ann was just twenty-one when she escaped from her violently abusive husband and fled across the country to seek refuge at her aunt's home in California. She was pregnant, and although she felt a lot of conflict about abandoning her husband, she knew she dared not remain in such a dangerous situation. The depth of the terror with which she lived in that marriage is evident from the fact that even today—more than thirty years after these events—Ann anxiously cautioned me to change her name and delete all identifying details from my account. She is still taking no chances that her ex-husband will ever find her again!

By the time she arrived in California, the young woman was falling apart emotionally, so her aunt hastened to arrange for psychotherapy with Dr. Santini. A major focus of their therapeutic work together was helping Ann decide what to do about the baby. Now, it had always been Ann's dream to be a wife and mother, but sadly, after months of discussion with all of the important people in her life, she concluded that she was in no position to give her child the kind of life she would want to. Destitute, jobless, and emotionally traumatized by her abusive upbringing and nightmarish marriage, Ann recognized that she had little to offer her unborn child. With Dr. Santini's help she reluctantly arranged to give her baby up for adoption at birth. It comforted her to think that her child would find loving parents who could give her the advantages Ann could not.

The unhappy young woman saw her daughter only briefly the day she was born. With an aching heart, Ann watched her baby carried away to a foster home, wrapped in the white blanket she had lovingly crocheted for her. It was a tragic moment in a young life that had already been repeatedly blighted with unhappiness. Severely depressed, Ann turned to face an uncertain future.

It was about a month later when Dr. Santini began urging his young patient to attend his Tuesday evening group therapy session. He said that there was going to be someone there he wanted her to meet—a man he thought would be perfect for her. Too despondent to take an interest in much of anything, Ann resisted for several weeks. But Santini was nothing if not persistent. In the end, she agreed to go.

Ann disliked Andrew virtually on sight! At Dr. Santini's invitation, Andrew began the session by telling the group a bit about himself. When he was through, Ann chimed in to make the point that this was *exactly* the kind of man she couldn't stand! For his part, Andrew remembers being distinctly underwhelmed by her.

"She was sitting there sprawled in a chair with her arms folded across her chest, and a scowl on her face, wrapped up in this awful baggy, brown coat she had made herself. She was just so closed off and hostile! When she started carping about me, I was very put off."

"What do you think made you so instantly antagonistic toward Andrew?" I inquired of Ann.

"Truthfully?" she replied with a sheepish look. "I think it was because some part of me recognized that he was going to be my husband. It doesn't make much sense, but there was something within me that registered Andrew's arrival in my life as if it had been expected. I wasn't fully conscious of it at the time, but at some level I just knew that we were going to be together from then on.

"Now you'd think that would make me happy, but my first reaction was to feel coerced and resentful. I mean, I'd been praying to God to send me a good, kind man who would not be abusive, and here he was. But I just didn't feel ready to settle down yet.

"Remember, I'd just gotten out of this horrible marriage, and given up my baby. At some level, I guess I thought I was owed a little romance and excitement. And I knew instinctively that Andrew wasn't going to be exciting that way—just kind and loving and dependable.

"You see, I'd always been attracted to dangerous men. I was fascinated by tough guys who were emotionally unavailable and kept me off balance. My idea of a good time was to pick some attractive loser and go through all the game-playing and melodrama you go through with a guy who won't be honest with you. Andrew's arrival on the scene meant I'd never get to do any of that again, and I responded childishly."

"It's a wonder anything *ever* developed between you, after such a miserable beginning," I remarked. "When did your feelings for each other change?"

"It didn't take long at all," Andrew beamed. "When the group ended, Ann needed a ride home, and it turned out that I was the only one with a car going in her direction. It was a bit awkward after what had happened between us in the group, but I really didn't have much choice about giving her a lift. On the way to her aunt's house, we decided to stop off for coffee at a diner. As I was sitting there looking at her over my coffee cup I heard a voice in my head announce, 'This is the next Mrs. Butler.'"

"What on earth did you make of that?" I asked. "Ann couldn't have been very attractive to you at that point!"

"That's true," Andrew agreed. "But at the same time it just seemed right. When the voice said that, I experienced a deep conviction that what had been said was true. It's hard to explain. There was a feeling of great comfort in being with Ann. It was like settling into something familiar."

"Yes," Ann agreed, "everything seemed so natural and easy between us, it was amazing. It was like being with an old friend— you feel you can say or do whatever you want. As I had watched the situation develop at Dr. Santini's office, I had this growing sense of inevitability about our being together. I wasn't really surprised when it turned out that I had to get a ride home from Andrew. It felt like we were being thrown together by fate. But I just wanted to dig in my heels and say to God, 'Hey, don't push!'"

"Still," Andrew added, "it wasn't until our third date that I really knew that the voice had had the right idea. Up until then Ann always wore dark colors. She was very depressed and didn't seem at all attractive physically. On our third date she appeared dressed in bright yellow, and she was an *absolute vision of loveliness!* And I think I even said out loud, 'Oh, I guess the voice was right.' That's when I told her about what the voice had said."

"Things between us developed really quickly after that," Andrew continued. "It was a few weeks before Ann told me about the baby, but Dr. Santini had already spilled the beans about her by then."

"Yes!" Ann exclaimed. "When I finally got up my nerve to tell Andrew I'd recently had a baby and given her up, it turned out he already knew! And the first thing he said was, 'I want that baby!' It was just unbelievable. Here, I'd been so afraid to let him know about my past, and it turned out that he not only already knew, but he didn't mind! I couldn't believe it when he said that he wanted to marry me and adopt my baby!"

"She thought it was too late to get the baby back," Andrew broke in eagerly, "but I knew from Dr. Santini that it wasn't. He'd told me that the baby was still in foster care, and hadn't yet been released for adoption. And he also told me why.

"You see, Dr. Santini had intentionally messed up the paperwork for the adoption on his end so that it couldn't go through as planned. He knew it would take the agency in charge months to figure out what was wrong, and that when they did, they'd have to go back to Ann to get her to sign new papers. Santini told me that Ann would shortly have to make the decision to give up her daughter all over again. Except that now I was there to look after them both, and there was really no longer any question of her letting little Alice go!"

Although they had only met for the first time in December, by January Andrew and Ann had decided to reclaim Alice and marry as soon as her divorce could be finalized. "The day we went and got Alice back was probably the greatest moment of my life!" Ann told me with tears in her eyes. "When her foster mother handed her over to me in that same white blanket I'd made for her, it was like a miracle. I guess it *was* a miracle. I felt that all my prayers had been answered!"

Ann took Alice and headed for Reno, Nevada, to establish residency and obtain a quick divorce. Even then, despite the violence she had endured at her husband's hands, Ann wondered whether she was doing the right thing ending her marriage this way. As she showered on the morning of the day she was to sign her final divorce decree, Ann prayed for guidance, asking God if she should turn back before it was too late. In response, she heard a voice in her head say, "You go forward with this." She did. Ann and Andrew were married in Reno the following day.

Thirty-odd years later, Andrew and Ann continue to rejoice in their relationship. Despite the inevitable ups and downs of married life, they seem as happy together as any couple I've met. They've raised two children of their own in addition to Ann's little girl, and their work on behalf of world peace takes them all over the globe. Ann's life today appears to offer sufficient challenge that she does not miss the sick excitement of trying to cope with a hostile, abusive husband!

Ann may have felt that she was being rushed into a relationship with Andrew, but she really had no time to waste chasing a succession of fascinating Mr. Wrongs before settling down with Mr. Right. Her guide knew something her ego didn't—that if she moved quickly, she could still get her daughter back. Her companion spirit also knew that the partner her ego rejected as "dull" was the soulmate who would bring her a lifetime of joy, adventure, and fulfillment.

If you have any connection to the practice of psychotherapy, you are probably as stunned as I was to hear of Dr. Santini's high-handed tactics. He seems to have been following his own inner guidance, and everything certainly worked out for the best in the end, but ethically, he had an obligation to conceal the identity of his patient, keep her disclosures to him confidential, and expedite the paperwork for Alice's adoption. As a psychologist, I find it disturbing to think that some divine plan for the happiness of Andrew, Ann, and Alice, might have hinged upon the willingness of a psychotherapist to violate the ethical code of his profession. Yet if Dr. Santini had not intervened as he did, how else could this happy ending have been achieved? I was delighted to discover an answer to this troubling question in a book by Brian Weiss, M.D., where he describes his own role in uniting two soulmates who were patients of his.

As background, I should tell you that Dr. Weiss is, among other things, a past-life therapist. He became interested in this unusual approach to healing when he was chairing the Psychiatry Department at Mount Sinai Hospital in Miami, Florida, and a series of extraordinary hypnotic regressions he did with a patient led him to the conclusion that past lives are real. Since then he has regressed thousands of people to what appear to be prior existences, and has come to believe that this type of therapy can be very valuable in healing emotional and psychosomatic disorders that do not respond to more traditional techniques.

The theory behind past-life regression therapy is that we are eternal beings that incarnate over and over again in order to learn the lessons in love that will allow us to evolve spiritually. This means that it is possible to encounter in this life, individuals we have known and loved in prior existences. In the view of Weiss and many others, our soulmates are beloved former associates with whom we've incarnated again on purpose. For example, the immediate sense of recognition Ann felt upon meeting Andrew, and their instant familiarity and comfort in each other's presence, could well have been the result of past-life associations and a shared intention to be together again.

Pedro and Elizabeth

In his fascinating book *Only Love Is Real,* Brian Weiss tells the story of soulmates Pedro and Elizabeth.* Pedro was a wealthy young man from a politically powerful family in Mexico. Elizabeth was a Miami businesswoman who had grown up on a farm in the Midwest. Both sought past-life therapy from Dr. Weiss at about the same time in connection with complicated grief reactions to the deaths of deeply loved family members. "Coincidentally," both were single, and both were troubled over their inability to find someone to love and marry.

After conducting numerous hypnotic regression sessions with each, Dr. Weiss began to notice certain intriguing correspondences between the past lives these two patients unearthed. In several cases, they appeared to be describing *exactly the same*

---

* From *Only Love Is Real* by Brian Weiss, copyright © 1996 by Brian L. Weiss, M.D., by permission of Warner Books Inc.

scenes from two different points of view! Weiss was shocked to realize that Elizabeth and Pedro had incarnated together repeatedly, and shared an abiding love for each other. Surely, he thought, there must be a reason these two had come to him for the past-life therapy that would uncover their soul connection.

Indeed, this psychiatrist found himself in much the same position as Dr. Santini. He knew of two lonely people who he felt were meant for each other. But despite his desire to bring them together, he had an ethical obligation not to interfere in any way. As Weiss puts it:

> I was severely constrained by the "laws" of psychiatry, if not the more subtle rules of karma. The strictest of the laws is that of privacy or confidentiality. If psychiatry were a religion, breaching a patient's confidentiality would be one of its cardinal sins.

Weiss agonized over this situation. He was convinced that Pedro and Elizabeth were soulmates and that if they could only meet, they would spark to each other. And since Pedro was soon to return home to Mexico for good, time was running out. Why, he wondered, would destiny have arranged this odd circumstance unless he was meant to play some role in bringing Pedro and Elizabeth together? But professional ethics made it impossible for him to introduce two patients, or discuss one with the other.

In the end, Dr. Weiss decided that there was one thing he *could* ethically do to promote the match. He scheduled Pedro's last two therapy sessions back-to-back with Elizabeth's. He knew that if Pedro was on time for his appointment, he and Elizabeth would at least see each other as she passed through the waiting room on her way out. As Weiss explains:

> During Elizabeth's session, I worried that Pedro might not come in for his appointment. Things happen — cars break down, emergencies arise, illnesses develop — and appointments are changed.

He appeared. I walked into the waiting room with Elizabeth.

They looked at each other, and their eyes lingered for longer than a moment. I could sense the sudden interest, the hint at worlds of possibilities lying under the surface. Or was this just wishful thinking on my part?

Elizabeth's mind quickly reasserted its customary mastery, telling her she needed to leave, cautioning her about appropriate behavior. She turned to the outside door and left the offices.

I nodded to Pedro, and we walked into my office.

"A very attractive woman," he commented, as he sat down heavily in the large leather chair.

"Yes," I answered eagerly. "She's a very interesting person, too."

"That's nice," he said wistfully. His attention had already begun to wander. He turned to the task of terminating our sessions and moving on to the next phase of his life. He had pushed the brief meeting with Elizabeth out of his mind.

The psychiatrist's high hopes for a real meeting between these two patients were similarly frustrated at Pedro's final session. Again their glances lingered on each other as she passed through the waiting room, but no one spoke, and Pedro made no further mention of her. Weiss had done all he could to bring these two soulmates together, and apparently, it had not been enough. But all was not lost. As Weiss put it:

Fortunately minds more creative than mine were expertly conspiring from lofty heights to arrange a meeting between Elizabeth and Pedro. The reunion was predestined. What happened afterward would be up to them.

A series of "coincidences" subsequently brought Pedro and Elizabeth together in an airline boarding area. They recognized each other from Weiss's waiting room, fell into conversation, and decided to arrange to sit together on their flight. The rest, as they say, is history!

Today, these two soulmates are happily married and living in Mexico, where Elizabeth cares for their young daughter, and Pedro has taken over his family business and become involved in politics. I'm sure they are as grateful to Dr. Weiss as Andrew, Ann, and Alice are to Dr. Santini. I am grateful too, for the knowledge that our guides will find a way to bring soulmates together, despite all the difficulties that lie in the way. In Weiss's reassuring words:

> Never worry about meeting soulmates. Such meetings are a matter of destiny. They will occur. After the meeting, the free will of both partners reigns. What decisions are made or not made are a matter of free will, of choice. The less awakened will make decisions based on the mind and all of its fears and prejudices. Unfortunately, this often leads to heartache. The more awakened the couple is, the more the likelihood of a decision based on love. When both partners are awakened, ecstasy is within their grasp.

GUIDELINES FOR ACTUALIZING A SOULMATE RELATIONSHIP

1. Don't be so sure you can tell someone's soulmate potential at a glance.
2. Take periodic vacations from your ego's thoughts, in order to contact your soul's feelings.
3. Relax! You'll meet your soulmate when the time is right for both of you.

10

Revising Your Romantic Plans

*If you both agree at a conscious level that the purpose
of your relationship is to create an opportunity, not an
obligation—an opportunity for growth, for full Self expression,
for lifting your lives to their highest potential,
for healing every false thought or small idea you ever had
about you, and for ultimate reunion with God
through the communion of your two souls—
if you take that vow instead of the vows you've been taking—
the relationship has begun on a very good note.*

—*Conversations with God,* Book 1

As enchanting as the whole idea of soulmate love undoubtedly is, the concept raises some perplexing questions. For one thing, how can people be destined to be together if both have free will? Helene, you'll recall, believed that she heard the voice of God say, "This is the husband I am giving you." But if Gideon was God's "gift" to Helene, where did that leave him? Didn't he have any choice in the matter? Then, too, if a relationship is "meant to be," *who* is it that means it to be? Fate? God? The angels? The souls of the two lovers?

When superhuman entities like *angels, fate,* and *the will of God* are invoked as the guiding force behind a love relationship, it is usually assumed that nothing could have prevented the two individuals from fulfilling their joint destiny. Many Jews, for example, believe that certain romances are *beshert*. This Hebrew word means *fated path,* and it suggests that soulmates couldn't deviate from the divine plan for their union if they tried. One or the other may delay, or try to resist, as Ann resisted loving Andrew, and Gideon, Helene. But their reluctance will eventually be overridden by some greater will—that of God, or the angels, or possibly some deeper and truer expression of their own individual wills. As Hollywood tough guys so eloquently put it in the films of the 1930s and 1940s, "Don't fight it, Baby! This thing is bigger than both of us! We've had this date right from the beginning!"

Nothing Is for Sure

Personally, I find the idea that the union of soulmates is inevitable unconvincing. The problem is this: How do we really know that people who are meant for each other *always* happily unite in the end? We "know" it from the fact that the couples we observe with soulmate relationships *have* happily united. But if two lovers don't elect to combine forces, we never imagine that they might have been soulmates who failed to fulfill their joint destiny. When things don't work out, we conclude that the two must not have had a date with destiny in the first place. Would Andrew and Ann be calling each other soulmates if they had parted in anger thirty years ago? Would we believe them if they did?

I don't think the mere fact that a relationship *doesn't* work out means that it *wasn't meant* to work out. Nor do I believe that there is any sort of higher power in the universe interested in dictating how we live our lives—not our guides, destiny, or the angels, and certainly not the Creator who gave us all free will. Free will means that *you* and *I* get to decide what kind of lives we will have, and to change our minds whenever it suits us. Unfortunately, it also means that the individual you planned to have as your life partner, may not, in the end, choose to be with you.

It Takes Two to Tango

It seems terribly unfair that one person's choices should be permitted to blight the happiness of another. Just how are you supposed to find personal fulfillment if your soulmate refuses to love you back—or has wandered off into the sunset with someone else before you even arrived on the scene? While it may be comforting to think that there is someone out there who is made just for you, the distressing corollary is that there may be only *one* such person.

Where does that leave you if your meant-to-be love dies, or marries someone else, or doesn't agree that you are the answer to his or her prayers? Are you supposed to settle for an inferior substitute—and in the process use up some other unfortunate soulmate's one-and-only? Or do you, like old Miss Havisham in *Great Expectations,* just mooch around your darkened mansion in rotting wedding garments until death puts a merciful end to your loneliness?

What this question comes down to is: Can there be more than one *perfect* partner for a given individual? Is there some sort of cosmic contingency plan for soulmates who keep their dates with destiny, only to discover that their intended didn't make it? Happily, I believe there is.

Second Chances

I am convinced that we can have soulmate relationships with a number of different people. The loss of one ideal partner doesn't mean that we cannot have the wonderful relationship our soul desires—it just means that we can't have it with *him* or *her.* For example, here's what my friend Carmen's guide replied when she asked if a man who interested her was her soulmate: "You want to know if Adam is 'The One.' I say he is a total possibility. But there are other men around who could join you on your path of holiness. You are nesting, and various holy friends who are, so to speak, at your level, will approach you. No matter who you choose, or who takes you as a partner, you both will be joyous in the same measure."

So while it may be great fun to reunite with a beloved former associate, don't forget that you have *many* beloved former associates. And if none of them happens to be available, you are quite capable of learning to love someone new. After all, every present friend was once a stranger.

I think the conviction that there is only one right partner for each of us is unnecessarily depressing and dangerous when a promising romance turns out badly. Folks who believe they've missed out on their sole chance for love in this life may regard suicide as their only remaining option. And I'm not just talking about consciously intended suicides where someone scrawls "Good-bye cruel world!" on a scrap of paper and downs a bottle of sleeping pills. I suspect that a great many people who have given up all hope of finding love unconsciously arrange to end their lives through accidents and illnesses.

Romantic disappointments will be a little easier to bear if you remain focused on the idea that your real objective is a particular *kind* of relationship, rather than a relationship with a particular *person*. What each of us truly wants is an intimate association in which we can safely let down our defenses and be ourselves. We want to feel accepted, valued, supported, appreciated, and understood. We want to know that we are of use to our partner, and to feel the delight he or she takes in our bond.

We're all looking for someone wonderful, but we do well to remember that who that someone will turn out to be is an unknown quantity in the equation of our happiness. Your soul and your guide know *who,* added to *you,* equals *fulfillment.* You only get into trouble when you fixate on a particular individual with whom you imagine bright possibilities, and refuse to accept the love and support you want from anyone else. Take Rob's experience for example.

Rob and Nicole

Rob, who describes himself as "a sort of Methodist Sufi," had been fervently praying for guidance about what he should do with his life. He felt that he found his answer at a Methodist religious conference where he heard a missionary couple talk about the miraculous work their church was doing in Brazil. Rob was so excited by their account that the very next day he went to his mother and announced that the following summer he was going to Brazil, "to see the Kingdom of God unfolding." He prayed daily that an opportunity to go would be provided, and was so focused upon the trip that when he encountered a friend in the church parking lot one evening, Rob's first words were "Hi! Do you want to go to Brazil with me?"

The friend gave Rob a strange look, and then asked if he was aware that their pastor was organizing a trip to Brazil. Volunteers were needed to build a church in Espiritu Santos, and three members of their own congregation would be sponsored. Needless to say, Rob lost no time in signing up.

Two life-changing experiences occurred for Rob in Brazil. One was that he fell in love with a fellow volunteer named Catherine. The other took place when Rob encountered some impoverished refugees from the drought-stricken northeast. This ragged band of squatters, consisting mostly of children, were being terrorized by a wealthy landowner's private militia. Let me continue the account in Rob's own words:

"One child in particular caught my attention. She looked to be maybe five, and had the distended belly that indicated malnourishment and parasites. She had a bacterial infection in her eye that just a drop of medicine would have cured, yet no doctor would dare treat this child or any other for fear of retribution from the landowner.

"As we stared deeply into each other's eyes, I heard clearly inside the following challenge: "What do you do now that you've confronted me in the flesh? When you help the least of these my children you are helping me. How will you live your life now that you've met me?"

Rob felt that Christ himself was inviting him to make the wretched children of the earth his special concern. He had asked for guidance about his calling, and here it unmistakably was. Rob continued his story as follows:

"I returned to the States with a new relationship developing with a woman I'd met on the team, the job that I'd always coveted was unexpectedly offered me at my firm, and in general, everything I'd previously wanted was waiting for me. However, as I sat at my new desk each morning with a smug look on my face I would remember the eyes of that nameless Brazilian child and the challenge presented me that day."

Catherine was of tremendous help to Rob in sorting out his priorities. With her support, he made the decision to leave his job and do a three-year stint overseas working for Habitat for Humanity International. When he returned, he and Catherine would marry, and he would enter a seminary.

Rob went off to Americus, Georgia, for Habitat training, eagerly looking forward to his first overseas assignment. As he informed his instructors, there were only two places in the world he *wouldn't* go—Zaire, because of the notorious bureaucracy, and the Philippines, because of all of the horror stories he'd heard about death squads and guerrilla activities. Nevertheless, he ended up posted in the Philippines.

"Now I thank God each day that I was given the chance to work in the Philippines. I found such a sense of community and love there that I am a much better person. I'm reminded of the scripture that says that whatever you may give up in following the cross will be returned a hundredfold. This was certainly so for me in the Philippines. I have more friends and family there than I'll ever have in the U.S."

While he served in the Philippines, Rob kept in close touch with Catherine through letters and occasional visits. They continued to plan for a life together, and Catherine's letters were full of designs she was considering for her wedding dress. Everything seemed perfect until, as Rob tells it, "One night I woke up with a great heaviness on my heart. I could not explain what was bothering me, so I started praying as I'd never prayed before. I prayed that if Catherine and I were not to marry, she might meet someone else who would be better for her. I then prayed that if my time in the Philippines was up, the door would shut and I'd be moved to another assignment. I then felt at peace and went back to sleep."

Within a few weeks Rob received a "Dear John" letter from Catherine. She had indeed met someone else. Shortly thereafter, the Philippine government issued an arrest and deportation order for him. Rob was ejected from the country and banned from re-entry for a year. After serving out the remainder of his three-year commitment to Habitat International in Armenia, Rob found himself back in his old job in Alabama, more confused and discouraged than he had ever been in his life.

"My mother refers to this period as my 'year in hell,' since I was certainly out of purpose. One night in February of 1992 I prayed for guidance about vocation and clearly heard the words, 'Help others have the same experience that you had in Brazil.'"

An opportunity to coordinate Habitat's short-term volunteer program—then known as Global Village Work Camps—was soon offered to, and accepted by, Rob. While taking a group of volunteers to build housing for poor people in Peru, he met Nicole.

Rob and Nicole agree that there was some low-level attraction between them right from the start, but both were emotionally reeling in the wake of failed relationships and neither was "looking." For his part, Rob says that he was struggling to come to grips with the distressing possibility that he might *never* find the soulmate for whom he longed. Maybe it was not just an accident that all of his relationships with women kept falling through. Perhaps God intended him to be celibate!

The Habitat team was working in Urubamba, near Machu Picchu, one Sunday when altitude sickness forced both Rob and

Nicole to stay behind at the hostel. As Rob put it, "We were sitting by a river reading from the book of Isaiah when I heard in my heart that Nicole was to be my wife."

Stunned and confused, Rob kept quiet about this inner communication. But he was forced to own up to it later that day when Nicole came over and asked him point blank if he'd heard from God during the morning. It seems that she had been told the same thing he had!

By the end of the trip, both Rob and Nicole had happily accepted the idea that they were to be husband and wife. After a year-long engagement, they married, and went off to work for Habitat for Humanity in Bolivia, where inadequate housing is one of the major causes of infant mortality and illness. The two have since returned to the United States and taken up positions with a Christian nonprofit organization called Little Children of the World, Inc.

I asked Rob how it had felt to be with Nicole once their guidance had made it clear that they were meant for each other.

"Once we were out of the fishbowl atmosphere of Peru," Rob replied, "it was completely natural. I remember the first time I visited Nicole in Chicago. I was engulfed in a tremendous sense of peace that I hadn't felt in years. I think the reason it was so easy was that we both felt, and continue to feel, that God brought us together. Also, at critical times we would receive confirmation when it was most needed.

"Yes, we are both still convinced that we are on the right path and have found purpose for our life together. One key to our happiness has been daily prayer together. There have been bumps in the road, but I think that is natural. We're both still learning the culture and language of marriage."

I also asked Rob whether he felt he would have been equally happy if his relationship with Catherine had worked out. He answered, "Before meeting Nicole I often wondered if I would have been happy if Catherine and I had stayed together. But the one constant in my life has been my desire to work internationally, and I now realize that while Catherine may have had the desire, she did not have the constitution for this work. She was constantly ill, and therefore unhappy, in Brazil and the Philippines. So I think that ultimately we would not have been happy together, and that it was providential that we broke up when we did."

I see no reason to doubt that Rob's relationship with Catherine was "meant to be," and of tremendous benefit to both. But at some point, things changed. Perhaps it was simply time for these provisional soulmates to move on to new partners better suited to the next phases of their lives. As long as working overseas was just a three-year interruption to his life in the United States, Catherine may have been perfect for Rob. When helping disadvantaged children in foreign lands became his life's work, he needed a new soulmate who was ready, willing, and able to embrace the kind of life he now had in mind.

As we grow and change, what we require from our relationships changes too. I suspect that many of us plan to be with different soulmates at different stages of our lives. The individual who is perfect as our high school sweetheart may not be equally well-suited to our needs in middle age. The lover you missed out on at twenty-five might have needed to be replaced at thirty-five in any case.

But the fact that a relationship is not *forever* should not lead us to minimize its value. As with any course of study, certain lessons in love must be mastered before others can be attempted. The individual who teaches us to read will not be the one who conducts our high school class in creative writing. Nevertheless, if our elementary education had not instilled basic skills, self-confidence, and a love of literature, we would not be adequately prepared to appreciate and succeed in the more advanced course.

GUIDELINES FOR ACTUALIZING A SOULMATE RELATIONSHIP

1. Be flexible. If a relationship doesn't work out as you had hoped and expected, trust your guide to find you someone else.

2. Focus on finding a partner who wants to share the kind of life you want, rather than adjusting your desires in order to be with some particular person your ego thinks would be perfect for you.

3. Don't assume that just because someone is your soulmate, the two of you are destined to marry and remain together forever.

11

You Are the Pearl

Love does not consist in gazing at each other
but in looking together in the same direction.
—Antoine de Saint-Exupéry

If there are actually a number of potential soulmates out there for each of us, where did we all get the idea that we have but a single "one-and-only"? I suspect that this popular misconception comes from confusion between the concept of *soulmates* and that of *twin flames* (also known as *twin souls*).

An ancient Hebrew tradition holds that each soul divides into a male and a female aspect when it first takes on physical form. These separated half souls then incarnate repeatedly, learning lessons in love during each sojourn on earth. The process is said to continue throughout many lifetimes until—having gained sufficient knowledge and experience—the divided soul prepares to reunite with its Creator. Only then do the separated male and female halves joyously rediscover each other, and link up for a final marriage of transcendent joy and mutual accord. Upon their physical deaths, the twins are said to triumphantly merge back into a single, complete being.

At first glance, the twin-flame concept is very appealing. After all, it holds out the hope that each of us will someday (although not necessarily in our present lifetime) find a romantic partner with whom we'll be able to enjoy uninterrupted bliss.

Surely our "other half" will cherish us above all others and understand us in a way no one else possibly could. No more arguments. No need to compromise. No fear of rejection.

Nevertheless, I have a number of reservations about this concept. For one thing, I don't care for the implication that the best relationships necessarily involve a male and a female. I've seen quite a few gay and lesbian couples whose unions seem every bit as loving, mutually supportive, and meant-to-be as the best heterosexual marriages.

Michael and Dick

Dick was a school teacher and Michael, a production assistant on a television show, when the two were introduced at a dinner party in New York. Both say they knew that very first evening that they'd found their life partner. Not three months later, they went down to the bank together and opened a joint account so that they could begin saving for the beautiful home they planned to share someday.

Today these two have a lovely house in West Hollywood, where they are active in the gay community. Like any relationship, theirs has had its ups and downs—Michael jokes that the only thing worse than living with Dick is *not* living with him. Nevertheless, their conviction that they were meant for each other hasn't wavered in the thirty-odd years they've been together. Dick loves his teaching work at an inner city school, Michael loves his bicoastal job in film production, and both continue to love each other.

I've known these two for some fifteen years, and if there is a happier, more united couple in Los Angeles, I'd like to meet them. I certainly don't know any other pair of lovers who can honestly claim that they were together for ten years before they had their first argument!

As gay men, Michael and Dick can't qualify as twin flames, but there's no doubt in my mind that they are soulmates. Of course, proponents of the twin-flame scenario could say that in some future life, both of these men are destined for heterosexual marriages that will be even more harmonious than their present relationship. I suspect that this is only wishful thinking.

After all, if your ego was going to come up with a fantasy of perfect love, isn't the twin-flame scenario exactly the fantasy it would create? Your false self is fundamentally incapable of caring about anyone but itself in any case. What could be better, from its point of view, than a romantic partner who would—in some mysterious, semimystical way—*be* itself? Whatever else can be said about it, the twin-flame notion is certainly a narcissist's dream come true!

Then, too, if you wanted to keep someone seeking, but not finding, love, it would be hard to beat the strategy of sending this person off in search of an ideally compatible "other half" who didn't exist. I'm afraid that the twin-flame concept encourages us to hold out for a kind of idyllic, trouble-free union that is neither possible nor desirable. If you go through life rejecting everyone who confronts, frustrates, and challenges you, you may miss out on many—and perhaps all—of your opportunities for true love.

Twin Flames Versus Soulmates

Do effortless, perpetually harmonious twin-flame alliances really occur? How would *I* know?! If such relationships do exist, they are—by definition—the exclusive domain of a few fully enlightened beings. I personally have very little idea what the lives and relationships of such people would be like.

Further, it seems to me that unless *you* happen to be fully enlightened yourself, it isn't something you need to be worrying about at this stage of the game. For all we know, there may really be a blissfully harmonious heterosexual marriage awaiting each of us at the end of our path of spiritual evolution. If there is, that's fine! But let's not waste any of our precious opportunities for soulmate love in the meantime.

It's important not to confuse twin-flame unions with the soulmate alliances we're considering in this book. Soulmate relationships *always* require us to wrestle with differences. Indeed, teaching us to deal with the anger and frustration our ego generates whenever our interests seem to conflict with those of our partner is, in some sense, their very *raison d'être.*

You see, the ability to love another unconditionally is a *learning objective* of soulmate relationships, not a talent with which people enter them. Our meant-to-be loves are our learning partners in a curriculum designed to awaken us from fearful illusions. As such, it is their job to hold our feet to the fire whenever our false self prompts us to act from fear rather than love.

Far from being blissfully harmonious, soulmate unions can be intensely conflictual. This sort of domestic strife resembles the prying open of an oyster to reveal the priceless pearl within. Ego-mates do little more than bang up against the shells of illusion our false self constructs to insulate us against love. But our soulmates have knives that are very sharp indeed, and if we hold still long enough, they will find just the right places to insert them, and pry our defenses apart. From the point of view of the oyster, this process is agonizing and, eventually, fatal. To the pearl, it is a tale of liberation and triumph. When you start feeling as if your soulmate is tearing you apart, it may help to remember that you are the pearl and not the oyster!

Far from being perfect lovers, soulmates generally start out dividing their allegiance between their partners and their own egos. Sometimes they are generous, tender, and supportive, but periodically they succumb to panic and try to withdraw from, or control, the relationship. In successful pairings, however, trust gradually comes to take the place of fear. Episodes of ego possession become less frequent, and don't last as long. The lovers eventually come to see separation from their mate as the *problem,* and not the *solution.*

If soulmates stay the course, they ultimately discover that love is safe, and that their egos' tantrums over not getting to control everything aren't *their* problem. They transfer their loyalty to their partners, and abandon their self-images to their fates. It is only then that these "matches made in heaven" begin looking the way most of us intuitively expect them to—joyous, mutually supportive, and harmonious. But never forget that on the way to that happy state of affairs, a river of frustrated tears may be shed, and a great many doors slammed in anger!

Good Relationships Are Not Found, But Made

The twin-flame concept implies that true love will be a done deal once we find our "other half." All we have to do is connect with Mr. or Ms. Right, and our romantic troubles will be over. However, as a psychotherapist, I'm convinced that good relationships are not found, but made. What we can reasonably hope to *find*—assuming we allow our soul or our guide to direct our search—is a willing partner who functions at a similar level of consciousness, genuinely wants to create a committed love relationship with us, shares our purpose in living, and has the unique qualities necessary to complement our own.

But whether the resulting relationship fulfills its promise depends upon what both decide to do. As my guide told me when I asked whether Arnie and I were right for each other: "You get along well, you are dedicated to a common purpose, and you both want someone to love, and be loved by. Why not decide to be that for each other? . . . Whether or not it works out would depend upon what you both do. You could be good partners for each other if you decide to be."

The thing that distinguishes soulmates from couples who wind up feeling more like cell mates is not perfect mutual understanding and agreement, but their willingness to go on loving in the face of periodic disappointment and misunderstanding. For example, I once saw Ruth Graham, the wife of the Reverend Billy Graham, being confronted by the host of a TV show about what he took to be her sanitized account of an ideally loving marriage to the famous evangelist.

"Come on, now," the interviewer prodded skeptically, "are you really going to try to tell us that you've been married all these years and you've never *once* thought about divorce?!"

"I really never considered divorce," Mrs. Graham replied with perfect composure. "Murder, yes! Divorce, no."

Now if even that nice Billy Graham could inspire the odd homicidal impulse in an otherwise devoted wife, how likely is it that any of the rest of us are going to enjoy the effortless domestic bliss said to characterize twin-flame alliances? The fact is, as long as we have an ego, we'll need a life companion who'll get in our face whenever we give way to egotistical behavior.

Soulmate unions exist for the benefit of those of us who don't yet know how to love without conditions but want to learn. The fact that these alliances of all-too-imperfect human beings are never free of disagreement and conflict doesn't mean they can, or should, be bypassed in favor of some hypothetical twin-flame union that purports to be more ideal. If you've been holding out for a fairy-tale perfect romance, it's time to get your head out of the clouds before life passes you by.

How Soulmates Deal with Anger

The prevalence of conflict in soulmate alliances may make you wonder whether they are really any improvement over the kinds of relationships our ego sponsors. But the consequences of anger are a function of the way it is handled, and it is handled very differently depending upon whether our true self or our false self is in charge of the process. In one case anger stimulates growth, and in the other, it acts as a slow poison.

The ego's first line of defense against anger is to push it out of awareness. By dissociating everything that interferes with its romantic fantasies, our false self is able to idealize a chosen partner, and generate infatuation. Unfortunately, disowned resentments continually fester in the unconscious mind, and eventually grow to the point where they can no longer be ignored. Without warning, righteous indignation explodes into awareness, obliterating everything in its path. The lover who once could do no wrong now can do no right.

But while anger is a time bomb waiting to blow the ego's relationships to kingdom come, it poses no real threat to the happiness of soulmates—just as long as they stick to the strategy of quickly deactivating it through forgiveness. Best-selling author Dr. Wayne Dyer aptly compares anger to the bite of a snake, and resentment to the venom a poisonous viper injects. He points out that no one dies of the snake bite itself, which creates only minor puncture wounds that would quickly heal. What people die of is the venom—unless, of course, they are able to quickly block its destructive action with an injection of antivenom. In human relationships, anger is the bite, resentment is the venom, and forgiveness is the antivenom.

True and False Forgiveness

Given the vital role of forgiveness in sustaining love relationships, it should come as no surprise that the ego encourages us to avoid it. In the opinion of our false self, a forgiving attitude betrays weakness. If you insist upon forgiving despite your ego's dire warnings, it proposes that you use instead its specially formulated forgiveness substitute—a concoction of condescension and moral superiority from which all of the relationship healing properties of true forgiveness have been carefully removed.

True forgiveness eliminates all of the conditions we've been placing on our love. It amounts to a decision to go on caring for the other person—*no matter what*. In the alchemy of love, true forgiveness is the philosopher's stone that transmutes the base metal of conditional love into the gold of unconditional love.

Your ego contends that this constitutes an open invitation to others to walk all over you. To understand why this isn't so, you need to be clear about the fact that unconditional love is due to *beings,* not to their *actions.* Forgiving others doesn't mean that you condone their behavior. It doesn't even mean you are prepared to let them continue behaving that way. It just means that you've chosen to regard their behavior as *a mistake* that calls for *correction,* rather than as *a sin* that calls for *punishment.*

True forgiveness rests upon the realization that hurtful people are frightened and misguided rather than evil, and that everyone is entitled to love, no matter how badly they behave. It says to another, "Your true worth is beyond question, even if I don't understand or approve of what you do. I may decide not to hang around you if you continue behaving like this. Indeed, I may argue with you, divorce you, fire you, fine you, sue you, or even put you in jail, if there are no better ways to prevent you from hurting me or others. But I will respect you and wish you well, regardless, hoping for a day when we can reach a better understanding."

The Transformational Power of Forgiveness

No one who is prepared to forgive needs a twin flame in order to sustain a deeply meaningful intimate relationship. No one who is unprepared to forgive is *capable* of sustaining a deeply meaningful intimate relationship. Indeed, an attitude of true forgiveness is necessary before we can even see who our partner really is. Until we discard the role of judge, it simply isn't safe for others to step out from behind their defenses and be themselves in our presence.

Of course, if we were idealizing our partner to begin with, the more realistic view of them that follows on the heels of forgiveness may well be disappointing. For instance, when I forgave Brent for not living up to my ego's expectations, I had to face the fact that he was never going to be the kind of partner I needed.

But surprisingly often, it turns out that the problems in our relationships are caused not by true incompatibility, but by the insecurity our own judgmental attitude has been generating. In cases where we've been threatening to revoke our love at the first sign of trouble, true forgiveness can make apparently "irreconcilable differences" disappear right before our very eyes. When I decided to love Arnie without conditions, I discovered that he was my soulmate!

Lest you think I am overstating the miraculous power of forgiveness to heal troubled relationships, I'd like to illustrate this point with an experience I once had with a dog. I think you'll agree that my decision to forgive Kobi made all the difference.

Kobi and Me

Kobi was an Irish Setter puppy who belonged to my roommate Helga, and he was a holy terror. From the day he moved in, he began destroying everything he could get his paws and jaws on, every time he was left alone in the apartment. We'd come home after a day's work to find curtains ripped off windows; potted plants lying smashed on the floor, furniture gutted; and books and items of clothing chewed almost beyond recognition.

Helga, of course, felt terrible about inflicting this hellhound on me, but she loved the puppy to distraction, and couldn't bear to give him away. Being an animal lover myself, I couldn't help but sympathize. Anyway, we comforted ourselves, the problem was only temporary. It would stop as soon as she was able to train Kobi not to do these terrible things.

Helga assembled an impressive array of books on dog training, each of which guaranteed a well-behaved pet if one would only follow its recommended procedure religiously. No one could have been more conscientious than Helga, yet one technique after another failed. Kobi simply developed still-more ingenious techniques for opening doors, getting into sealed garbage cans, and detaching breakable items from high shelves.

YOU ARE THE PEARL

When Helga had to leave town for a week, I was left to carry on alone. The current technique hinged upon whipping the dog lightly with his leash for five minutes—no more, no less—in the presence of the mess he had made. The strokes were to be only symbolic taps. It was the duration of the punishment that was supposed to do the trick. I faithfully promised Helga to carry on in her absence.

I came in from a party late in the evening of the day she left, and there was that demon dog standing defiantly amid the wreckage as usual. My pleasant mood evaporated instantly. Dutifully I got out the leash, informed Kobi that he was a "bad dog," and sat down on the floor to begin the whipping. Kobi just lay there beside me, submitting to this indignity with a sigh of resignation.

All I can tell you is that at some point in the five-minute process, I was simply overcome with shame and self-disgust. There was no getting around the fact that I had never liked Kobi—there wasn't much to like as far as I could see. The quality of my life had deteriorated precipitously since he'd moved in. Still, it was pretty pathetic carrying a grudge against an animal. And now here I was whipping a dog who was obviously too stupid to learn to behave better.

Now, I knew I wasn't hurting Kobi physically, but the whole thing just seemed so degrading! Ever since Kobi had come into our lives, he'd been doing mean things to us and we'd been doing mean things to him. He was still little more than a puppy, yet his life had become variations on the themes of rejection and punishment!

And then it occurred to me that Kobi wasn't going to change. It was time to face the fact that this was who Kobi was, and that as long as he lived in our apartment, this was what we could expect. Since I knew that Helga could not bear to give him up, and since I wanted to continue having her as a roommate, I was going to have to live with the problem too. So far as all of that was concerned, there was nothing I *could* do that I was *willing* to do.

But there *was* one thing I could change, I realized. I could change my attitude. I looked down at this miserable sinner of a dog, and felt my heart open to him. Poor jerk—too stupid to learn not to chew things up—too stupid to avoid these tiresome punishments that punished Helga and me as much as they did him! I actually found myself weeping with compassion for this pathetic canine moron. I was unutterably ashamed of myself for having added to his misery.

I threw aside the leash and dragged Kobi's huge bony head into my lap, sobbing out an apology I knew very well he couldn't understand. "Kobi, I am so ashamed of the way I've treated you. You can't help being the way you are, and if Helga and I aren't going to give you away, we're just going to have to accept you. Please forgive me for hitting you, and yelling at you, and hating you. I promise I'll never do it again!"

By now the dog was alert, gazing into my eyes with real interest. "From now on, Kobi," I continued "you just do any damn thing you want and I'll deal with it. Tear the place up if you have to! I'm through trying to change you. I'm just going to try to learn to like you. And I'll see if I can get Helga to give up on all this dog training stuff, too. We can't make you do anything you don't want to do when we aren't here to control you. Not without hurting you a lot more than we'd be willing to do. So let's just be friends, okay?"

Kobi panted up at me with that wide, clueless Irish Setter grin and I had to duck out of the way of a wet kiss. Following this exchange of civilities, I tidied up the mess—complimenting Kobi on the extremely thorough job he'd done on the wastebaskets—and took him out for a late run. In the morning when it was time for me to leave for work, Kobi walked me to the door as usual. "Okay, kiddo!" I said, giving him an affectionate ear ruffle. "Have at it! You might want to start with the sofa today. I think there might still be a little stuffing left in that middle cushion. See you later."

When I climbed the stairs that evening it was with a sense of relief that I no longer had to upset myself about the mess Kobi would have made in my absence. But my front door opened on a very unfamiliar scene. There was Kobi standing in the middle of a perfectly clean, intact room. His head was up, and his tail was wagging. He looked me proudly in the eye and grinned. I burst into tears.

This "dog from hell," whose intelligence I had so often maligned, had responded to my friendly overture with one of his own. I suddenly realized that he had understood me very well the night before. His destructive behavior had been his way of paying Helga and me back for withholding our love. We withheld love as a punishment to get him to stop destroying our stuff, and he punished us for withholding it by destroying even more of our stuff. The problem wasn't that Kobi was too stupid to understand what we wanted. He had always known exactly what we wanted him to do—he just wasn't going to do it until we gave him what *he* wanted! Unconditional love.

I am happy to report that in the rest of the time Helga and I shared the apartment, Kobi was a model of canine decorum. It may seem strange that the change I had tried to extort from Kobi by force was given me as a gift once I decided to accept him without conditions. But then, isn't that always the way it works? Even animals know better than to settle for conditional love.

Sure, your soulmate is going to drive you crazy from time to time. That's what he or she is there for! Your job is to stand your ground and continue to love in the face of all the reasons your ego can manufacture to justify counterattack or withdrawal. Just keep flushing the resentment out of your system with forgiveness, so that whatever is wholesome in the relationship will have a chance to grow.

GUIDELINES FOR ACTUALIZING A SOULMATE RELATIONSHIP

1. Your problem may be less about your partner's apparent shortcomings than your refusal to forgive them.
2. Stop holding out for a relationship that is effortless. Intimate relationships are frequently hard work, even when the other person is a soulmate.
3. Remember that even good relationships contain bad patches.
4. It is only when we accept another "for better or for worse" that the "better" part begins to predominate.

12

What's Love
Got to Do with It?

*First, make sure you get into a relationship
for the right reasons. . . . I mean "right" relative
to the larger purpose you hold in your life.*
                    —Conversations with God

We've already seen that the thing that makes someone your soulmate isn't the fact that you are madly infatuated with her or him, but it may surprise you to learn that soulmates aren't selected on the basis of true love either. First of all, you must remember that the ability to love another unconditionally is a *learning objective* of soulmate relationships, not a prerequisite for entering them. As we have seen, these unions often begin as tentative alliances between two fearful people. Trust and mutual understanding may build slowly over a period of many years, and there are undoubtedly some soulmate couples who *never* (in this life) fully appreciate the gifts their partners have brought to them.

Then, too, expanding our capacity to love increases our ability to love *everyone*. There is no limit to the number of people you can cherish; yet, despite the heroic efforts of certain Hollywood celebrities to prove the contrary, you really can't *marry* everybody!

So the fact that you truly love someone is not a sufficient reason to embark upon a life partnership with him or her, and the fact that you aren't sure how much you care isn't always a good reason to duck a commitment. *The defining characteristic of soulmate relationships is shared purpose.* What makes someone your ideal mate is neither love nor infatuation, but rather the fact that being with him or her is in alignment with your soul's reasons for being here.

Perhaps you've already been struck by the way a number of the soulmate couples we've discussed evolved into highly efficient, two-person teams dedicated to performing a specific service for humanity. The fact is that meant-to-be lovers don't just mean to *be* together, they also mean to *do* something together. Their alliances are spiritual laboratories in which two people unite to jointly discover and create the meaning of their lives. Further, the love soulmates cultivate for each other is eventually destined to overflow the bounds of their relationship and nurture a thirsty world.

There are certain experiences each soul desires to have as part of its process of awakening, and we require partners who have as much to gain from those experiences as we do. Rob, for example, sees service to the world's disadvantaged children as the thing that will give meaning to his life. Thus, he needs a partner like Nicole, who shares not only his general desire to learn to love unconditionally, but also his specific intention to achieve it by living and working among the poor. The reality is that while we can love a lot of people, we can't persuade very many of them to relocate with us to an economically depressed area of the Third World.

Teamwork and the Value of Diversity

Understanding the importance of shared purpose in soulmate relationships helps us make sense of the unusual degree of diversity that seems to characterize these unions. Egos gravitate toward partners they take to be like themselves—individuals from similar backgrounds whose attitudes and interests are much the same as their own. But when our souls are in charge of the mating process, we frequently select partners who—superficially at least—are very different from us.

Just as it would make no sense to assemble a baseball team where everyone was a pitcher, and no one could bat, run, or catch, soulmate teams are typically composed of individuals with common objectives, but diverse areas of insight and expertise. If we are to fulfill our purpose in living, we need life companions capable of compensating for our weaknesses rather than simply duplicating our strengths. The result is that intellectuals often find themselves with partners who give more weight to intuition than to book learning, while idealists may wind up yoked to those with a relentlessly practical turn of mind. For example, in his book *Grace and Grit,* transpersonal theorist Ken Wilber contrasts himself and his soulmate Treya as follows:*

> I took feelings and related them to ideas; Treya took ideas and related them to feelings. I moved from the particular to the universal; Treya moved from the universal to the concrete. I loved thinking; she loved making. I loved culture, she loved nature. I shut the window so I could hear Bach; she turned off Bach so she could hear the birds.

I suspect that this need for complementarity is the reason soulmates frequently seem so *mismatched* from the ego's point of view—African-American and Pakistani, Jew and ex-Nazi, Mexican and Midwesterner, and so on. But while differences in background and outlook tend to swamp relationships in which egos compete with each other for specialness and control, they only strengthen soulmate unions based on a shared vision. In Ken and Treya's case, two highly self-sufficent people found themselves enjoying the unfamiliar luxury of a partner who supplied vital insights and resources they themselves lacked.

---

* From *Grace and Grit* by Ken Wilber, copyright © 1991. Reprinted by arrangement with Shambhala Publications, Inc., Boston.

A Meditation About Me and Arnie

The value of diversity was beautifully symbolized for me in the images of a meditation I had early in my relationship with my future husband, Arnie. At the time, I was wrestling with the question of how two such oddly assorted individuals could possibly be right for each other. Despite the fact that we were both psychologists and students of *A Course in Miracles,* we were very different kinds of people.

At the same time I had been a campus activist organizing opposition to the Vietnam War, Arnie had been directing research for the C.I.A. so covert that he couldn't acknowledge its very existence. While I was cutting sugarcane in Cuba, he was putting together corporations and taking them public. What on Earth was a formerly left-leaning, acid-dropping Yippie like me doing with a pillar of the military-industrial complex like Arnie? I demanded of my guide.

In meditation I watched as a woodland scene began to unfold before my mind's eye. I saw Arnie and me staggering exhausted into a forest clearing with a stream running through it. We approached this grassy open space from different directions, arriving at the same time and place as if by prearrangement. Both of us were toting identical, heavily laden backpacks which we wearily shrugged off the minute we arrived.

At first, the scene held no message for me. When I examined it more closely, however, I noticed that our backpacks were not really identical. They contained very different things.

My pack, I now saw, was completely filled with food. Arnie's was stuffed with camping equipment: A tent, canteen, flashlight, hatchet, bedroll, pots and pans, knives, matches, and so forth. I was being shown that we were fellow travelers who had met by prearrangement on our way to the same destination. While the things we brought to our relationship were completely different, each came equipped with exactly what the other needed. If we decided to travel together and pool our resources, we would both be well nourished, comfortable, and safe. If we chose to go our way alone, both would suffer needless deprivation.

Does this mean that "opposites attract"? Not really. It continues to be true that "birds of a feather flock together"; it's just a matter of what is seen as constituting commonality. Soulmates are highly similar to each other in that they function at the same level of consciousness, share a strong commitment to self-realization, and agree on the means by which they've chosen to pursue it in this life. But their backgrounds, and the skills they bring to the fulfillment of their shared mission, tend to vary. Maybe this complementarity, and not twin soulship, is the real reason why so many soulmate couples feel as if their partner is their "other half."

Our Gift to Others Is Often the Fruit of Our Own Suffering

Soulmate couples tend to have a shared mission, and that mission is often influenced by the nature of the problems each has had to overcome individually. Through confronting adversity, humans often develop extraordinary strength in the very areas where they once felt most wounded. Please understand that I am not touting the nobility of suffering. I'm just pointing out that every experience we have can be turned to good account when we approach it in the right spirit. Dealt with creatively, misfortune sculpts the soul and turns it into an instrument uniquely attuned to the special needs of those suffering in similar ways.

Thus, the missions soulmates unite to perform often evolve out of the hard lessons life has taught both of them as individuals. I believe that people become eligible for a soulmate relationship by virtue of first having taken their own growth and healing as far as they can on their own. Meant-to-be lovers then use their relationships to heal and grow still further, each one gaining personally through providing the encouragement, insight, and support the other requires to release fear and embrace a more expansive worldview. Yet no lesson in healing is complete until it has been shared. For that reason, soulmates generally make it their business to extend a helping hand to those a step behind. Take Connell and Gloria, for example.

Connell and Gloria

In his late twenties Connell began searching in earnest for his soulmate. A Protestant whose spiritual faith had long been the linchpin of his life, Connell wanted a wife who would share his devotion to God. Unfortunately, the small Virginia community in which he lived offered few opportunities to meet like-minded singles.

Undaunted, Connell approached the priest of the local Catholic Church and obtained his permission to begin an interdenominational Christian singles group. From the first, these meetings drew hordes of attractive young women. Connell quickly found himself hip deep in eligible females. As he puts it: "I thought I had died and gone to heaven when they elected me their group leader. There I was, a single male surrounded by women desiring me to be their leader! Still, none of the ladies interested me when we discussed spiritual matters. Things simply didn't seem to click."

Despite the lack of immediate results, Connell was not discouraged. The singles who attended the group were constantly giving him the names and numbers of prospective members to contact. It wasn't too long before he was handed a scrap of paper with Gloria's number on it.

Connell felt an instant connection from the moment Gloria picked up the telephone. That first conversation was far-ranging and went on for hours. Definitely interested, Connell invited Gloria to have dinner with him a few days later. As he put down the receiver, he was ecstatic. "Finally, someone I could relate to on a spiritual level!"

He was no less enthusiastic when the two met in person. "Carolyn, this woman was *the absolute personification of beauty!*" Connell raves today. Although he couldn't yet be sure that his delightful new acquaintance was really the partner who was meant for him, he fervently hoped she was. "I was saying to myself and to the heavens, 'God, let this be the one!'"

Notice that Connell had given up on the notion that he could decide for himself, at the level of his ego, which woman would be best for him. Gloria seemed to be everything he was looking for, and there was no lack of infatuation. But despite his enthusiasm, he was still prepared to invite guidance on the issue.

That guidance came in the form of a startling coincidence. Some weeks earlier Connell had extended his search for a soulmate to the personals column of a local newspaper. On his way to pick Gloria up for their second date, he stopped off at the post office to check for replies to the anonymous ad he had placed. There was a single letter waiting in his box, and as he read it, a chill went through him. It was from Gloria!

"She, of course, had no idea that she was writing to *me*," he explained. "And a large portion of the letter was speaking of this nice man who had recently called to invite her to become a member of a local singles group!"

The coincidence that had led Gloria to choose Connell's ad to answer, and the fact that she had been so impressed by him on the phone that she'd confided her enthusiasm to a complete stranger, convinced Connell that this was more than a physical attraction. He was so overjoyed that he had trouble keeping a straight face when he picked her up at her apartment a few minutes later.

"You certainly are acting funny!" Gloria remarked as they got into his car. With a devilish grin Connell leaned over and whispered in her ear, "I have a post office box!" Gloria was so startled by the realization that it must have been Connell's ad she'd answered that she leaped right back out of the car!

Fifteen years later, Connell and Gloria have no doubt about the fact that they were truly meant for each other. As Connell puts it, "Gloria is one with my soul. I owe my very life to her. Every fiber of my being is intermingled with her being . . . with her soul."

Nevertheless, as in the cases of other soulmate couples we've seen, the fact that these two know they were meant for each other has not resulted in a married life devoid of conflict and challenge. As Connell says: "We have shared many happy moments, but we have also shared our battles and disagreements. We have discovered that two people brought together by divine intervention may not always have days full of bliss and joy. God often uses the two to bring out the best in each other. To discard old negative patterns and behaviors is often very painful, but so richly rewarding afterward."

And like many other soulmate couples, it seems that Gloria and Connell also share a joint spiritual mission that is evolving out of their own personal concerns—in this case, concerns related to liberation from the effects of mental illness, social stigma, and limiting self-concepts. As Connell explains: "I was born in Stuart, Virginia, to the town drunkard and a mother who abandoned me for New York City the day after my birth. I lived with my grandmother until the age of three, when my mother returned with a military man who supposedly offered financial and emotional security. The financial security consisted of nickels and dimes—spare pocket change promised to a four-year-old in return for sexual favors. Whatever emotional security I experienced came only with the discovery and mastery of psychological dissociation.

"Broken promises and tortures that ranged from cigarette burns to immersion in scalding water eventually broke my personality into fragments. A bedroom closet became my refuge.

"When I grew old enough to escape, I spent several years simply drifting. Along the way, I had the good fortune to meet a number of compassionate fellow travelers who helped me regain sight of my destination. The most compassionate of these was my wife, Gloria, who held me in her arms during hundreds and hundreds of sleepless nights as I worked through the emotions of the past.

"With only limited help from society, but with a hope and faith in miracles, I ultimately overcame the torment of extreme childhood physical and sexual abuse, and reintegrated the multiple personalities I had created to deal with the trauma. I have wept in a solitary cell, while the professionals stood outside saying, 'There is no hope. . . . He is too far gone.' Yet after my graduate work at Duke and Vanderbilt led to a doctoral degree in Divinity, I climbed into the church pulpits to preach a message of hope and miracles to those same professionals."

Connell has recently entered a doctoral program in psychology and, inspired by their firsthand knowledge of the beauty that lies dormant in even the severely emotionally disabled, Connell and Gloria now work together to help other "hopeless cases" find their way back to productive roles within society.

"Gloria and I are in the process of creating the Michelangelo Project," Connell told me. "It's a nonprofit corporation designed to enter state and federal institutions (mental hospitals, nursing homes, prisons, and so on), to free those in oppressive mental states through counseling and education. The name of our organization comes from an incident in the life of the artist Michelangelo.

"According to tradition, on a morning stroll Michelangelo passed a builder's yard that contained several discarded pieces of marble. Inquiring of the owner as to why these stones had been cast aside, the artist was told that they contained major defects and thus were worthless. Michelangelo eagerly directed the mason to move all of the discarded stones to his studio. When the surprised builder asked why anyone would want these useless chunks of marble, Michelangelo is said to have replied, 'Because within each stone is trapped an angel, and I can set it free!'"

I have a feeling that, before they're done, Connell and Gloria are going to free a lot of angels too.

Guidelines for Actualizing a Soulmate Relationship

1. Decide what you want to accomplish in this life, and then look for someone who shares your enthusiasm; soulmate relationships have a joint purpose.
2. Don't imagine that you are meant to marry someone just because you truly love each other. Love is a necessary, but not a sufficient, condition for soulmates to unite.
3. No one is so damaged that healing is no longer a possibility.

13

What about Divorce?

Try not to confuse longevity with a job well done.
Remember, your job on the planet is not to see
how long you can stay in relationship,
it's to decide, and experience, Who You Really Are.
　　　　　　　　　　—Conversations with God

By now it should be clear that when we are identifying with our ego, romantic mistakes are not only *possible*, but practically *inevitable*. Convinced that the partner who fits our ego's specifications is someone *we* want to marry, we are all too likely to vow eternal devotion to a person who has little to offer us at the level of our soul. What are our guides doing while we are galloping off to the altar with Ms. or Mr. Wrong? If Sarah's experience is any indication, they are screaming the house down!

Sarah

"It's kind of embarrassing to admit," a publishing executive named Sarah told me ruefully, "but I married my first husband largely because I couldn't come up with a good reason *not* to.

"Ed and I were both Buddhists, and we'd been dating for two years, and living together for six months. We got along well enough, and although I didn't feel much passion for him, I figured that I probably just wasn't a very passionate person. So when Ed proposed, I said yes, and started planning the wedding. And when he suggested that we speed things up by racing off to Reno to have the civil ceremony performed immediately, I said yes to that too.

"But Carolyn, even as my mouth was saying yes, there was a voice in my head shouting *'No!'* so loud I was actually kind of surprised Ed didn't hear it himself! I now know that it was the voice of my guide and that I should have listened. But at the time it didn't make any sense to me, so I just blocked it out.

"I think I was dimly aware even then that I didn't really *want* to marry Ed, but it just seemed so irresponsible to refuse him without a good reason. After all, he was a nice guy. He didn't yell, or hit me, and he wasn't an alcoholic or a drug addict or anything. And if I was going to marry him in a religious ceremony in five months anyway, there just seemed to be no good reason not to marry him right away.

"Part of the problem was that while I had done a lot of spiritual work, I really hadn't done any psychological or recovery work," Sarah continued. "I knew the kind of person I wanted to be, but I couldn't acknowledge or accept the person I actually was. Besides, it was clear to me that I didn't want a volatile relationship like my parents had, and I thought the fact that Ed was kind of bland and unemotional meant that we'd be happy together.

"If my self-esteem had been higher, I'm sure I wouldn't have considered settling for this relationship. But at the time it seemed as if I ought to be grateful that *anybody* wanted me. So I married Ed, and when I woke up the morning after our wedding with no arrangements to fuss over, it finally hit me what I'd done. I've never felt such a sense of doom!

"I wound up divorcing Ed twenty months later. And he *was* a nice guy. Still is! I just didn't love him, although I didn't realize that until much later, when I learned what love actually felt like. Unfortunately, that didn't occur until after I'd made a *second* disastrous marriage—again in the face of clear guidance not to. And this time I married a guy who wasn't even nice!

"I met my second husband, Phil, through a personals ad, and from the minute we started talking on the phone, I thought he was really obnoxious. I didn't want to meet him, but he was so damned insistent about wanting to meet *me* that I finally gave in. I thought, 'What the hell! It can't hurt to just go have a drink with this guy!' Wrong!

"When we were arranging the meeting, I'd made some remark to the effect that he'd better be there with bells on. Well, as soon as I walked into the bar, there was this 6' 2" guy wearing bells around his neck, so I knew instantly that he must be the one I was there to meet. And my gut reaction on seeing him was, 'I am *terrified* of this guy!'

"Did you ever meet someone who just scared you to death? My intuition was operating just fine, and if I'd had any sense at all I'd have turned around and walked out then and there without identifying myself. But I was arrogant enough to think the fact that I had nothing but contempt for Phil would eliminate any possibility that I'd ever get involved with him. No such luck!"

"What changed your mind about him?" I asked.

"A couple of drinks!" Sarah replied with refreshing honesty. "I was drinking pretty heavily at that time. I belted back a couple and wound up going home with Phil that night. And somehow, I got hooked. I still didn't *like* him, but I *fell in love* with him. Soon I was hooked so bad I couldn't be without him. Shortly thereafter, much against my better judgment, I agreed to marry him.

"I was able to ignore the fear I felt of him throughout our engagement. I was so busy living in a fantasy of wedded bliss that I just zoned out on the fact that I was about to marry a guy who was capable of terrifying rages and endless demeaning remarks. A therapist friend of mine told me later that he was borderline — one of those people who love you one minute and want to kill you the next. Turns out ours was his *ninth* marriage. You'd think that would have been a clue, wouldn't you?

"My marriage to Phil lasted twenty months, just like my first, but this one was hell to get out of. Phil made the divorce just as difficult and expensive as he possibly could. He even tried to sue me for spousal support on the grounds that I'd taken away his 'will to work'!

"But there was one good thing about being with Phil—it got me into AA. He was a recovering alcoholic, and I used to go to meetings with him all the time. I'd be sitting there hearing these stories, and I'd suddenly find myself thinking, 'My God! That's me they're talking about!' I got clean and sober as a result, and that's made a tremendous difference in my life.

"Now I'm happily married to a wonderful man. I met John through the personals too, but my first reaction on seeing him was 'What a nice guy!' If I'd paid attention to the warnings my guide was trying to get through to me, I'm sure I could have avoided those first two marriages. Maybe there's an easy way and a hard way to get where you're going. I guess I just kept picking the hard way.

"I think there are a lot of people like me who have clear guidance not to pursue a relationship with someone, but go ahead and do it anyway. I can't get over the fact that I knew so clearly that I shouldn't marry either Ed or Phil! So be sure to tell your readers that not being able to get in touch with their guidance isn't the only problem they have to look out for. Sometimes your guidance is coming through loud and clear and you just go ahead and do something stupid anyway! For guidance to do you any good, you have to be willing both to *listen* to it, and then to *act* in your own best interest."

I suspect that a lot of sadder-but-wiser divorced people can relate to Sarah's story. Our ego can lead us into the most egregious errors while loftily dismissing the protests of our inner teacher on the grounds that they "make no sense." And indeed, guidance often does seem to make no sense—*at first*. That's because what is really going on in the situation bears no relationship to what our ego has been telling us about it.

Emotions Versus Feelings

Your soul has a response to everything you experience. But then so does your ego. For purposes of this discussion, I'm going to call the responses of your soul *feelings,* and those of your ego, *emotions.* I regard *feelings* as communications from our inner being that *give rise to* the realistic thoughts of our true self, and *emotions* as reactions that *follow from* the distorted thinking of our false self. Emotions are essentially knee-jerk reactions to the untrue things our ego is telling us about what is going on, whereas feelings represent our authentic response to the situation itself.

Although most people use the terms *emotions* and *feelings* interchangeably, psychotherapists have recognized a need to make some distinction between them. For example, there are therapies designed to help people "get in touch with their feelings." The underlying assumption is that feelings are honest, realistic, and informative, albeit somewhat elusive and hard to identify. Many mental health professionals would agree that our true feelings point us in the direction of our highest good.

There are other therapeutic approaches designed to deal with emotional reactions that have become so exaggerated and inappropriate as to be distressing and maladaptive. Cognitive therapists, for example, teach clients to control pathological emotional states like panic, anxiety, chronic anger, and depression, by helping them understand that these overblown reactions come from entertaining thoughts that are both frightening and irrational. Clients learn to identify the "stinking thinking" that leads to emotional upset, and to substitute more realistic ideation. By focusing on "the truth, the whole truth, and nothing but the truth," troubled individuals discover that they can reason their way back to a calmer and more balanced outlook.

So, while few psychologists would agree with my contention that feelings come from the soul and emotions from the ego — polls indicate that most psychologists don't believe people *have* souls — it is nevertheless widely accepted that (a) thoughts cause emotions, (b) persistent irrational thinking can lead to crippling emotional disturbances, and (c) the cure for this lies in a conscious effort to withdraw attention and belief from distressing possibilities that are not provably true. In addition, many of my colleagues would agree with me that (d) feelings help us identify the true personal significance of events, while (e) emotional reactions tend to cloud the issue and make it more difficult to figure out where our best interests really lie. So at the risk of oversimplifying a very complex subject, you won't go too far wrong if you think of your feelings as *revealing* the truth, and your emotions as *concealing* it.

Let Your Feelings Lead the Way

Feelings are the language of the soul, and as such, they are an invaluable asset in your search for a soulmate. You meet one person, and your heart soars. You think about being with another, and something inside you seems to darken and shrivel. How many times have you looked back upon some disappointing outcome and said, "I just *knew* this was going to happen! I had a bad feeling about this right from the start"?

When you meet someone who is not right for you, as Sarah did, your true self tries to warn you not to get involved. If you are in conscious contact with your true self, you'll calmly recognize that there are good reasons why you shouldn't attempt a relationship with this person. However, if you are identifying with an ego that has a very different take on the situation, it may attempt to persuade you that this individual is exactly what you've been looking for. It will do this by drowning out your negative feelings with strong positive emotions.

In this situation, your true self is broadcasting one message through your feelings, and your false self is broadcasting the opposite one via your emotions. The result is inner conflict, and this often leads to the sensation of visceral tension known as a "gut feeling." Gut feelings can range from vague uneasiness to outright disgust. Think, for example, of Sarah's revulsion when she first laid eyes on her second husband, Phil! These visceral tensions are a sure sign that our false self is trying to put one over on us.

However, even if we are unaware of any gut feelings, the presence of powerful positive or negative emotions—in and of themselves—should tip us off that our ego is trying to convince us of something that isn't true. The false self is like a high-pressure salesperson whose glib, persuasive patter is intended to ensure that we don't read the fine print before signing the contract. Whenever you find yourself in the grip of powerful emotions, it's a safe bet you're on the brink of making a bad decision. Don't commit yourself one way or the other until you've calmed yourself down by actively searching out the false, irrelevant, or exaggerated things your ego is telling you.

For example, when her fiancé, Ed, suggested they marry quickly, Sarah's ego generated a lot of complex emotions by telling her things like: "This is probably the best offer you're ever going to get." "You love this man—what else could it possibly mean that you get along with him and appreciate the fact that he doesn't abuse you?" "You're going to marry him sooner or later anyway, so it might as well be now." "Being married will prove that you are a worthwhile, lovable person." "Refusing him would be unconscionable." I'm sure Sarah could have found the flaws in these arguments if she'd put her mind to it, but the point is that she *didn't* put her mind to it. Instead, she allowed powerful ego-generated emotions to drown out her true feelings and the voice of her guide.

I find the circumstances of Sarah's second marriage particularly interesting since they demonstrate the ego's ingenuity at winning arguments without resorting to any sort of logic at all. Unable to marshal *any* plausible reasons for becoming involved with Phil, her ego simply persuaded her to drown her feelings in alcohol, and then maneuvered her into a position where escape was sure to be difficult.

Physiological research indicates that when females are caressed and stimulated sexually, their brains secrete a hormone called *oxytocin* that promotes emotional bonding. An infant nursing at the breast, for example, releases a flood of oxytocin in the mother, and this leaves her feeling fiercely devoted to her offspring. It is now known that something similar happens when women engage in sexual behavior, and this is probably why so many of us have enormous difficulty keeping "casual sex" casual. Sarah is not the first of her gender to wake up the morning after what was supposed to have been a one-night stand emotionally bonded to a guy who may not even have been all that good in bed. No wonder she felt "hooked"!

Divorce Among Soulmates

Clearly, neither of Sarah's first two marriages represented a soulmate match, and I expect that most readers will agree that she was sensible to divorce these men—inasmuch as she was certainly *not* behaving sensibly when she married them! But, it's one thing to say that a marriage entered into by our ego against the wishes of our true self may need to be dissolved, and quite another to suggest that true soulmates might appropriately divorce. If soulmates can't count on living happily ever after, who can?

But the fact is that even meant-to-be lovers sometimes *do* divorce. Indeed, I suspect that this is sometimes the logical consequence of the successful completion of their joint mission. Having accomplished whatever they came together to do, soulmates may find themselves with nothing more to contribute to each other, and appropriately decide to go their separate ways in search of new challenges. Just because a relationship is meant to *be* doesn't mean that it is meant to be *forever*. Unconditional love entails loyalty to the best interests of one's partner, and if it becomes necessary to release that partner to seek greater fulfillment elsewhere, this is what soulmates do.

This idea that no-fault divorce might be something more than a convenient legal fiction runs counter to the teachings of many religions. Christians, for example, often cite the fact that Jesus condemned divorce as the last word on the subject. However, I think it is important to remember that in the patriarchal Jewish culture of Jesus' time, marital dissolution inevitably inflicted great hardship on women. Where divorce deprives a wife of her children, leaving her disgraced with no respectable way to earn her living and no realistic prospect of remarriage, it is cruel indeed.

In our society, where the burdens of divorce no longer fall so disproportionately upon the shoulders of one sex, I don't believe that it is necessarily wrong to dissolve a marriage that has fulfilled its purpose. Although this will be a disturbing idea to some readers, I suspect that our soul and our guide don't just draw our soulmates to us, they also sometimes pull relationships apart so that we can seek further growth and fulfillment elsewhere. Even a soulmate marriage is not necessarily our final resting place. Consider the following case.

Marianna, Jim, and Robert

My friend Marianna and I had been talking about possible past-life associations in marriage, when she mentioned that she'd been told by a psychic that she'd known her first husband, Jim, in a previous existence. Supposedly, he had been a slave owner and she his slave. But my friend wasn't at all sure she believed in past lives, and she felt that even if they were real, the psychic had probably been wrong about this one.

"My relationship with Jim didn't have the slightest hint of a master-slave dynamic," Marianna told me. "In fact, it was very much the opposite. Jim deserves a lot of the credit for turning me into a liberated woman!

"I was raised in this very close, somewhat overprotective Jewish family in Beverly Hills where I was encouraged to think that one of the greatest successes I could hope for as a woman was to grow up and marry a nice Jewish doctor. And that's the way I thought about things until I met Jim. He was the undergraduate assistant for the section of a sociology course I was taking at UCLA. I was attracted to him immediately, and I knew within a few weeks that I would someday marry him.

"Jim didn't have a sexist bone in his body. He looked upon me as a complete equal and saw no reason why I shouldn't achieve anything I was willing to work for. I liked the idea of university life and I'd always thought it would be nice to marry a professor. Now for the first time I realized that I didn't have to *marry* a professor—I could *be* one.

"Jim and I married three years after we met, and it was a time when everyone was rethinking gender roles. With Jim's support I let go of a lot of outworn, sexist concepts that weren't really serving me. I'm not sure I'd be a university professor today if he hadn't encouraged me to be all I could be."

I suggested to Marianna that perhaps the unusually liberating effect her first husband had had upon her, actually constituted evidence that the psychic had been *right* about their past-life association.

"If in one life Jim enslaved you, perhaps he felt he owed it to you to come back into your present one and liberate you from whatever was still holding you back. It sounds like you two might have had some unfinished business together that was completed in this life by his encouraging you to reach for your dreams. In fact, maybe that was the main reason the two of you were together. Once you were off and running—thinking of yourself as the equal of anyone—maybe Jim's obligation to liberate you was complete, and both of you were ready to move on to other partners."

"Well, that's an interesting way to look at it," Marianna mused. "What the psychic said was that because Jim had enslaved me in a former life, this time I had to be the one to leave him. This time around I escaped my 'bondage' by divorcing him. But yes, he did help me grow to the point where I had the strength and self-respect to do that, so in a sense he did facilitate my liberation.

"I decided to divorce Jim because, despite accepting me as an equal, he was intensely critical of me as a person. He didn't totally appreciate me the way I was, and he was constantly after me to change and be better. In fact, maybe there was some hint of a master-slave relationship after all. I know that I was always a little afraid of Jim's temper.

"For instance, for the first few years after I married my second husband, Robert, I'd kind of cringe every time I screwed up—broke something around the house, forgot to mail the mortgage payment—things like that. I kept expecting Robert to get mad and yell at me the way Jim did. But Robert thinks I can do no wrong, and it would never occur to him to try to make me feel guilty over a silly mistake. I eventually realized that it wasn't normal for a wife to be so afraid of displeasing her husband.

"Even though leaving Jim was very hard for me, it was really the best thing I could have done. Because once I gave up on our marriage, I fell in love with Robert, and he is absolutely the love of my life! We've been together for eighteen years now, and I just never tire of being with him. Talk about a soulmate!

"From the first, Robert has always loved and accepted me unconditionally. The foolish man thinks I'm perfect just the way I am!" Marianna laughed. "I simply adore being adored, and since Robert adores adoring me, it all works out perfectly!

"Of course Robert and I have a very liberated relationship too. In fact, for several years we completely reversed the traditional gender roles. I supported the family while he stayed home and worked on his art. I brought home the bacon, and he did the cooking, the laundry, the bills, and all that stuff.

"Now we're both working and we try to share the household duties equitably. He still does most of the cooking, because he doesn't mind that job, and I do most of the cleaning because—well—my standards of neatness are a little higher than his.

"So maybe Jim and I parted right on schedule. Maybe we'd done what we needed to do together and were both ready for new partners. I certainly couldn't be happier about the way things turned out!"

I suspect that Jim and Marianna were meant to be together, but perhaps only long enough for her to decide not to put up with his oppressively critical attitude toward her. Jim encouraged her to recognize her abilities and options, and in so doing, set the stage for his own divorce.

We create our lives through our choices, and since we learn from every choice we make, there is a sense in which we never make a bad one. It is said that a young man once consulted the ancient Greek philosopher Socrates about whether he should marry. The sage, who was very unhappily married himself, replied that he should. "If you and your wife are compatible, you'll wind up having a wonderful life together," Socrates explained. "And if not, you'll become a philosopher!"

If we journey down one path, we'll encounter certain things we wouldn't have experienced walking on another, but every experience we have adds to our store of knowledge. Perhaps Sarah's first two romantic mistakes prepared her to choose better when it came to John, and Marianna seems to have needed Jim, if only so that she could eventually decide against putting up with a partner who didn't love her unconditionally.

Many of our relationships turn out to have been stepping-stones to better ones. Yet the mere fact that they are temporary need not be a cause for regret. While I believe that committed, monogamous relationships are the framework within which most of us will find our greatest fulfillment, I don't think these commitments necessarily are—or even *ought to* be—"until death do us part."

Some unions, like that of Marianna and Jim, seem to involve a certain planned obsolescence since their success eliminates the very needs they were designed to meet. A paternal older man, for example, may lovingly nurture a younger wife until she gains more self-confidence. To the degree that he is successful, however, she may eventually mature to the point where she craves a more equal relationship, or one in which she gets to play the role of mentor. Some marriages end because they are not working, while others end because they have worked so very well.

Partners sometimes have to revise their plan to travel through life together if significant disagreement arises about the direction they wish to take, but the duration of layovers can be a source of conflict as well. All of us occasionally need to pause for rest and recuperation before turning to face the challenges waiting around the next bend. Indeed, many people's lives seem to alternate between frantic attempts to cope with rapid change, and periods of relative tranquillity where life may even seem a bit humdrum. Exhausted, and sometimes even traumatized by the stresses we've been through, some of us cling to the predictability of a stable phase long after our partners are eager for new adventures. Take the case of Hiro and Judy.

Hiro and Judy

Hiro, an Asian-American dermatologist, made an appointment to see me at the request of his wife, Judy. He explained that the two of them had been happily married for sixteen years, but that she was now considering divorce. Not that she had ceased to love him, he added. It was just that, over the years, their interests had moved in different directions, and she was beginning to think they might be happier apart.

Judy was a therapist, and like me, she was fascinated with the whole transpersonal movement in psychology. She devoured books and lectures on metaphysics, channeling, and past-life therapy, and her idea of a good time was attending conferences where she and Hiro would meditate, learn yoga, or study mind-body relationships.

But consciousness studies left Hiro cold. He explained that his only real enthusiasm outside of his medical practice was golf. Hiro's concept of a great vacation was to visit an exotic resort where he and Judy could relax in romantic surroundings, golf, swim, and dine in elegant restaurants. Yet now that they could finally afford many of the finer things in life, he ruefully confided, all she wanted to do was sit on the floor and meditate!

Both missed the intimate companionship they had enjoyed earlier in their marriage when they had been focused on common goals. At that time this interracial couple seems to have shared a very dynamic alliance. The understanding and support they offered each other had been vital in bridging their different cultures, establishing their careers, and making them psychologically independent of their respective families. But over the years they had grown apart, and although they continued to love each other, Judy at least, was no longer sure she wanted to continue the marriage.

Judy had asked Hiro to see me in the hope that, through our work together, he might develop an interest in the transpersonal thinking she found so fascinating. At first I was reluctant to take the case, since I didn't want to be in the position of indoctrinating Hiro in a perspective that didn't feel right to him. But Hiro was eager to save his marriage if he could, and he felt that if there was some way he could come to share Judy's point of view, he wanted to explore it.

"Maybe I'm missing something here," he said. "It would be wonderful if we could get back on the same wavelength again, and if she can't get on mine, maybe I can get on hers."

It was a pleasure working with Hiro—he was so very bright, and insightful, and willing to try anything. He struck me as an unusually well-balanced, and personally effective individual with no pressing psychological problems. Together we explored the idea of past lives, used the principles of manifestation to achieve some of his personal goals, and discussed the meaning of life. Nevertheless, at the end of a few months I had to agree that consciousness studies weren't Hiro's "thing." The transpersonal dimension just didn't capture his interest, and there seemed to be no point in pursuing the issue any further.

Hiro agreed. He thanked me for my efforts, but acknowledged that it just wasn't working. Untroubled by existential angst or any inner pressure to search for ultimate answers, he longed for a peaceful, companionable, country-club sort of life, and an affectionate, unreflective wife with whom to share it.

"If Judy doesn't want to stay married to me, I guess I'll have to look for someone else," he reluctantly concluded. "Maybe divorce really would be best for both of us. I'll always love Judy, and no matter who she eventually marries, she'll always be able to count on me if she ever needs anything. But maybe we would be happier with companions who want the same things we do."

In a final session with Judy, I cautioned her that she would be taking a big risk divorcing a good man like Hiro. "Are you sure you want to separate from such a loving and supportive husband just because he doesn't share your enthusiasm for exploring higher consciousness?"

"Oh, I know!" she agreed. "He's a terrific husband. Any woman would be lucky to have him!"

"If you throw him out, someone else is going to snap him up before he hits the pavement," I added.

"I hope someone will." Judy sighed. "He deserves to be very happy with a woman who wants what he wants out of life. Hiro will always be my dearest friend, and I'll always want the very best for him. But I just don't think that I *am* what's best for him anymore, or that he is what's best for me. We'll always love each other, but I want a partner with whom I can share the things that stir my soul. Hiro is a very spiritual man in his own way—deeply good and generous and very, very grounded—but our interests just don't coincide anymore."

I always think of Judy and Hiro as the poster children for soul-mate divorce—two loving partners who reluctantly concluded that they would both be happier pursuing their interests individually. If they had had common goals beyond helping each other become successful, fully autonomous adults, they might have been very happy working on them side-by-side for the rest of their lives. But these two seemed to me to be like devoted lab partners who had helped each other complete a difficult course of study. Once their project was finished, Hiro craved a period of peace and predictability so that he could consolidate his gains, while Judy longed for further challenge. They were simply no longer in synch, and their desire to be together was not equal to their desire to have the lives they knew they needed.

I believe that the desires of our soul are divinely inspired. We couldn't change them if we wanted to, and when we try to behave as if these passionate yearnings didn't exist, we only wind up living sterile, inauthentic lives that benefit neither ourselves nor those around us. Sometimes the longing is for union with a soulmate, and sometimes for a certain kind of work, or a particular manner of life. Whatever their object, our soul's desires represent a divine calling that draws us in the direction of our highest possibilities.

Unfortunately, few of us have the courage to dissolve a good marriage just because it has ceased to be deeply fulfilling. We would feel too guilty to leave a devoted spouse without a darned good reason like infidelity or abuse. Perhaps this is why so many breakups occur only after a new romantic interest has captured the attention of one partner.

I suspect that our guide sometimes orchestrates an encounter with a new soulmate we'll find irresistible because that's the only way to get us to leave a relationship that has outlived its usefulness. In such cases, it generally looks to outsiders as though some heartless home wrecker destroyed an otherwise happy marriage. But the truth is that no third party can snare the attention of anyone who is deeply stimulated by his or her spouse. In retrospect, the marriage partners themselves often realize that the new love interest was incidental, and that the real problem was that they had ceased to engage and challenge each other since the joint purpose that had brought them together had already been fulfilled.

GUIDELINES FOR ACTUALIZING A SOULMATE RELATIONSHIP

1. Trust your heart. Trust your gut. And trust the inner sense you have when the energy closes down around some involvement. Be willing to consider change when some aspect of your life has ceased to be fulfilling.
2. You need never feel guilty about doing what is best for you, because what is truly best for you will ultimately benefit everyone.
3. You don't have to be mad at your partner to leave.
4. Sometimes releasing a lover to seek greater fulfillment elsewhere is the highest expression of love.

14

Dealing with
Your Fear of Love

*The day came when the risk to remain closed in a bud
became more painful than the risk it took to blossom.*

—Anaïs Nin

As we saw in the previous chapter, there are good reasons to leave a relationship. But there are bad ones too, and since coming up with excuses to escape from love is your ego's stock in trade, you need to be intensely suspicious of your own motives whenever you are tempted to pull away. Otherwise, fear, masquerading as good judgment, is liable to get the better of you.

Further, while *conscious* reservations about intimacy and commitment can be serious stumbling blocks, *unconscious* ones pose an even greater threat. When fear goes underground, it emerges in disguised forms that seem unrelated to its original object. At that point, it can look to us—and everyone else—as though we are trying our best to establish a loving bond when we are really doing just the opposite.

Ambivalence is the psychological term for this conflicted mental condition in which we consciously desire something we are unconsciously afraid of getting. Let's begin with an example unrelated to romance—that of a businesswoman who is eager for a promotion at work, but intimidated by the additional effort and responsibility the new job would entail. As long as her fears are conscious, she can make a rational decision about whether or not she really wants to try for the position. But sometimes people find it too embarrassing to admit—even to themselves—that they are afraid of something they think they ought to want. In this case, they push their fear out of awareness, and pretend it isn't there.

But it is. And once it has been rendered invisible to the conscious mind, it is free to operate autonomously in pursuit of ends quite different from the ones the individual is aware of embracing. Thus, while one part of the woman in our example definitely wants the new position and works hard to earn it, other subpersonalities—operating outside her awareness—may sabotage her efforts, causing her to miss important deadlines or blow up at her boss. *Self-defeating behavior is the hallmark of ambivalence.* When we are unconsciously afraid of getting what we consciously want, we unwittingly work at cross-purposes with ourselves.

Of course, ambivalence can be understood in metaphysical, as well as psychological, terms. The universe is set up in such a way as to fulfill our soul's desires, but that fulfillment must be delayed when those desires are strongly opposed by ego-generated fears. When we seek a thing some part of us would be unwilling to find, we don't put the necessary energy and effort into manifesting it.

The trick to creating the soulmate relationship you truly want, then, is *to truly want it.* To desire it—not desperately—but *wholeheartedly,* and without reservation. The problem is that since egos are inherently afraid of love, ego-identified individuals can't help being leery of it too. At the same time our false self argues that we can't live without the support and validation of a romantic partner, it is grimly warning that it would be idiotic to believe that anyone really *could* love us, and instructing us to keep our guard up at all times.

The situation is all the more confusing because there are times when achieving a soulmate union requires us to leave a partner with whom a deep love is not presently possible. It isn't always easy to tell whether our reservations about a relationship are well founded, or simply the product of our ego's irrational fear of love. However, since romantic ambivalence is so common and so destructive, it is never a good idea to ignore the possibility that it is operating.

Looking at Your Lover through a Distorting Lens

I've said that the ego is really just the unique spin each of us places on reality to distort our perception of the simple truth. When we let our false self do our thinking for us, various *possible* ways to perceive what is going on in our relationships occur to us—none of them perfectly consistent with reality, and some of them extravagantly fanciful. Because practically anything can *seem* possible, our ego-filtered perceptions of a lover can take us in an instant from adoration to abomination.

It's a little like looking first through one end of a telescope, and then through the other. As long as we are gazing at our beloved through the rosy filter of an infatuated subpersonality, we throw ourselves into the relationship with all the verve of a child doing a cannonball off a diving board. But then a fearful subpersonality takes the helm, and unrealistic confidence gives way to equally unrealistic doubt. Reacting to imaginary slights and betrayals, we begin angrily distancing ourselves from the person who seemed just perfect only a short time before. And the ironic part is that it always looks to us as though our *partner* is the one who changed, never we ourselves!

How Ambivalence Manifests

The ego's fear of love can be played out in direct, or very indirect, ways. Some individuals, for example, never actually reject potential partners. Instead, they maneuver the other person into rejecting *them*. Extreme examples of this would be a man whose lack of personal hygiene makes others shun intimate contact with him, or a woman who rationalizes her biting sarcasm as a lively sense of humor. Such indirect strategies for avoiding love allow us to pretend we are actively pursuing intimacy, while running as hard as we can in the opposite direction. When others point out the inconsistency between what we say we want and the way we behave, our ego comes up with elaborate rationalizations to justify our self-defeating behavior.

But love-avoidant patterns can also be extraordinarily subtle, leaving friends, family, and even therapists just as baffled about our romantic misfortunes as we are. It *looks* as though we are doing everything we possibly can to make our relationships work, but somehow they just don't. For example, if Karen and Pat had gone their separate ways years ago, those of us who heard her version of the story today would probably have no more insight into the real reason they'd failed to click than she did. We would very likely be agreeing with Karen that Pat was a nice enough guy, but just a little too conventional for someone who preferred life in the fast lane. What a pity that such a beautiful, caring woman never found anyone to love!

The Flight from Love

People who are secretly afraid of love often pursue partners until they've achieved a certain degree of intimacy, and then sabotage, or flee the relationship. They *think* they are leaving because they are bored, or have found serious flaws in the other person, or have sighted someone much better on the horizon. But often the real reason is an ego scared to death of the love that threatens to engulf and obliterate it.

Sadly, the partners we abandon may very well be the ideal mates for whom we've been searching. It's all too easy to make this mistake, since the true soulmate potential of another is seldom apparent until our decision to embrace him or her in unconditional love calls it forth. Take Sam's experience with Susan for example.

Sam and Susan

Sam was attracted to Susan the minute he saw her across the room at a public lecture. "Excuse me," he interrupted the acquaintance with whom he'd been speaking. "I have to get over there and talk to that girl before some other guy does!" Whether this initial fascination was coming from his ego, his soul, or both, is hard to say, but it seems clear that much of his subsequent courtship behavior was directed by his ego.

Over a period of several months Sam and Susan dated, and the bond between them deepened into a sexual relationship that grew progressively more intimate and exclusive. All very satisfactory, one would have thought. Yet Sam, who is now a psychologist himself, says that by the end of the third month he was shopping around for an excuse to break up with the woman he was later to recognize as his soulmate.

"I don't get it," I said, puzzled. "Why did you want to leave Susan?"

"I guess I just thought that it was *time*." Sam shrugged. "That was my M.O. in those days. I'd meet some nice girl and begin a relationship that would go on for a few months. And then the issue of commitment would begin to loom, and I'd find some excuse to distance myself and run out on her. It was what I *did*.

"But just as I was getting scared, Susan underwent some surgery that resulted in serious complications. She wound up being hospitalized for nearly a month, and I figured I ought to put off the decision to leave until she got better. I mean, what kind of a heel would break up with his girlfriend when she was in the hospital? I decided to stick around until she was well again, figuring that then I could decide without guilt."

"So when did your feelings for Susan warm up?" I inquired.

"It happened while she was still in the hospital." Sam beamed. "She walked me to the elevator one evening, and kissed me goodbye. *And what a kiss it was! Whooee!* I can still feel that kiss twenty-six years later!

"Somehow Susan got in under my defenses that night, and I was done for! I fell madly in love with her at that moment, and I've been madly in love with her every moment of the twenty-six years we've been together since. That kiss changed my life!"

Note that if his ego had had its way, Sam would never have hung around for that soul-shattering kiss. After three months spent looking upon his ideal mate through the sightless eyes of his false self, he was thinking of moving on in search of someone better. Had he done so, he would probably today be lamenting that he'd never found anyone he could really love, and doubting that such things as soulmates even exist.

The problem is that we don't get any more out of our relationships than we put into them. As long as Sam was holding back—offering his soulmate only conditional love and waiting to see whether she would prove worthy of the little he was giving—she seemed to fall short. How was he to know that it was his own participation in the relationship that was really falling short? Only in the instant when he opened his heart to Susan did he discover that she was perfect for him—*and had been all along.*

Probing for Unconscious Ambivalence

The only way to put a stop to unconsciously motivated, love-avoidant behavior is to bring our fears back into awareness where we can reconsider them. But this is more easily said than done. When we consign information to our unconscious mind, it is as if we've instructed a trusted subordinate not only to hide it from us, but also to deny its very existence. If you have buried fears of love, it's probably going to take a certain amount of ingenuity and persistence to persuade your unconscious mind to cough them up.

The situation is rendered all the more confusing by the fact that we tend to fall in with partners whose fear of love is a perfect match for our own. When the other person is holding back too, it's tough to tell who's doing what to whom. Am I afraid to commit because he's investing so little in the relationship? Or is he investing so little because he realizes how lukewarm I am about him?

When a relationship stops growing, there's a strong temptation to point the finger of blame at your partner, and to either leave or else set to work trying to change him or her. But if you want more love in your life, you needn't change anyone but yourself. (This is fortunate, considering that you are the only one you *can* change.) Only by resolving your ambivalent feelings will you be able to resume forward movement toward the deeply loving union your soul desires, whether with a present partner or a new one.

If you want to probe your unconscious mind for hidden reservations about love, insight-oriented psychotherapy can be extremely helpful. However, I'm convinced that the ideal therapist for each of us is our guide, who already knows where our problems lie, and how to correct them. What could be more convenient and economical than to enlist the astonishing therapeutic expertise of your companion spirit?

How might you go about this? You can start by inviting your guide's assistance in bringing any hidden fears of love you might have into awareness. Begin with a declaration of your intent such as: "I don't know whether I have any hidden fears of love, but if I do, I want to know what they are so that I can reconsider them. I ask my guide to direct my awareness to any and all aspects of my thinking and behavior that are not in alignment with my goal of a soulmate relationship, and I authorize him or her to bring relevant insights to my attention by any means that will work, including books, films, the advice of friends, family, or therapists, and all sorts of lucky coincidences and serendipitous discoveries."

Then begin to systematically search your mind for any ideas, beliefs, attitudes, or behaviors that might be holding you back. Here are some hints to help you start the self-examination process.

List All Possible Fears

It often helps to take an oblique approach to hidden fears. Instead of asking yourself what *you* are afraid of where intimacy and commitment are concerned, ask instead what *somebody*—let us say, a person far less psychologically sophisticated than you are—*might conceivably* be afraid of. After all, you probably made the original decision to hide your fears back when you were much younger and less aware than you are today.

For example, just because you see nothing frightening about sex now doesn't mean that you didn't have sexual fears as a child or an adolescent. You may still have badly frightened subpersonalities that didn't have an opportunity to mature because they were split off from consciousness early in life. Don't assume you aren't unconsciously afraid of something just because it now seems to you to be a ridiculous thing to worry about.

Come up with an exhaustive list of possible drawbacks to love that includes not only disastrous outcomes (e.g., marrying someone who subsequently murders you for the insurance money), but also minor inconveniences (e.g., having to spend holidays with boring in-laws). When you've put down everything that occurs to you, invite your guide to direct your attention to items that are especially significant for you, and ask for help in understanding how these fears might make you hesitant about getting close to anyone.

"What I Can't Stand about Women (Men)!"

Another approach to identifying hidden sources of ambivalence is to search your mind for the things you *don't like* about members of the sex that attracts you. While it is embarrassing to confess our fears, it is usually much easier to identify things that really bug us. Yet the reason we dislike those particular qualities is precisely because we feel threatened by them. Every antipathy has a fear at its foundation, so whenever you get in touch with a pet peeve, you're in an excellent position to track down the underlying source of ambivalence.

If you're a guy who resents women for being fickle, there's a good chance you are really worried about being man enough to hold a woman's attention. If you are a woman who complains that men are too aggressive or controlling, perhaps you lack confidence in your ability to assert yourself effectively.

In my experience, most folks can readily generate a long list of bad qualities they believe to be more prevalent among members of the opposite sex. "Men only want one thing." "Women won't look twice at a guy unless he has a fancy car and a fat bank account." "Guys are insensitive." "Inconstancy, thy name is Woman." And so on.

You might think it would all be a lot easier for gays and lesbians who are relating romantically to members of their own sex, but that doesn't seem to be the case. For one thing, most of us harbor negative stereotypes about our own gender as well as the other. Then, too, many gays and lesbians absorb some measure of homophobia from the larger culture, and this also tends to limit their expectations for lasting happiness in a same-sex alliance.

"Well, Isn't That Just Like a Man (Woman)!"

Another way to access any negative stereotypes you might be harboring is to take note of your reactions to things others say about *their* relationships. When a friend tells you that her husband is completely faithful, do you instantly feel a bit skeptical—as if she *could* be right, but may well be kidding herself? When a prosperous male friend remarks that he's finally found a woman who loves him for himself alone, is your first thought that she has probably pulled the wool over his eyes?

Negative stereotypes point to an ingrained mistrust of those we seek to love. It's not enough to pray and search for a soulmate; we must also work to reduce the fear that our lover will take advantage of us if we let our guard down. How eager could any of us really be for an intimate relationship with someone we suspected would eventually turn critical, demanding, boring, unfaithful, or whatever?

Most important, don't be fooled into thinking that your conscious opinions of men and women are the whole story. Take me, for example. Before beginning my inner work with my guide, I would have sworn that I was just *crazy* about men. Yet my companion spirit soon showed me that I actually had a very negative view of them. In some hidden recess of my mind, it seemed clear to me that women were the good sex, and men, the not-so-good one. After all, women were kind, loyal, sensitive, helpful, and patient, while men were selfish, arrogant, inconsiderate, violent, and irrational. Or so it seemed to me.

Once my guide helped me to critically examine my prejudices, I discovered that while I had been holding men responsible for a great deal of my unhappiness, few of my relationships had really been the way they had looked to me at the time. I realized that many of the things I'd blamed the men in my life for doing to me, I had imagined, or brought on myself. Indeed, some things I'd thought they were doing to me, *I had actually been doing to them!* Gradually, I learned to stop regarding men as the source of my troubles, and began to truly respect and admire the ways in which they are different from women.

You may be wondering how someone with so many prejudices could even become a psychotherapist, but you must remember that the mistrust of which we are speaking is *unconscious,* and all of us have our share of it. If *we* aren't aware that we don't entirely like or trust a particular group, those around us usually can't tell either. Our speech may be as politically correct as anyone could wish, but that is no guarantee that we will not tacitly assume that less is to be expected of certain people. And while therapists are trained to be on the lookout for such biases, we don't always succeed.

In the course of some twenty years spent training psychotherapists, I've become convinced that many of my colleagues suffer from the same sort of ambivalence about love that I discovered in myself. Many female counselors are a little too quick to regard their women clients as the innocent victims of their fathers, husbands, and boyfriends. A great many male counselors have a tendency to dismiss the concerns of their female clients as hysterical exaggerations.

Because unconscious gender stereotypes distort the thinking of so many therapists, I urge you to consult your guide even if you are in therapy. Professional helpers are only human, and they have egos just like the rest of us. The best ones have learned to tune in to their own inner guidance (intuition), and use this source of insight to help their clients. But in the absence of guidance, "unhealed healers" have little chance of helping others solve relationship problems they haven't been able to solve themselves.

Whenever you seek advice about love—professional or otherwise—let me suggest that you give special weight to the opinions of people who have created happy, long-term relationships themselves. If you were training for the Olympics, you'd naturally give more credence to the words of successful athletes than to those of couch potatoes, and the same principle ought to apply here. Don't jeopardize your romantic future by taking your lead from the embittered casualties of multiple failed relationships. An ounce of sound advice is worth a pound of prenuptial agreements.

Fear Gives Rise to Self-Fulfilling Prophecies

Of course, even when you've become fully conscious of your fears about relationship, you may still find yourself reluctant to part with them. Many of us mistakenly believe that fear serves a valuable protective function. We imagine that a wary attitude will keep us from getting hurt. Ironically, just the opposite is true.

As we shall see later in this book, we all have a tendency to find in any situation whatever we *expect* to find. When we anticipate trouble with some individual or class of people, our low opinion of them subtly provokes them to behave just as badly as we thought they would. For example, if you half expect a lover to turn down some request you regard as perfectly reasonable, you're likely to make that request in querulous tones that communicate the resentment you're already experiencing in anticipation of refusal. Your partner may well be offended by your attitude, and become recalcitrant as a result. Of course, you'll see this as evidence that you were right to expect to be let down "as usual," instead of realizing that your negative expectations caused the whole problem.

Our fears don't keep us out of trouble—they get us into it! Perhaps I can best illustrate this point with an incident that occurred early in my marriage.

Thanksgiving Dinner

The year Arnie and I married, I prepared an elaborate Thanksgiving dinner for his mother, his son and daughter, and a few of our friends. It was to be our first holiday meal together as a couple in our new home, and as I gaily shopped, and cooked, and cleaned, I experienced poignant resonances of childhood Thanksgivings— memories more often bitter than sweet.

Miller family gatherings had been the occasions for some of my alcoholic father's worst craziness. I could not remember a holiday meal at our house that had not been spoiled by his drunken antics and unpredictable rages. But now I had a family of my own. Now, finally, I was going to be at the center of a peaceful, joyous holiday celebration. Now Thanksgiving would be just as it *should* be—I would see to that!

Our guests arrived in high spirits and when the meal was ready, I called everyone to the table, proudly producing one fragrantly steaming dish after another. However, before we could begin eating, Arnie leaped up from the table and told everyone to wait. He had to find something. He dashed into the junk-filled walk-in closet that opens onto our dining room and began rifling the contents.

I was at first surprised, and then annoyed. The food I had worked so hard to prepare was getting cold. Those of us at the table tried to fill the delay with conversation, but it was clear that everyone was hungry and wanted to begin the meal. "I'm sure he'll be back in a moment," I assured them pleasantly. But he wasn't.

Now we could hear the sounds of falling objects and muttered oaths coming from the closet. Arnie's teenage son Rob got up nervously and offered to help his father look for whatever it was, but since there was room for only one person in the closet, all he could do was stand helplessly by the door and watch. A minute later he had to dodge out of the way as large objects started flying through the air! Arnie had begun pitching things out of the closet and onto the dining room floor. This was really too much!

I had a growing sense of having been overtaken by a nightmare. My hostess smile froze on my lips as the minutes wore on. There was a painful knot in my stomach, and I could see the strain in everyone else's face as well. The violent sounds of yanking and muttering in the closet only escalated as my beautiful dinner grew cold.

How could Arnie have so little respect for me and our guests— so little gratitude for the effort I had put in to make this meal a memorable occasion? Wasn't that just like a man? I thought grimly. At that moment I had the eerie impression that my new husband had somehow metamorphosed into my irrational, alcoholic father. This was just the sort of thing Dad would have done, disrupting everyone's dinner to go off on some absurd tangent without a thought for anyone else's convenience—blundering around drunkenly and working himself up into an ugly temper over his inability to find what he wanted. Arnie didn't drink, and wasn't ordinarily temperamental, yet here he was acting exactly the same way! I felt as though I'd fallen down a rabbit hole into some bizarre alternate reality where I was condemned to repeat the misery of my parents' marriage.

I was soon so furious with Arnie for ruining our holiday like this that I didn't trust myself to speak. Obviously I was trapped in a marriage with a lunatic. Probably all of my holidays from now on would be like this. After all my hard work, this was my thanks!

At that point I became aware of how toxic my thoughts were becoming. This growing sense of righteous indignation I was feeling toward Arnie could not possibly be appropriate to the holy relationship we wanted to build. I realized with dismay that already there was a part of me that wanted to justify my anger against my husband by having it turn out that Arnie really was behaving inexcusably. I actually *wanted* him to be a jerk so that I could play out my role as his innocent victim and receive the sympathy of all our guests as my mother always did when my father had made a spectacle of himself.

I saw the road to my parents' marriage stretching out before me. How could this be happening to Arnie and me, I wondered?

It couldn't, I decided. This appalling transformation of my husband into my father must be an illusion thrown up by my own ego. *A Course in Miracles* suggests that we respond to this sort of attack on our peace and sanity by centering our minds and asking for a holy instant we can share with the person who has unexpectedly taken on the aspect of an enemy, so that's exactly what I did. Then I stilled my simmering thoughts to listen for guidance.

My inner teacher urged me to simply suspend judgment about what Arnie was doing—to stop dragging in the past and imagining that I knew what was going on when I didn't. This was Arnie, not my father bent on demonstrating his power to make everyone else miserable. Whatever was going on with my husband, we could sort it out later. For now, I needed to trust that whatever he was up to, he was doing it for some good reason that I did not presently understand.

I took a deep breath and fought to stay in the present. Everything was fine. Dinner was a little delayed, but what did that matter? I made up my mind that I was going to remain peaceful and enjoy my day whatever Arnie chose to do.

Forcing myself to smile around at our guests, I managed to make some good-humored remark about Arnie's eccentric behavior. A ripple of relief ran around the table as everyone saw that whatever was going on with Arnie, at least I was not going to lose my cool and make a scene. I was surprised to realize that *I* was the one they'd been watching with concern. They weren't offended by Arnie's behavior—just afraid that I was going to lose my temper over it, as I very nearly had.

Arnie's daughter Julie quickly joined in with a witty remark of her own, and all of the remaining tension went out of the situation as we began exchanging humorous speculation as to what on earth the man could be doing in that closet! It dawned on me that Arnie's peculiar behavior was not ruining anyone's good time, but that my horrified reaction to it might very well have done so. Was it possible that all of those holiday dinners back home would have gone more smoothly too, if my mother had not been quite so intent upon using my father's absurd antics as the evidence of her martyrdom?

A few minutes later Arnie victoriously emerged from the closet with his prizes held high. He had dug out his camera and all of its indispensable lenses and attachments. With his photographic equipment finally organized, the ill humor I had imputed to him had magically disappeared—if indeed it had ever been there at all. My husband was simply bubbling over with joy! I had done such a wonderful job with the meal and the table had looked so beautiful, he explained, that he just had to capture it all on film. His pride in me brought tears to my eyes. All of our guests graciously forgot their hunger to take part in a series of exuberant group photos around the table.

Far from having no consideration for all of the effort I had put into our holiday feast, Arnie had been so impressed with the job I'd done that he'd wanted to immortalize it on film. How had I ever thought this dear man an unappreciative lunatic? How had I ever imagined that he was anything like my father? And what did it matter if the food had to be reheated as long as my husband adored me? We had a terrific Thanksgiving that year, but alongside the fond memories I cherish of it, I can still see the dark road to my parents' marriage that my ego very nearly seduced me into walking that day.

Rethinking Your Fears

After emphasizing how difficult it can be to get in touch with unconscious fears of love, you may be thinking it will be even harder to deactivate them. Actually, that part is a piece of cake. All you have to do to defuse fearful thoughts is to look at them squarely and recognize that *they aren't true.* It isn't even necessary to deny that there is any truth in them. All you really have to do is recognize that negative stereotypes are only generalizations, and that no generalization applies to everyone.

For example, there's no harm in believing that *some* men are dishonest, or that *some* women care about nothing but money, as long as you mentally emphasize the point that they aren't *all* like that. This allows you to expect the best from the people you meet, and shifts your mental focus from your fears to the positive qualities you want to attract into your experience.

Finding and defusing the fears that prevent you from freely giving and receiving love may involve some work, but it brings tremendous rewards. For one thing, as you express more unconditional acceptance, you'll actually become much more attractive! After all, love is the most attractive thing in the universe. As you "let your light shine," the men and women you meet will pick up on the fact that you genuinely respect, trust, and appreciate people like them, and they'll hasten to return the favor.

GUIDELINES FOR ACTUALIZING A SOULMATE RELATIONSHIP

1. If love seems to be avoiding you, consider the possibility that you may actually be avoiding it.
2. Actively search out your own sources of ambivalence so you can *act,* and not merely *react.*
3. Explore the things that annoy, depress, or infuriate you about the gender that attracts you, and consider the possibility that you are overgeneralizing.
4. Attack your fear, not your partner.

15

Holding Out for
What You Really Want

You've got to know when to hold 'em,
and know when to fold 'em.
Know when to walk away,
and know when to run.
—"The Gambler," song by Kenny Rogers

It often appears that we can do nothing but wait and hope and
pray for the relationship we want, while a capricious universe
takes its own sweet time finding us an appropriate mate. But it
only *looks* this way because we are unaware that *we ourselves* may
be the ones holding things up. There is an old saying: "When the
student is ready, the teacher appears." Since our soulmates *are* our
teachers, the maxim applies equally well to them.

In the previous chapter, we saw how the ego can prevent us
from finding love by manufacturing reasons to walk out on ideal
partners the minute real intimacy becomes a possibility. But self-
defeating behavior can take other forms as well, including that of
misplaced loyalty. Our false self can disrupt our love life just as effectively by persuading us to continue working at relationships
that are fundamentally unworkable. There are times when it is appropriate to stand by our man or woman through thick and thin,
and there are other times when it is sensible to let go and move

on. But in the absence of some sort of guidance, it can be very difficult to know *when* to "hold 'em" and when to "fold 'em."

Knowing When to Quit

If there is one thing that clearly distinguishes effective courtship behavior from the self-defeating variety, it is the discrimination to quickly identify and release partners who lack real soulmate potential. It seems obvious that as long as you are involved with Person A, you are not available to explore your possibilities with Persons B, C, D, or E. Yet many would-be soulmates persist in believing that it is better to hang onto any sort of relationship at all, than to risk being alone. Nothing could be farther from the truth!

For one thing, bad relationships are profoundly demoralizing. Spend enough time in the company of a lover who doesn't love you very much, and you'll begin to doubt your own worth and attractiveness. But the worst part is that when you occupy your time with non-soulmates, your meant-to-be love has no alternative but to look elsewhere.

If you hope to achieve a wonderful intimate relationship, you are going to have to learn when to say no, as well as when to take no for an answer. Remember, individuals who maintain an unswerving faith in their destiny with another, despite all evidence to the contrary, are not called *soulmates*; they are called *stalkers*. Clinging to Mr. or Ms. Wrong not only ties up someone else's soulmate, it also needlessly delays the moment when you'll find your own.

Don't Hesitate to Release Partners Who Aren't Right for You

Unfortunately, the ability to release unsuitable suitors gracefully doesn't come easily to those of us raised without good parental role models for discrimination and assertiveness. Some people find it excruciating to terminate a relationship, even when they know perfectly well that it has no future. If this is a problem for you, it may help to remind yourself of the following:

First, the universe is set up in such a way that when you do what is truly best for you, you are simultaneously doing what is best for everyone else. If a particular partnership is wrong for you, it cannot possibly be right for the other person either (although she or he may not yet have realized this). Besides, the sooner you release someone you're going to release in the end anyway, the more considerate you are being.

Also remind yourself that you have no obligation to display any more loyalty than you've agreed to. Casually dating one person doesn't mean you should not simultaneously date others, nor is there any good reason to agree to exclusivity unless there is a mutual understanding that if things work out at this level, a deeper commitment is to follow. Too many people commit unilaterally "on spec," assuming that if *they* invest heavily in the relationship, their partners will feel too guilty to do otherwise. Unfortunately, even if you convince your intended that she or he owes you a commitment after "taking the best years of your life," there's no way to build a loving relationship on a foundation of guilt.

It's all very well to be charitable in other areas, but intimate relationships are only viable when both parties feel they are (a) benefiting equally, or (b) getting the best of the bargain. Your soul expresses itself through feelings, and if you don't feel comfortable, stimulated, and uplifted when you are with this person, that's really all there is to say about it. Of course, it's always a good idea to check with your guide, just in case you are confusing ego-generated emotions with your true feelings. But don't make the mistake Sarah did, and pursue a partnership that doesn't *feel* right, just because your ego insists it *ought to.*

And finally, remind yourself that while the lovers you leave behind are entitled to be disappointed, they have no legitimate reason to behave as though they've been injured or insulted by your decision to look elsewhere. Your pool of potential soulmates is a very exclusive club indeed, and it is not demeaning to anyone to suggest that he or she is not a member of it. The world is teeming with good, kind, intelligent, attractive people who needn't think any less of themselves just because you or I don't want to marry them!

Confronting Your Fear of Rejection

But perhaps you are less afraid of rejecting others, than of being rejected yourself. If you're holding back from dating because of such fears, you need to see that your ego has you blowing things way out of proportion.

First of all, remind yourself that being rejected often says less about you than it does about the person doing the rejecting. As we saw in the last chapter, there are a great many reasons for aborting romantic involvements that have absolutely nothing to do with the individual being left behind. Remember Sam, whose standard operating procedure was to develop a promising relationship with some nice woman, only to disengage as soon as he felt that things were getting too serious? Some of the lovers he dropped probably wondered what he thought was wrong with them, but Sam just didn't want to get involved. As he would be the first to admit, the only "crime" these non-soulmates committed was being so charming and attractive in the first place!

How can being rejected mean that you are unworthy of love when nearly *everyone* gets rejected at one time or another? Why, my glamorous friend Karen, whose romantic adventures we considered in a previous chapter, can be amusing for hours on the subject of the scoundrels who once broke her heart! If highly attractive people like Cary Grant, Princess Diana, and Marilyn Monroe all had to endure painful romantic disappointments, is it realistic to go on hoping that everyone who makes your heart beat faster is going to return your affection?

Most people discover that the best way to get over an exaggerated fear of rejection is to actively court disaster. For example,

Dr. Albert Ellis, the founder of Rational Emotive Therapy, says that as a young man he cured himself of his pathological diffidence concerning the opposite sex by strolling around Central Park asking every woman he met for a date. Naturally, most of them brushed him off rudely—this was New York, after all! The point is that after being turned down dozens of times in a row, he began to get it that rejection was really no big deal. Besides, there was the occasional gal who said yes!

"All I've Got to Do Is Dream!"

Loyalty to a dead-end relationship, and an exaggerated fear of rejection, are excellent ways for our ego to persuade us to waste the time and energy we'd otherwise devote to finding true love. But our ego has another trick up its sleeves as well. Sometimes it offers to compensate us for a grossly unsatisfactory love life by keeping us entertained with daydreams and erotic fantasies. Many people discover early in life that they can have a pretty good time by themselves, fantasizing about the wonderful things that might someday happen. The less rewarding their real relationships, the greater the temptation to escape into a delightful dream world populated by nubile nymphomaniacs and dashing corporate buccaneers.

Unfortunately, this sort of temporary relief from loneliness comes at a high price. Our mind brings our soul's desires into manifestation through concentrated attention and belief, coupled with purposeful action. When we are content to entertain ourselves with fantasies, it short-circuits this process, draining off the energy we'd otherwise use to create *real* relationships.

If love stories, soap operas, daydreams, or pornographic websites are major sources of satisfaction for you, *your dedication to imaginary lovers may be preventing you from attracting real ones.* It's time to put down the trashy novels and adult videos and start reaching out to living, breathing people in your immediate environment before life passes you by. Opportunity does not bother

knocking at the doors of those who are obviously too busy elsewhere to answer the summons.

Beware your ego's spurious argument that "half a loaf is better than no bread at all." It may encourage you to believe that
there's no harm in holding onto the benefits of a rich fantasy life,
or a partially fulfilling relationship, while waiting for true love to
come along. But there is! We meet our soulmates when we are
ready to give them our undivided attention. If our interest is otherwise engaged, we send out a psychic signal that we are not fully
available for new involvements, and this discourages anyone who
is in the market for a serious relationship.

When in Doubt, Ask Your Guide

Now when I say you shouldn't tie yourself up with attachments
that have no future, I don't mean that you should drop a present
lover just because there are problems in the relationship. If uninterrupted domestic bliss were the criterion for sticking together,
soulmates would be divorcing each other left and right! But do
try to be realistic about whether the most serious problems you
face as a couple are likely to improve. For example, if your partner doesn't even *want* to change some totally unacceptable behavior, it may not be sensible to go on expecting that he or she
will. And when you are knee-deep in broken promises, it's time
to consider the possibility that the next vow you hear isn't going
to be worth any more than its predecessors.

Certainly, there are instances where a romantic long shot
romps across the finish line at the head of the field. Gideon, for example, offered Helene very little encouragement before actually
proposing marriage. But Helene persisted because her guide was
telling her that the situation was not as it appeared—and indeed
Gideon later confirmed that he'd been in love with her ever since
their first opportunity to spend time together in Jerusalem. If you
are in doubt about the wisdom of continuing a relationship, why
not do what worked for Helene and consult your guide?

It takes courage to refuse to settle for less than you want, but would-be soulmates must be prepared to go it alone for as long as it takes to find an eligible, like-minded individual who wants to share the kind of relationship they have in mind. In the next story, we'll see how one man set the stage for the entrance of his meant-to-be love by ringing down the curtain on an ego-sponsored infatuation that was draining his energy and wasting his time. The speed with which he then encountered his soulmate suggests that the love for which he had been longing was simply waiting for him to decide against settling for less.

Rick, Shari, and Lois

Rick is the man mentioned in an earlier chapter who broke up with Lorraine soon after starting therapy with me. Together we explored the insecurities that had made him so desperate for love that he had ignored the many warning signs that he and Lorraine were not right for each other. He eventually realized that their affair had been doomed from the start by the fact that they had not really respected each other's values, or wanted the same things out of life

Rick also realized that he had contributed to the downfall of this and other romantic affairs by pretending to be someone he wasn't. In an effort to impress women, he would act supremely self-confident, easy-going, and undemanding. Later, when his human flaws and vulnerabilities began to emerge, his lovers often felt they'd been deceived.

As his awareness and self-acceptance grew, Rick found the courage to present himself to women as he really was, instead of pretending to be what he thought they wanted. He dropped the phony act he used to put on, and started just being himself. Unfortunately, the immediate results of this change were not very encouraging. Now that he was no longer coming on like the answer to every maiden's prayer, the women he met seemed to find him decidedly resistible!

"It's like I'm dipped in shit, Carolyn!" Rick lamented on more than one occasion. "Now that I'm not acting like Mr. Cool, the kind of women who used to fall all over me step around me like I was roadkill! It's all very well 'being myself,' but the women I'm attracted to don't seem real impressed with 'myself.'"

I, of course, pointed out that women who were attracted to his act rather than to him were not ones he could hope to love and marry in any case. Rick could see that that was so, and he did not waver in his commitment to being honest and direct in his dealings with the opposite sex. Nevertheless, we were both eager for the "dipped-in-shit" phase to be over.

Rick's new relationship skills were put to the test when he met Shari in an acting class. A moderately successful actress who was often recognized on the street from her recurrent role in a long-running television series, she was beautiful, vivacious, and talented. Further, unlike Lorraine, Shari was a real kindred spirit. She and Rick found it easy to confide in each other, and she seemed to return his regard. Finally, an attractive woman who appreciated Rick for himself!

The problem, Rick discovered, was that Shari was in a live-in relationship with a boyfriend she said she hoped to marry. My client was disappointed to learn that she was not open to exploring a future with him, but he was able to be philosophical about it, merely remarking to me, "It's too bad Shari isn't available. She's exactly the kind of woman who would have been perfect for me." So far, so good. Rick was being admirably realistic.

However, for a woman who was more or less engaged to someone else, Shari began giving Rick an awful lot of encouragement. At her invitation they worked up romantic scenes for their acting class, and neither seemed to have much trouble making their stage kisses truly convincing. Shari invited Rick to accompany her to films, play golf, and sing with her, and the two spent hours each day talking on the phone. Despite the explicit message that she was not interested in developing a relationship with him, Shari was acting like someone who might become available if Rick just played his cards right. The spontaneous warmth of her behavior toward him made it increasingly difficult for my client to accept the idea that he could not hope for more.

I was delighted when Rick decided to deal with these mixed messages in a straightforward manner. Instead of consulting his ego to find out what her ambiguous behavior meant, he asked Shari. She reaffirmed that she was committed to her fiancé, and said that she just really enjoyed having Rick as a friend.

Rick accepted the situation with good grace, and the two continued doing things together whenever Shari's boyfriend was not available. My client often picked her up at her house, and occasionally would have a drink with Shari and her fiancé before taking her off to some engagement. He commented that it was a lot like stopping in to meet a girlfriend's father before taking her out on a date.

But proximity was only serving to feed Rick's infatuation with Shari. The more he squired this desirable young actress around town, the more he found her on his mind. Further, there was no room for any other woman in his life while he was spending all his free time with her. When I raised this issue and suggested that he see less of Shari so that he could get on with his own life, Rick objected that he might as well enjoy her company until some more interesting woman came along.

"The problem is," I told him, "you aren't going to find anyone else while your energy is tied up in this relationship. If what you really want is to find a soulmate to love and marry, yearning after Shari is only going to waste your time. It might be best to put some distance between you until the attraction dies down. While this arrangement is serving her needs, it really doesn't seem fair to either you or her boyfriend."

"Yeah, but she's just so perfect for me." Rick sighed. "We have such a great time together, and her boyfriend really doesn't seem to mind. I just hate to give all of that up to go back to being dipped in shit."

"I'm not really worried about your getting hurt here," I explained. "You're taking an emotional risk, but I can see that you've got your eyes wide open, and I think you'll be able to deal with whatever happens. I'm just concerned that you're wasting your time in a dead-end relationship when you could be looking for someone who is really available. Shari has made it perfectly clear that this isn't going to go anywhere. If you want a real partnership, you're going to have to create the space for it by getting your mind off her.

"And I also think you should look more closely at this idea that Shari would be perfect for you if only she were available," I went on. "This is a woman who is essentially dating you at the same time she is going to couple's therapy to work out her problems with her boyfriend. Would you really want to marry someone who would react to conflicts in your relationship by drawing in an admirer? Even if she is being completely honest and open, and the whole thing is entirely platonic, doesn't that seem like an odd way to behave if she's as serious as she says she is about making her current relationship work? Besides, it isn't very considerate of her to lead you on this way when she knows how you feel about her. Intentionally or not, I think she's using both of you."

Rick acknowledged the truth of all this, but was nevertheless reluctant to give Shari up. He left our session still undecided about what to do. That evening, the two of them went to a screening together and then stopped off for drinks afterward. The warmth of her behavior prompted Rick to remark once again, "I can't help wishing you were available for something more than movies and golf. I'm really attracted to you, and I wish we could have a chance to see where things might go between us."

"Oh, don't let's get into *that* again!" Shari laughed, skillfully sidestepping his advance. She turned the conversation to other topics. Soon she began talking about her past relationships.

Rick had known that before her current boyfriend there had been a famous actor who had divorced his wife to be with Shari, only to have her quickly move on. What he learned now was that

that lover hadn't been the first to leave a wife in the mistaken be-lief that Shari would marry him if he did.

"As she spoke about each of these old boyfriends," Rick told me at our next session, "I had this odd sensation that she was shrinking right before my eyes! It was the strangest thing. She'd tell me about one guy she'd kind of strung along without really meaning to, and *zoop!* Some of the glamour I'd been seeing in her would just vanish. Then she started in on the next one and again—*zoop!* Smaller still!

"And at some point—*poof!* It was all gone! All of the glam-our I'd been seeing in her vanished, right along with the infat-uation I'd been experiencing. Suddenly she was just this kind of screwed-up friend sitting across the table from me. I still cared about her and liked her and all, but it suddenly seemed obvious that I could never have the kind of relationship I want with someone who treats men the way she does. The spell was broken.

"And you'll never guess what happened the very next day!" Rick continued jubilantly. "I hit the *jackpot!*

"You see, Shari and her boyfriend have been looking for a place to move to, and so have my roommate, Liz, and I. The next day Shari called me up and said she'd just looked at a house that wasn't right for them, but would be perfect for Liz and me. She gave me the number of the woman who was trying to sublet it, and suggested I get over there to see it right away. So I called for an appointment and went.

"Well, the minute this woman opened the door, I was ab-solutely dazzled! The only thing I could think was 'Damn! It's too bad she's so beautiful or I could ask her out!'"

Lois was a Canadian actress who needed to sublet the house she was renting in Los Angeles because she was scheduled for six months' work on a television series in Vancouver. Did I mention that Rick was a Canadian citizen, or that he was an aspiring writer/director involved in negotiations to shoot his first feature-length film in Vancouver?

Rick found Lois enchanting, and she seemed to like him too. They managed to drag out their discussion of the sublet for two hours. When Rick still couldn't quite get up his nerve to ask this stunning woman for a date, she took the initiative, suggesting that he drop over some time for a game of Scrabble.

Rick went home to collect his roommate Liz, and the two returned that evening to firm up the deal for the house, which Liz agreed was perfect. Then the three of them went out for pizza to celebrate. When Rick left the table to wash up, Liz played matchmaker.

"So, Lois, I think Rick really likes you," our youthful yenta casually remarked. "Do you like him?"

"He seems great!" Lois replied a little shyly. "It's too bad I'm leaving the country in three weeks."

By the time Rick returned, Liz had managed to spread herself and her belongings all over one side of the booth they were sharing, forcing Lois to sit pressed up against Rick on the other. Nobody seemed to object to this arrangement—least of all Rick! After dinner the three stayed up talking until 4:00 AM. No one could believe how late it had gotten when the two roommates finally dragged themselves away.

The following afternoon Rick and Liz returned to sign the sublease. Then Liz pleaded exhaustion, and Rick took Lois out for a bite to eat and a game of pool that lasted until midnight. When he took her home, Rick shyly asked if it would be all right if he kissed her. She said yes, and, as my client put it, "It was like we burst into flames! I've never experienced anything like it!

"We celebrated our one-week anniversary yesterday," Rick went on happily, "and we're already trying to figure out how we're going to get through the next six months while she's in Canada and I'm here. I'll have an excuse to make some trips up to Vancouver to scout locations. It's all settled that I'll be staying with her while I'm there, and I'm going to drive her up when she moves in two weeks.

"We know it's probably crazy to be so sure about each other so quickly, but we both really feel that this is it for us. We've already discussed our thoughts about having kids—we both definitely want them, but not right away. We have similar interests, values, and spiritual views. And can you believe it—a beautiful woman like that and she hasn't so much as dated anyone in the past year? She's just been working on herself in therapy and praying she'd find a guy who'd done his own psychological work.

"I just can't believe this has finally happened to me!" Rick marveled, grinning from ear to ear. "And I *especially* can't believe the way it happened the very next day after I released my infatuation with Shari! You said I'd have to let her go if I wanted to find someone who was really right for me, but I never thought it would work that quickly. And with Lois leaving town so soon, I hate to think what might have happened if I hadn't gotten over Shari when I did!"

Today, two years after these events, Lois and Rick are happily married. Only time will tell if they will be right for each other for a lifetime, but having made a wonderful start on an honest and mutually supportive relationship, I see no reason why they won't make a go of it.

It may seem like a striking coincidence that Rick would encounter a soulmate within twenty-four hours of becoming disillusioned with Shari, but I don't think there was anything random about it. Rick met the essential qualifications for this sort of relationship the night he recognized the difference between love and infatuation, and decided in favor of the former. He *could not* have recognized his soulmate before making this choice and, having made it, what need was there for further delay? It looks to me as though Rick and Lois found each other just as soon as they possibly could have.

There appear to be certain realizations people must achieve before they become capable of true love. For example, I achieved the prerequisite level of honesty and awareness when I finally brought myself to confess my manipulative behavior to Brent, and then release him. That and my decision to henceforth be direct and realistic in my dealings with men were the things that allowed me to connect with my soulmate a few weeks later. If I had continued trying to manipulate Brent into loving me, or entertaining false hopes for our relationship, I suspect that I would not have found Arnie when I did, and that my life might have taken a very different course.

Rick seems to have gone through a remarkably similar process. First he developed the determination to be honest, direct, and vulnerable with women who interested him romantically, and he stuck with it despite the fact that it initially appeared to be a step in the wrong direction. Once he stopped pretending to be someone he was not, he had to weather a period of withering romantic rejection that went on for months. Yet, despite the fact that his prospects for love seemed to be receding into the distance, he did not revert to the deceptive tactics that had won him feminine admiration in the past.

Having demonstrated his determination not to deceive women, Rick met Shari, who confronted him with the need to stop deceiving *himself.* This glamorous actress was an ideal target for infatuation, but Rick ultimately faced the fact that if it was love he wanted, he would have to look elsewhere. Confronted with a choice between an unattractive *reality*—that Shari was only leading him on as she had many others—and an enchanting *illusion*—the fantasy that he might be the lucky guy who would win the hand of this glamorous princess—Rick had the good sense to withdraw his emotional investment.

Let's pause for a moment to take a closer look at Shari's behavior. Like a lot of people who fear intimacy, it may be that this woman finds ways to distance herself from men at the same time she tries to boost her self-esteem by making romantic conquests. She seems to assuage any guilt about this by remaining sexually faithful to her boyfriend, and being completely honest with the other guy about her intentions.

But, having laid her cards on the table, she then feels free to send her admirer a very different *nonverbal* message, probably

173

without consciously recognizing what she is doing. If some guy gets the crazy idea that she might be willing to leave her boyfriend for him despite everything she's said to the contrary, it can't very well be her fault, can it?

And in truth, it *isn't* her fault. All Shari is doing is offering selected men an opportunity to delude themselves if that is what they would like to do. Those who prefer their ego's fantasies to reality will wind up the worse for it. But when their castles in the air come tumbling down, they'll have no one to blame but themselves. Shari gave them fair warning.

Always be leery of any relationship in which you are getting mixed messages. A lot of ambivalent people *say* they are available to make a commitment while their behavior suggests otherwise. Perhaps they never get around to introducing you to their family and aren't interested in meeting yours. Or they don't want to make plans with you that presuppose you'll be together next week, next month, or next year.

Others, like Shari, tell you frankly that they aren't available, and then proceed to flirt with you in a manner that suggests their hearts belong to you alone. Fortunately, Rick saw what Shari was doing and declined to waste any more of his time. He no sooner made the decision to hold out for real love than that is what he found.

It seems clear that the timing of this opportunity depended upon Rick, since Lois had evidently already prepared herself to move forward with a soulmate relationship. If he had continued to delude himself about his possibilities with Shari until Lois moved back to Canada, her guide might very well have decided to find her someone else. In that case, a longed-for opportunity for true love would have passed Rick by without his ever knowing what he had missed!

Your meant-to-be love may be right around the corner. But you won't actually turn that corner until you are ready to be completely realistic and honest. It's time to stop *waiting* for love, and start actively moving toward it.

GUIDELINES FOR ACTUALIZING A SOULMATE RELATIONSHIP

1. If you want true love, don't settle for anything less. Work hard to improve your current relationship, but if it becomes clear that it is not going to evolve into the kind of soulmate union you want, move on.
2. If you want to know someone's intentions, ask! And, having asked, make sure the person's behavior is consistent with what has been said.
3. Remember, *loyalty and optimism are not virtues when they are misplaced.*

16

When You Don't Look,
You Find

When human love relationships fail . . .
they fail because they were entered into
for the wrong reason.

—*Conversations with God*

We've just seen how important it is for would-be soulmates to stop tying up their time and energy with ego-based infatuations. But if you've been paying close attention, you may have noticed that individuals who achieve soulmate unions often don't just give up on particular relationships that are not going anywhere—there is a sense in which many of them seem to give up on finding true love altogether. In one story after another we've seen people who were desperate for an ideal partnership reluctantly face the possibility that their dreams might never be realized. They accepted that they might have to live as best they could without a soulmate, only to find the man or woman of their dreams pulling in on the next bus.

Take me for example. I had spent my whole adult existence in a frantic search for Mr. Right, only to be blindsided by him as soon as I realized I could have a reasonably satisfying life on my own if I had to. Helene was pitilessly realistic about her chances of finding the kind of husband she wanted, and Rob was trying to come to terms with the possibility that God intended him to be celibate when he found Nicole. Ann was actually a little disappointed when she realized that the exciting single existence to which she'd been looking forward was not to be.

Make no mistake, all of us very much *wanted* a soulmate. What had changed was that we were now prepared to be more realistic about our chances of finding one, and to make the best of an existence that didn't include this blessing. Life without true love was still regarded as a state of affairs to be avoided, but no longer as one to be avoided at all costs. We wanted a loving life partner, but not badly enough to delude ourselves that we had found one when we hadn't, or to try to induce another to love us by pretending to be someone we weren't.

It may seem ironic that you have to stop frantically searching for a soulmate in order to actually connect with one, but then again, this insight isn't exactly new. Folk wisdom has long held, "When you stop looking for love—that's when you find it." Take Madeline's experience with Richard, for example.

Madeline and Richard

"I don't remember exactly where or when I first became aware of 'the face,'" Madeline told me. "It might have come to me in a dream, or maybe I saw something like it in a book or a movie. But around the age of ten or eleven I became aware of a face that I associated with the guy I'd someday love and marry.

"The man of my dreams was dark, with Mediterranean features. He had a rather long face, and a Semitic nose with a mole beside it. Do you know that actor Sam Elliot? Well, this face was a little like his. Rugged, but sensitive. It's not one that everyone would consider handsome, but I felt sure it was the face of my soulmate. I could see him very clearly in my mind's eye, and I grew up expecting him to appear at any moment.

"Every time I met a man who looked a little like the guy in my imagination, I thought, 'Maybe he's the one!' I've had a lot of relationships in my life, and the really important ones were all with guys who bore some resemblance to my mental picture. They all had a dark Mediterranean look, and Semitic noses with moles beside them. But they weren't really 'the face,' and I'd soon realize that they weren't my soulmate. It wasn't until I was thirty-six that I actually met the man I'd been dreaming about in person!

"What happened was that a friend of mine in Alcoholics Anonymous invited me to go to a meeting with him so that he could introduce me to his sponsor, who was scheduled to be one of the speakers. Well, the minute I laid eyes on Richard, I knew that he was the man I'd been visualizing all those years. And when he opened his mouth, I realized that there had also been a voice associated with the set of features in my mind—soft, deep, and strong. Richard not only had 'the face,' he had 'the voice' as well! Here in the flesh was the man I'd been seeing in my dreams since I was a little girl. I was practically speechless!

"But it was all so crazy! I'd always assumed 'the face' would turn out to be that of my soulmate, but it was obvious that Richard and I were not meant to be together. I was happily married to someone else, and I soon found out that Richard was engaged himself. Talk about confusing! And it became even more so when he came to work at the alcohol recovery center where I'm a therapist.

"Richard had been a scientist, but he'd changed professions and was then studying to be a social worker. He did an internship at the agency where I'm an alcohol counselor, and we were soon working together doing outreach in jails and prisons. We became good friends, although I always had to struggle to suppress the attraction I felt toward him. From my position as a friend and co-worker, I could see that he was kind of a ladies' man, and that the women he seemed to like weren't anything like me.

"After his internship ended, Richard moved on to another agency. I'd run into him occasionally at A.A. meetings and events, and I felt the same old fascination every time I did. But he certainly wasn't on my mind. I had long since given up on trying to figure out what it meant that he was 'the face.' He obviously wasn't my soulmate.

"Several years passed, and my marriage fell apart. It wasn't the first one that hadn't worked out. I got yet another divorce and decided it would probably be best if I just gave up on marriage.

"It isn't that I didn't want to find a soulmate—I did! I just didn't think it was going to happen. I was forty by then, and as far as men went, my choices so far had all been way off base. Not that the problems were all of their making, of course. But I could see that I didn't know how to choose someone who'd really be right for me. And now that I'd found 'the face' from my girlhood dreams, and he wasn't the one either, I figured I just had a broken 'picker,' and I'd better quit while I was ahead.

"So I decided that from now on I was just going to look after myself, and enjoy being single. I didn't plan to be celibate or anything. I knew I'd probably have affairs. But I was no longer looking for my one true love. It seemed like a good time to stop messing up *my* life, and I figured it would be a kindness to the men I'd be sparing.

"After my divorce was final, I bought myself a nice condo on the Inland Waterway, and then took myself to Europe. And when I came back, I decided to throw a little party to celebrate my newly liberated outlook. I had invited the friend who first introduced me to Richard, and he brought Richard along. It turned out that Richard's engagement hadn't worked out, and he was now at loose ends. He asked if I was going to the party of a mutual friend the following night, and when I said I was, he suggested we go together.

"Now, even though he was 'the face,' I'd known him for seven years by then, and just thought of him as a friend, so our going somewhere together didn't strike me as a date. Besides, I was through with romance. We went to the party and wound up making a night of it, hitting an AIDS fundraiser afterwards, and then a late movie. We parted at my door without a kiss, but the next morning Richard called and asked if he could come over and study for his Boards at my house. He came, but he didn't get any studying done. We talked all day, and we've never been apart for long since.

"A little over a month later, Richard asked me to marry him. By then I knew that he was very sick with hepatitis C, and might not have that long to live. His proposal touched me very deeply. He said, 'Madeline, I don't have much, and I don't even know how much longer I have to live. But I'd like to spend whatever time I have left with you.' We married a few months later, on Thanksgiving Day, and have been together for the last six years, although so much has happened that it feels like twenty!

"One thing was that Richard nearly died of the hepatitis. He was so sick we were actually planning the funeral. But by some miracle he pulled through.

"Then the medical bills did us in financially, and I thought I was going to lose my condo. But some friends threw a fundraiser for us and got us back on our feet. In A.A. we say that religion is for people who believe in hell, but spirituality is for those of us who've been there! Richard and I are getting to be *real* spiritual.

"Richard is better now and has been able to go back to work. I don't know how long we'll have together, but I know one thing for sure—this is my last marriage. I've had the best, and I can't imagine ever wanting anyone else.

"Richard is the most loving husband I could ever imagine. After six years of marriage, he still sends me a greeting card every week telling me how grateful he is that we're together. And he's always doing thoughtful things. Each year for my birthday he designs a special piece of jewelry for me. We've been through some very rough times together, and heaven only knows what lies ahead, but I wouldn't have missed it for the world!

"There's a greeting card I gave Richard that he keeps on his mirror. It has a picture of eagles mating. Do you know about eagles? They mate for life, and once a year they take off together on a conjugal flight. They soar to an unimaginable height, and then in midair, they lock their talons together and plunge to earth, mating as they fall. If all goes well, they pull apart just before they hit the ground and soar away together. But sometimes they crash and one or both are killed. Well, that's what our relationship is like. We've mated for life, and we cling to each other in the face of immanent peril.

"I don't mean to make it sound like we have an ideal relationship or that we get along perfectly together," Madeline went on. "We have plenty of arguments, but we handle them better than I ever believed possible. Early in our marriage we made up our minds that we weren't going to repeat the mistakes we'd made in the past. We decided never to use demeaning language no matter how mad we got, and made a rule that if we have a fight, neither of us will leave the room until we've talked out our differences and arrived at some compromise. So we argue, but we always treat each other with love and respect.

"In fact, there are times I wish I didn't love Richard quite so much. It might be a little easier to cope with the prospect of losing him. But every time I look at that face I've loved for so long, I just melt!"

I asked Madeline about Richard's first impression of her.

"He tells me he was very intimidated by me when we met," she replied. "I guess I tend to hide my vulnerability beneath a brassy, street-wise manner. Working every day with low-bottom drunks who'll roll right over the top of you if they get the chance doesn't exactly encourage a gal to be demure!

"When we first met at the A.A. meeting, he thought I was attractive, but kind of a tough cookie. Then when he came to work at my agency and saw my office, he said he realized there must be another side to me. It's full of objects with spiritual significance, including a lot of Native American stuff from the Southwest. I feel very drawn to the indigenous peoples of Arizona and New Mexico, and so does Richard. You should see our house!

"Remember that line Ram Dass said he used to use to lure attractive prospects up to his apartment?" Madeline laughed. "'Come up and see my holy things'? Well it was a little like that.

Richard says that when he saw all my 'holy things,' he knew that there must be a lot more to me than he'd first thought. Still, he never looked on me as anything more than a friend until we finally connected after the party. We're definitely soulmates, but I really don't think I'm his type!"

I've pointed out that there seem to be certain things soulmates must accomplish on their own before being ready to unite. When meant-to-be lovers run into each other before their preparatory work is complete, they just don't seem to click. That may have been what happened when Herman and Roma met in Israel, and when Carrie and Norman brushed by each other without recognition on campus in Albany, and it seems to be what occurred when Madeline and Richard first became acquainted.

What was it these two soulmates needed to do before really sparking to each other? Well, it seems likely that completing their existing romantic commitments was at least a part of it. I suspect that our guides—acting in the service of our souls—are prepared to delay the recognition of our soulmates indefinitely if they would distract us from whatever issues remain to be worked on in our current relationships. It is usually best to get all we possibly can out of one liaison before embarking on another.

Maybe that's why people so seldom seem to find their ideal mates before disengaging from previous partners. I *have* heard stories of soulmates who fell in love while still married to other people, but they seem to be the exceptions rather than the rule. Perhaps these are cases where the marital bond has ceased to serve the deepest needs of either partner, but the two remain together out of inertia, or a misplaced sense of obligation. Some marriages are over long before either spouse is prepared to acknowledge that this is so.

I also wonder if Richard's arrival on the scene played any role at all in Madeline's dissatisfaction with her marriage. Not that she decided to divorce her husband so that she could fly to him. But I suspect that there are times when an encounter with someone we've loved since before our births stimulates an unconscious memory of the kind of unconditional acceptance that is truly possible, and makes us discontent with partners who aren't offering us everything our soul desires. Sometimes this dissatisfaction leads to an overhaul of the marital relationship, and sometimes to divorce.

Going It Alone

Be that as it may, I also think that Madeline's decision to give up on finding true love was the final piece of whatever puzzle needed to be solved before she could unite with Richard. Isn't it interesting that she was throwing herself a party to celebrate her new, permanently single status when Richard reentered her life to take up his role as her soulmate? Is it possible that both of them had just been waiting for Madeline to achieve the realization that she didn't really need a special man in her life? How interesting that she would discover her true love at the party she threw to celebrate her decision to quit searching for him!

Giving up on the idea that we *simply have to* find a soulmate may be a necessary prerequisite to actually finding one. For one thing, it amounts to a decision to dissociate ourselves from our ego's insatiable neediness and entitlement, and to be grateful for what life has given us already. Singer/actor/filmmaker Barbra Streisand and actor James Brolin, whom she believes to be her soulmate, both appear to have achieved this "attitude of gratitude" prior to their first encounter at a dinner party in 1996. Streisand, who had not dated anyone seriously for several years before meeting Brolin, told reporters from *People Magazine*:* "I was liking my solitude. I had been given so many blessings, [I thought] maybe a relationship was an area I could never have—and that was okay."

Brolin too seems to have made his peace with the single life prior to finding the love he'd always dreamt of with Barbra. In

---

* "Perfect Harmony," *People,* Kim Hubbard and Todd Gold, 3/9/98, pp. 78–84.

the same article, the twice-divorced actor reported that before meeting her, he had been quietly resigned to the idea of living the rest of his life alone: "All I needed was the newspaper, a great cup of coffee and a view of the ocean. For the first time I wasn't worrying about when I was going to find someone who made me complete."

Is it just a coincidence that so many people find true love only after achieving the realization that romance is not the be-all and the end-all of life? Or might this shift from desperation to grateful contentment be essential to the process? And if so, what is it about giving up on our romantic dreams that opens the door to a soulmate relationship?

GUIDELINES FOR ACTUALIZING A SOULMATE RELATIONSHIP

1. Realize that your happiness in life doesn't depend upon being loved, but upon loving. You can have a joyous, love-filled life even if you never find a mate.
2. Don't wait for someone else to "fill you up." Open up to your inner being and your life will feel so richly rewarding that even a soulmate will seem like the icing on the cake.
3. Be grateful for all the love you have, and all the love you can give, independent of whether you ever find a soulmate.

17

Of Saviors
and Soulmates

There is a way to be happy in relationships,
and that is to use relationships for their intended purpose,
not the purpose you have designed.

—*Conversations with God*

If you are troubled by a sense of neediness when it comes to romance, perhaps the desperation you feel is actually rooted in a misguided attempt to find in a relationship with a lover, the joy, security, meaning, and self-worth that can only be attained through reidentification with your true self. Just as the ego has to offer us a chemical high as a substitute for love, it has to distract us from the joy of self-remembering with the promise of a very special lover who'll somehow make it possible for us to live happily ever after within its dark world of frightening illusions.

Think for a moment about that standard fairy-tale formula "happily ever after." Doesn't this phrase suggest a state of perpetual joy and eternal safety—complete satisfaction multiplied by the knowledge that this satisfaction can never be taken away? Isn't it, in fact, suspiciously reminiscent of what religious folk call *heaven?* Your ego wants you to believe that lifelong infatuation with a very special romantic partner can compensate you for the eternal happiness and security you sacrificed when you dissociated your memory of who and what you really are. It can't.

Searching for the Love That Will Save You

If you want to overcome neediness, it helps to begin by reminding yourself that a sense of anxiety about finding love is a sure sign of ego identification. Only a deluded mind could imagine itself apart from love. When we are aware of our soul and spirit, we recognize that love is everywhere. At such times, the idea that we could lack anything essential to our happiness is seen as utterly ridiculous.

Nevertheless, when you look upon yourself from the fearful perspective of your ego, you certainly seem to have ample reason for anxiety and self-disgust. Your false self regards you as a vulnerable, inadequate, isolated creature, threatened with immanent destruction at the whim of a meaningless and uncaring universe. And it maintains that the solution to this existential dilemma is not to dismiss it as an illusion, but to conquer and annex some more fortunate being who will somehow possess the power, security, and love-worthiness you so obviously lack.

Existentialist philosophers refer to this as *the illusion of an ultimate rescuer*. When ego-based fantasies are introduced into our spiritual life, they encourage us to wait around for the messiah, avatar, or savior who is to someday magically deliver us from our self-created misery without any effort on our parts. When these distorted salvation fantasies bleed through into the romantic arena, they generate a yearning for an all-powerful, all-good consort who is somehow supposed to guarantee our safety, validate our worth, and redeem our otherwise miserable and meaningless lives. This ultimate rescuer, whose job it will be to save us from our ego's version of reality without actually calling it into question, is essentially the grown-up's equivalent of a fairy-tale prince or princess.

Have You Been Looking for a Savior Rather Than a Soulmate?

Is it just barely possible that you too have unwittingly been searching not simply for a loving helpmate with whom to share your life's adventures, but for a godlike being whose love would make your existence tantamount to heaven on earth? After all, your friends and relatives love you, but you aren't crazy enough to think that *their* love would make you live happily ever after, are you? But I think if you're honest, you may have to admit that you *are* crazy enough to think that your soulmate's affection is going to do just that!

Now some readers—and especially those who don't believe in any sort of spiritual dimension—will object that while they may indeed have been hoping for a little *magic* from romance, they are certainly *not* seeking eternal salvation in a lover's arms. But let's be clear about one thing: Not believing in a higher power doesn't make a person *less* likely to confuse a lover with love itself, but *more* so. People who understand that their salvation lies in the relationship of their true self to the universe are not likely to be seeking it through romance. The acid test of whether you've been searching for a savior rather than a soulmate is *the depth of your despair over the loss of a love.*

- If romantic rejection has ever damaged your self-esteem, you must have been imagining that your lover was uniquely qualified to be your judge by virtue of some sort of divine omniscience. Why else would this one opinion matter so much more than those of friends and family?

- If you've ever felt frantic or enraged when threatened with the loss of a lover, you must have thought your ultimate security and well-being depended upon him or her.

- If you have ever seen a sweetheart as *angelic* at the start of a relationship, only to have this angel later seem downright

187

demonic, you can be sure that you've been relating to your ego's projections, rather than to the reality of the other person.

- If you have entertained the thought that, having been rejected by this person, you would *never* find happiness, you must have imagined that winning the hand of this individual was the key to your eternal salvation.

- If you have ever considered killing yourself when a marriage or a love affair ended, you must have believed that more was riding on it than simply a rewarding association with a beloved friend.

Naturally, everyone is disappointed when a romantic affair doesn't work out. It's always sad to see our beautiful hopes for the future whirling down the drain. Nevertheless, people focused on finding soulmates can be relatively philosophical about such setbacks and quickly move on, while those who are unconsciously searching for a savior often feel so humiliated, defeated, and hopeless that it is difficult for them to face the imagined risks involved in forming new attachments.

Sadly, fantasizing that some particular lover holds the key to your eternal salvation has another unfortunate consequence. It encourages you to put up with things you otherwise wouldn't. After all, if you mistakenly believe that your eternal happiness is a gift that only one person can give you, you can't very well take your business elsewhere, can you? When you give your power away to others by idealizing—and even deifying—them, you effectively enslave yourself, and invite every sort of inconsideration and abuse.

The Lover as Savior

If you suspect that you may have been entertaining unconscious salvation fantasies about romance, you are certainly not alone. The tendency to confuse a lover with divine love is very common. Indeed, a cursory survey of popular music underscores the fact that infatuation is almost always clothed in spiritual metaphors.

In the grip of a grand passion, we all experience a strong temptation to swear "eternal" devotion, and to regard our sweetheart as our "special angel, sent from heaven above." Nevertheless, despite our euphoria, there are times when we can't help wondering whether the "divine" lover we "idolize" is really going to deliver "the love that will save us," or turn out to have been nothing more than "the devil with a blue dress on." Occasionally, we may even feel "possessed" by someone who puts us "in a spell" with "that old, black magic called *love*." But, "devil or angel," we put those we adore on "pedestals," and "worship the very ground they walk upon," — at least until the day we sadly discover their "feet of clay." Just as it is said that there are no atheists in foxholes, it would appear that there are no atheists in love!

Come on now, admit it! Haven't you secretly been hoping that your soulmate would turn out to be some extraordinarily glamorous, larger-than-life figure whose love would transform your existence, validate your worth, make you the envy of all your friends, and end all your earthly cares? Haven't you been thinking that this person would be, not merely "nice," but more than a little *divine?*

We've seen that the ego invariably leads us to *overvalue* the objects of its affection. Now we are in a position to understand *why* it encourages this idealization. For only by wildly exaggerating our lovers' virtues and blinding us to their faults can our false self hope to make their possibilities as our saviors seem in any way credible.

I think this also puts us in a better position to understand the appeal of twin-flame relationships. The ego induces us to feel inadequate and incomplete, and then promises us a solution in the form of a lover who will be our "other half," supplying all the inner worth we experience ourselves a lacking. When we are seeing ourselves through the eyes of our ego, it's easy to believe we are only half a person, and that our only hope for survival lies in inducing someone whole to complete us.

189

You Need to Save Yourself

Now let me say right here that I do believe our soulmates some-times function as our saviors. But because each of us has free will, the only way true salvation can be achieved is through learning to prefer reality to illusion. No one has the power to remove false and terrifying thoughts from our minds as long as we prefer to entertain them. Your soulmate may very well be your "savior" — and you, his or hers — if what you mean by that term is "honored teacher of love." But the only one who can free you of fear and make you live happily ever after is *you*.

Ultimately, each of us must *save ourselves*. We must dismiss the illusion that we lack something essential to our well-being and stop searching for what appears to be missing outside ourselves. When we rely upon others to meet our needs we feel helpless and dependent no matter how well we're cared for. When we learn to rely instead upon the creative power that resides within our true self, we discover that our fears were groundless, and be-come *self*-sufficient in a way we never thought possible.

If you've been imagining that you *need* an ideally compati-ble life partner — as opposed to very much *wanting* one — you can be sure that you've been seeking a savior rather than a soulmate. And because you are setting your lovers a task they cannot pos-sibly fulfill, you're destined to be perpetually disappointed. Last-ing security, love, and happiness are the result of self-realization, and self-realization necessarily involves *self-reliance*. People don't become soulmate material until they begin to put their faith in the creative power of their own inner being.

However, let me hasten to add that it really doesn't matter whether you think of this *self* upon which you are going to rely in spiritual or psychological terms. People who put their faith in God often feel *self*-reliant because they believe there is a higher power within them that validates their worth, directs their steps, and arranges for them to manifest the things they want and need. But there are plenty of happy and effective nonbelievers whose faith in *themselves* accomplishes the same thing. Out of their self-respect, self-confidence, and self-love, they manifest lives rich in pleasure, meaning, and accomplishment.

I believe that each self is an individual expression of God. Thus, as far as I'm concerned, to have faith in yourself *is* to have faith in God. To love yourself *is* to love God. To call upon your own creativity *is* to call upon the creative power of the universe. The thing that distinguishes people who live joyous, successful lives is not belief in some transcendent higher power, but belief in *themselves.*

Think, for example, of Marianna realizing that she didn't need to *marry* a professor; she could *be* one. This insight was not experienced as increased faith in God, but rather as increased faith in *herself.* She realized that she could *help herself* to the good things she wanted out of life. Perhaps this is the true significance of the expression, "God helps those who help themselves." Whenever we confidently rely upon our own inner resources, and make the best possible use of our personal talents and abilities, we are, in effect, calling upon "the God within," and we will be answered.

"Settling" for a Soulmate

Self-sufficiency enables us to quit searching for a lover who is "perfect in every way," and settle instead for one who is "perfect for us." However, this shift from outer-directedness to inner-directedness affects much more than just our romantic aspirations. It has ramifications in every dimension of our lives.

For one thing, it makes us much more realistic, and this inevitably brings us face to face with the possibility that what we have right now may be all we'll ever have. The realization that no fairy-tale prince or princess is going to come along and transform our existence is a little disappointing at first, but it eventually leads to the discovery of reasons to be grateful for what life has given us already. Think again of Barbra Streisand's comment: "I had been given so many blessings, [I thought] maybe a relationship was an area I could never have — and that was okay."

Self-sufficient individuals learn to savor the little things in life—in James Brolin's words: an ocean view, a newspaper and a great cup of coffee. Like Madeline, they stop deferring their happiness until they find the special someone who was supposed to confer it upon them. If they want to go to Europe, they go to Europe. If they want a nice place to live, they get one for themselves.

And, perhaps most important, they start seeking—and finding—solace and joy in their relationships with the seemingly "ordinary" people in their environments. As we relax into our natural roles as conduits through which divine love pours forth into the world, we find ourselves experiencing enormous fulfillment from even casual friendships. Further, because like attracts like, this decision to extend love freely attracts unconditional love from others and makes us very magnetic where our soulmates are concerned. Take Ellen's experience.

Ellen and Peter

Ellen's work as a foley artist at a major motion picture studio earned her a handsome living—so handsome, in fact, that by the age of forty-one this single woman was in a financial position to retire and pursue her interests in art, dance, psychology, and spiritual growth. In most respects, her proverbial cup was running over. She had met and exceeded her professional goals, she was enjoying many warm friendships, and she was delighted with the progress she was making in her meditation training at the Los Angeles Self-Realization Fellowship. The only thing lacking was a soulmate to share her happiness, and even that wasn't seeming like the problem it once had.

"I had looked for a soulmate for so long," Ellen told me, "but I had never found any man with whom I could feel that deep a connection. For a while, I even began to think that maybe God hadn't created a partner for me. Maybe I was destined to be single all my life. But fortunately I soon thought better of it. How small it was of me to try to make God so small! Nothing is beyond the power of God. If you can dream it, you can create it!

"When I left my job at the studio in May, it was a very exciting time. One of the first things I did was to visit a psychic who announced that I would meet my soulmate at a seminar I was scheduled to attend at the Esalen Institute toward the end of July. She said that he was going to really knock my socks off! According to her, he would be handsome, nurturing, and sensitive—someone who 'heals people with his words,' whatever that meant! I asked her what I had to do to connect with this paragon, and she said, 'Absolutely nothing!'

"It's funny, though. I'd been hoping and praying for a soulmate for so long, you'd think I'd be deliriously happy about this prediction. But at that particular time I was enjoying my life so much that it almost didn't matter to me whether I met him or not. I was meeting a lot of fascinating people, and I felt like I was falling a little in love with every one of them. Each seemed to nurture and satisfy some part of me. In fact, life was so delicious that I actually thought seriously about not going to Esalen! I was feeling completely whole and fulfilled, and I knew my life was going to continue to be a delightful adventure even if I never found a special man to love and marry.

"But of course I did decide to go. I was the last one to arrive for the workshop and when I walked into the room, thirty or more people were sitting in a circle on pillows on the floor. There was only one empty pillow, and it was right next to this guy who riveted my attention immediately. He was very good-looking, in just the way I like best. The psychic had said I'd meet my soulmate toward the end of July. Well, when I sat down next to Peter, it was after 8:00 PM on July 31st. You can't get much later in July than that!

"The minute I settled down beside Peter, I was aware of a powerful attraction between us. When the facilitator went around the room asking us to introduce ourselves, I tried to keep my feelings in check by telling myself that this intriguing man would probably open his mouth and say something really off-putting. But it wasn't like that at all. When Peter spoke about himself, I was moved by everything he said. For one thing, he told us that he had recently retired from a very successful career in business and that his focus now was on his own psychological and spiritual growth. Just like me! He also said that he was a poet. That got my attention because I love poetry.

"As the evening went on, I continued to be conscious of Peter in a way that made it very hard to focus on anything else. I remember there was one point during the workshop when we were sitting there side-by-side, with our bare feet only a few inches apart. I found myself absolutely longing to touch his foot with mine! It was all I could do to restrain myself because caressing him seemed like such a natural thing to do—except, of course, that he was a complete stranger. He later told me that he had been feeling exactly the same way!

"We got acquainted after the workshop disbanded for the evening. As things were breaking up, I turned to him and asked if he'd ever read my favorite poet, Rumi. He said he'd just bought his first volume of Rumi's work a few days earlier and was absolutely enchanted with it. Peter was just as eager to make contact with me as I was with him, so the conversation flowed on from there. It seemed as if we were on the same wavelength about everything. I felt completely free and easy with him. From the very first evening, it has felt like Peter is part of me—as if we couldn't separate if we tried.

"The thing I love most about Peter is that he lets me be everything I am. In other relationships, I always had a feeling that some parts of me were acceptable and others less so. Without realizing it, I guess I was always censoring myself in an effort to live up to the other person's expectations. But Peter has no expectations of me, other than that I be myself.

"With Peter, I feel free to explore my feelings and reveal myself completely, even when what I have to communicate is anger or disappointment over something that has happened between us. You see, it isn't that we never argue. It's just that we both prize our relationship so much that we work really hard to resolve the problem quickly, and get back into a good space together. Our happiness is connected. Neither one of us could be comfortable while the other was upset, so when problems arise, there's nothing to do but solve them as quickly as we can."

I asked Ellen if she had any tips for people who want to find a soulmate relationship of their own.

"Well, first of all, I believe that life is whatever way you think it is," she replied. "At one time I had become discouraged about ever finding the kind of love I wanted, and I was beginning to wonder if God had created a soulmate for me. But as soon as I realized how ridiculous that was—that of course God could find me someone perfect—I met Peter.

"I believe in the creative power of consciousness, and I think that what happens to us is whatever we *believe* will happen. That's why it's so important not to let the collective consciousness convince us to doubt that life can be truly wonderful. We should dare to dream our most extravagant dreams, because the things we dream eventually become our reality. If we're harboring the thought that we won't find someone wonderful to love, it could prevent us from doing so.

"The other important thing is feeling complete within yourself," Ellen continued. "Before Peter and I met I was really enjoying life and not feeling needy in any way. I think that by experiencing myself as whole, self-sufficient, and happy, I attracted someone with the same qualities.

"If you want a really healthy relationship, you have to get yourself straightened out first. For years before we met, both Peter and I had been pursuing our own growth and healing through psychotherapy, our spiritual disciplines, reading, growth groups, and so on. And both of us had achieved a certain level of professional success, psychological maturity, and financial independence. I think that's why things are so good between us now. Peter and I don't *pull on* each other, or make demands of any kind. We don't need each other to be anything other than what we are. We're here to share and have fun and be supportive. This is not a relationship fraught with issues and emotional baggage."

I think it's significant that Ellen didn't find Peter until she'd become content with the life she'd created on her own. Her increased self-reliance is evident from the pleasure she began to take in the non-soulmates she encountered. When relating to others out of a sense of neediness, her anxious gaze probably passed right over individuals who did not appear to be the ultimate rescuer she sought. But as she became more inner-directed and self-reliant, Ellen stopped living for future rescue and started making the best of the present, giving her loving attention to whoever was handy. And sure enough, the desperation she'd felt about finding her soulmate vanished as she awakened to the inner beauty of the people around her. What did she need with an ultimate rescuer once she discovered the joys of "falling a little in love" with everyone she met?

Ellen's story also points to another indicator that you've been searching for a savior instead of a soulmate: the inability to believe you'll ever really find what you seek. As long as Ellen was desperate for a special man to make her life worthwhile, she couldn't help doubting that there was any guy in existence capable of meeting all her needs. And of course, there wasn't! The kind of needs she had in mind could only be met through the relationship of her true self to the universe, not by another person, however good and powerful and loving he might be. Yet once Ellen realized she could rely upon her *self,* the whole enterprise of finding a soulmate began to seem much more doable. Ultimate rescuers are notoriously hard to come by, but if you're willing to settle for a soulmate, it needn't be all that difficult to find what you're looking for.

Guidelines for Actualizing a Soulmate Relationship

1. Turn within for the strength and wisdom to solve your problems and create the richly meaningful life you want.
2. Don't expect a lover to meet all your needs.
3. Come from strength, and focus on what you have to give others rather than on what you hope to get from them.

18

Place Your Case in Expert Hands

Therefore ask not of yourself what you need,
for you do not know,
and your advice to yourself will hurt you.
— *A Course in Miracles*

I've alluded to the way your thoughts and expectations influence the events that occur in your life, and hinted at the awesome creative power that resides within your true self. Indeed, there are metaphysical traditions throughout the world that maintain that we manifest whatever life circumstances are most consistent with our state of mind. The "laws of manifestation" are currently a hot topic within financial circles as well, where success gurus like Tony Robbins, Wayne Dyer, and Napoleon Hill teach people to attain their financial goals through positive thinking. Many contemporary scientists also believe thoughts affect the circumstances that manifest in the physical world. Physicist David Bohm, for example, concluded from his work in quantum mechanics that by focusing attention and belief on certain possibilities and ignoring others, we unwittingly select the particular possible future that will take shape in our lives. Yet many of us have trouble recognizing our vast powers of manifestation.

The thing that makes it so difficult for us to comprehend the power of our mind is the fact that it *looks* as if experience influences belief rather than the reverse. The conventional wisdom is that "seeing is believing." It seldom occurs to us that our personal beliefs may be causing things to turn out as we anticipate.

Thus, a heterosexual man who has never made much of an impression on the opposite sex tends to conclude that he must not have a whole lot of sex appeal. If *believing is seeing,* however, as the metaphysical view contends, the man in our example is confusing effect with cause. The real reason he doesn't attract women is that he thinks of himself as unattractive. This causes him to manifest experiences of rejection, and unwittingly to speak and act in ways that practically demand it. If he could learn to think about himself differently, others would begin to think about him differently as well.

Now, it isn't just that our beliefs and expectations produce related outcomes *automatically*—although they *do* do that. There is also a sense in which we actively bring about the states of affairs we anticipate. When we believe something to be true, we expect future events to be consistent with that belief, and we speak and act in ways that reflect our confidence that they will.

Thus, an adolescent embarrassed about his acne is likely to cut a pretty unattractive figure, slouching around and steeling himself against the rejection he anticipates. A woman enjoying the fantasy that she is fatally attractive to men is going to dress in a becoming fashion, and walk around with a certain air that draws attention to her sexuality.

Expect the Best

Because there are so many excellent books on manifestation techniques, creative visualization, positive thinking, and related topics, I'm not going to discuss this subject in depth here, except to emphasize the fact that confidently *expecting* certain things to happen greatly increases the likelihood that they will.

Film star Sophia Loren, for example, has often spoken of her unhappy childhood in war-ravaged Italy. Starving, fatherless, and stigmatized by her illegitimacy, little Sophia was also tormented by her peers for being such a skinny, ugly, ungainly child. How did she go on to actualize a future so very different from her past? She believes her grandmother had a lot to do with it.

Loren says when she was an infant, her grandmother made up a little song about all the wonderful things Sophia would someday be, and do, and have. It celebrated the idea that she would be extraordinarily beautiful, rich, happy, and adored. All of her dreams would come true. No blessing would be denied her.

The older woman would sing little Sophia to sleep at night with these happy images, and often used the song to distract her from her hunger, fear, and loneliness throughout the day. Loren believes that the constant repetition of these positive thoughts about a future rich in joy, success, and love profoundly affected her unconscious mind, encouraging her to believe in her possibilities and to reach for her dreams. By her early twenties, every word of her grandmother's song had come true!

The Problem with Trying to Manifest a Soulmate Intentionally

There's no doubt that thought is powerful. As *A Course in Miracles* puts it:

> *When you change your mind,*
> *you change the most powerful instrument*
> *that was ever given to you for change.*
> —A Course in Miracles

Conscientiously applied, the techniques of intentional manifestation may well bring you just the kind of partner you've been dreaming of. But then again, they may not. And even if they do, the man or woman you've "manifested," is not likely to be a real soulmate. The problem is that the "you" that thinks, speaks, and acts to create the future of your choice is not necessarily *you* at all. It may well be the false self that is controlled by your ego.

Again, we need to understand that each of us has two wills: one that our true self shares with the universe and all other beings, and a split-off individual will that is under the sway of our ego. *Free will* means that we are at liberty to obey our ego, doing things that conflict with our own *true will* for ourselves, and creating situations that are ultimately not in our own, or anyone else's, best interests.

To the extent that our mind is not in touch with either our guide or our inner being, none of us really *knows* what will make us happy — much less what actions on our part will lead to the outcome we desire. Under these conditions, we inevitably use the creative power of our consciousness in the service of our ego's agenda. And if you are working to actualize the romantic future your ego has in mind, *you* are not going to be very happy with the way things turn out.

Think, for example, of Karen. She was convinced that she knew *exactly* what to look for in a man, yet the length of time it took her to recognize Pat as her soulmate is evidence of how far off base her ego's concept of an ideal partner really was. Had she relied upon the power of her consciousness to manifest the lover of her ego's dreams, she might have spent the rest of her life becoming involved with one superficial, self-involved heart-breaker after another!

But happily, that's not what she did. If you think about it, that's not what *any* of the people whose meant-to-be relationships we've discussed did. Soulmates don't tell the universe what they need; they allow the universe to *tell them* what they need, through the medium of their soul's desires and their heaven-sent guide. If you hope to find a relationship that will truly fulfill your grandest aspirations, you have to step away from the illusion of autonomy offered by your ego, and be willing to be shown not merely *how to get* what you want — but also *what* to want.

Who Do You Want Pulling Your Strings?

Although it may seem a little insulting to suggest such a thing, we humans are a lot like puppets—incapable of making decisions for ourselves. Thus, all our vaunted "free will" really amounts to is the right to choose who will pull our strings: the ego, or the inner presence that speaks on behalf of God.

When we allow the ego to interpret what we see, we seem to look out upon a frightening, meaningless world where nothing we achieve ever satisfies us for long. However, we can instead choose to "surrender to our higher power," and make the happy discovery that *God's will for us is actually our own true will for ourselves.*

God is love. Your desire to experience love is divinely inspired, and the universe wills to support you in finding the soulmate relationship of your dreams. It even sent along a trusted emissary to make sure you'd succeed.

Your ego, on the other hand, wills that you perpetually seek for love, but never find it. Which of these two wills is more likely to be your own true will for yourself? Which do you want pulling your strings?

God's Will Is Ours

Now that I've introduced the idea that God's will for us is our own true will for ourselves, it may be a little easier to understand that somewhat odd quotation from *A Course in Miracles* Arnie hit upon when he asked for guidance that first evening we were together in my apartment.

> *You must ask what God's Will is in everything,*
> *because it is yours. You do not know what it is,*
> *but the Holy Spirit remembers it for you.*
> *Ask Him, therefore, what God's Will is for you,*
> *and He will tell you yours.*
> *It cannot be too often repeated that you do not know it.*
> —A Course in Miracles

Ironically, it is only through seeking to know God's will for us that we find out what *we* truly desire. For example, when I asked about God's will for Arnie and me, my guide suggested that we create a holy relationship. Not only did I have to be *told* what I truly wanted from Arnie, but even *after* I'd been told, I was still so confused by my ego that I had trouble believing that this was what *I* really wanted. Loving Arnie initially seemed like my guide's idea, rather than my own!

Should You Rely on Manifestation or Guidance?

Now, don't get me wrong. The mastery of manifestation techniques can be an important step along one's spiritual path. For one thing, it refutes the ego's assumptions that you are guilty and God is vengeful. After all, if there is a divine power within you that is ready, willing, and able to supply the things you ask for, you can't be as weak and helpless as your ego would have you believe, nor can God be as punitive and uncaring. Further, the fact that you can dramatically improve your lot in life just by thinking, speaking, and acting on the basis of more positive beliefs makes it hard to avoid the conclusion that your previous suffering was the result of your own misthought rather than God's lack of concern for your well-being.

Nevertheless, mastery of intentional manifestation is, at best, an intermediate step on the path to true awakening—and one you can skip over completely if you prefer to go directly to guidance. If there are ways you need to change your thinking so that the soulmate relationship you desire can manifest in your life, your guide will show you what to do. Unfortunately, when you try to use the techniques of intentional manifestation without benefit of guidance, your mind can easily slip over into negativity without your even noticing.

How Your Ego Subverts Your Efforts to Manifest a Soulmate

It's important to realize that when you put all your faith in positive thinking, you are implicitly affirming your belief that God cannot be trusted to give you what you need and want without prompting. You are imagining that it is up to your ego-identified mind to figure out what you need, and snatch a little happiness from an uncaring universe. Your ego's job is to make sure that you don't find the love your soul desires, and it can do this just as easily when you rely upon the techniques of intentional manifestation as when you don't.

While the laws of manifestation are ordinarily considered "spiritual," since they were discovered by spiritual adepts, the reality is that they are *natural laws,* and, like any other natural laws, they can be used for good or ill. They certainly pose no threat to the ego, which simply bends them to its own purposes. Indeed, egos take to positive thinking like ducks to water! What could be more attractive to your false self than the grandiose fantasy that it will eventually learn to control the universe, making everything turn out exactly as it has decided it should?

Where romance is concerned, your ego will do its best to keep you affirming and visualizing partners who possess the superficial characteristics it finds attractive, encouraging you to "manifest" a stream of beautiful heiresses or dynamic captains of industry who are every bit as sexy and charismatic as you may have hoped, but quite incapable of loving you or anyone else.

Then, too, your ego is equally adept at undermining your hope of finding love, even as it exhorts you to think positively. We've already explored the way it induces a sense of desperation by persuading you that you don't simply *want* a soulmate. No, you *need* a soulmate, *because life would be utterly insupportable without one.* Start thinking along these lines and your mental focus instantly shifts to fear and loneliness, causing you to manifest more of the same. Eventually, your ego convinces you that you're a hopeless case and that you fully deserve the misery that you get!

Relax!

How different the outcome would be if you forgot about intentional manifestation and instead allowed your guide to help you experience the great love the universe has for you! Just think how positive your thinking will be when you rest content in the certain knowledge that your creator will bring you everything that is truly conducive to your happiness. The moment you stop trying to control everything, and entrust your safety and happiness to a loving and supportive universe, you'll automatically suspend the fearful, ego-generated thinking that has been holding romantic fulfillment at bay. The results you achieve will quickly verify that you made the right decision!

Because God wills for you what you truly will for yourself, you can safely replace all of your positive affirmations with a single all-purpose prayer: "Not my will, but Thine be done." Simply give up on trying to do things "your" way—which is to say, your *ego's* way—and follow the instructions of your divine guide to the fulfillment God wills for you. Isn't that pretty much what we've seen one soulmate after another do?

If you absolutely *can't* bring yourself to believe that "Someone up there loves me," then by all means use the techniques of intentional manifestation as best you can to clarify your intention, increase your sense of love-worthiness and personal effectiveness, and create the future your ego says you need. But if you can—even tentatively—embrace the possibility that heaven has sent a wise and loving guide to show you the way to romantic fulfillment, wouldn't it make good sense to check out the short-cut to soulmate love your inner teacher is trying to show you? And don't worry if you have no faith in a higher power. Faith will come later, after you see what your guide does for you.

Your Guide Is Trying to Help

Now, I've pointed out that even if you've never been aware of your inner teacher's presence, you've undoubtedly received some of the help he or she has to offer all the same. When we don't tune in to guidance consciously, our companion spirits communicate instead with our unconscious minds—and with the unconscious minds of others with whom we interact. They orchestrate fortuitous encounters with people who can provide the answers we are not allowing ourselves to hear directly from them, and maneuver us into positions where we'll stumble upon important insights through books, radio and television shows, conversations overheard on the street, and so forth.

The problem with these indirect methods of communication is that even when our guides succeed in getting a message through to us, we may not know whether to trust it. After all, that author could be wrong. That friend could just be jealous. That therapist may have been locked away in his ivory tower for so long that he has no idea how things operate in the real world.

Unless you know that a suggestion is actually coming from your divine guide, you may hesitate to rely upon it. Take Robin's dilemma, for example. She was being bombarded by the same romantic advice from many different sources, but she was unwilling to act on it until she recognized it as coming from her inner teacher.

Robin

Robin was a member of a spiritual group I was conducting, and it became clear early on that her most painful issue was relationship. The torch she was carrying for the lesbian lover who had decamped a year earlier would scarcely have looked out of place on the Statue of Liberty! Indeed, Robin's stated intention in joining the group had been to improve herself to the point where Sue would want to come back to her. After all, she had made a mental list of all of her former lover's criticisms. Surely if she corrected all of these things about herself, Sue would *have to* love her again!

Having toted a few torches of my own in my time, I was convinced that nothing was going to get better for Robin until she released her ex and moved on. Sue was happily situated in a new relationship and had given Robin no reason at all to expect a reconciliation. It seemed to me that holding onto the vain hope that her former partner would come back was only preventing this young woman from finding the love she wanted elsewhere.

But it was very hard for Robin to hear my suggestion that she give up on Sue. In fact, she became quite angry with me one day in group when I urged her to forget this woman and move on. In the face of Robin's resistance, her therapist had conceded that the most sensible way for her to proceed was to surrender her obsession with Sue gradually, a little at a time. When I suggested that she just do it and get it over with, Robin felt offended and misunderstood.

"Don't you get it?" she protested, "I *can't* just let her go! What do you think I've been *trying* to do for the past year? Do you think I'm just stupid? I've tried everything I can think of to get over this relationship—psychotherapy, prayer, positive affirmations, spiritual rituals—and nothing works! I can't do it! I don't know *how!*"

"First of all," I replied, "of course I don't think you're stupid. I certainly don't think *I'm* stupid, and I've done exactly the same thing you're doing. This isn't about brains.

"As hard as it is to believe," I continued, "you *do* know how to let this go. You just haven't really wanted to. It's as though you're holding onto your obsession with Sue with one hand, while trying to push it away with the other. You continue to derive comfort from the fantasy that it might still turn out well. But there's no good reason to think it will. And the more time you waste waiting for something that isn't going to happen, the longer you're going to be lonely and miserable.

"You *do* know how to let go of this," I urged, as I mimed opening my fist, glancing at the imaginary contents without interest, and casting them aside. "Everyone knows how to release things they no longer want. The hard part is no longer wanting them. Sooner or later, you'll be forced to realize your dreams are not going to come true with Sue. Why not let that time be *now?* Why not face the fact that she doesn't choose to be with you, and start looking around for someone who does?"

Robin left the session still experiencing a lot of conflict, so when she bounced in the following week, I was glad to see that all traces of negative feeling seemed to have vanished. In fact, she looked very much like the cat that ate the canary!

"Are you surprised that I came back after last week?" she began with an impish grin.

"Not at all," I laughed. "I knew you were upset with me, but I didn't think that you'd quit the group over it."

"Well, just wait till I tell you what's happened since then," Robin went on eagerly.

"First of all, I was so disturbed by what happened between us last week that I made an appointment with my therapist the next day to talk it over. I understood that you were trying to be helpful, but it seemed so unfair of you to insist I had a choice about something I didn't feel I could control. As I was sitting in my therapist's waiting room, I kept thinking about how you'd said I could just let this thing with Sue go if I wanted to, and I couldn't see how that could be true.

"But then it began to seem to me that I was hearing the voice of Jesus in my head, telling me that what you'd said was true . . . that I *could* release Sue immediately if I wanted to, and that it really would be the best thing if I did. I didn't know if it was really Jesus talking to me, but I couldn't help thinking it was.

"When I went in to see my therapist, I talked it over with her. She'd been suggesting that I just try to give up my obsession with Sue little by little, since I didn't feel I could do it any faster. But I sat there thinking, 'What if that really is Jesus telling me I could let go this minute? What if Carolyn is right that delay will only wind up hurting me more?'

"As we discussed it, I finally achieved the willingness to release Sue once and for all. Then my therapist took me through a visualization in which I severed all connection to my ex. It was a big relief, actually! It made me sad of course, but I also felt free, and kind of exhilarated.

"When I left my therapist's office," Robin continued eagerly, "I went straight on to the bar where I always meet my friends for Western dancing on Thursday nights. Well, at first the evening wasn't going very well. I danced for a while but I couldn't really get into it. So I was standing at the bar feeling kind of bummed out, and I was thinking maybe I should just go home, when this woman I've never seen before walked up to me and asked, 'Where's Robin?'

"Of course, I understood that she was referring to my friend Robin, who was in the next room dancing. So I told her where the other Robin was, and the next thing I knew, she threw her arms around me and started hugging me! And I've gotta say, it was just about the best hug I've ever had! There I was, in the embrace of a total stranger and *loving it.* The two of us stood there rocking in each other's arms for maybe a minute. And the whole situation just seemed so crazy that all I could do was laugh.

"And I finally said to her, 'I don't know who the hell you are, but you feel so good, and you smell so good, *I don't even care!'*

"So then she said to me, 'Didn't you get my message?'

"And I said, 'What message?' And she explained that Robin had given her my number and told her to call me, and that she'd left a message on my machine that afternoon about meeting me later at the bar.

"Then the penny dropped. I remembered that last week, Robin had been telling me about this friend of hers she thought would be just perfect for me. She'd said Lillian had seen me at a party and was very interested in meeting me, and that I ought to give her a call.

"But of course, last week all I could think about was Sue. I'd explained to Robin that I didn't want to meet anyone, but she wouldn't stop nagging me about how I needed to start dating again. Finally—just to get her off my back—I'd said that this Lillian could call *me* if she wanted to, but that it wouldn't do any good—I just wasn't interested. So here she was in my arms, and I was completely blown away by her!

"I don't know whether Lillian will turn out to be my soul-mate," Robin went on. "All I know is that in the week we've been seeing each other she seems like everything I've ever wanted, and she's just as enthusiastic about me as I am about her. We're taking things real slow because neither of us wants to make the same mistakes we've made in the past—rushing into a sexual relationship before we really get to know the other person. But we talk for hours every day, and the better I know her, the crazier I am about her! I've been walking around on my own little cloud all week. I haven't felt this good in over a year!

"And I know perfectly well that I'd never have connected with Lillian this way if I hadn't released Sue first. If I'd continued hanging onto her, I'd have seen Lillian the same way I've seen dozens of women I've met in the past year. She would have been just another pretty face who couldn't hold a candle to my ex. So I really want to thank you for not letting up on me last week, and I really want to thank Jesus for keeping after me, too. Can you believe I found someone new only a couple of hours after releasing Sue? That's gotta be a new record!"

Although Robin did not forge a lasting bond with Lillian, their brief romance served as immediate reinforcement for her decision to release Sue, and convinced her that she *could* love again. She has since resumed dating and has never again felt nearly as bad as she had during the year when she was living for the return of her ex. I think you can see that the universe is amazingly quick to reward every step we take in the direction of love.

Note that Robin hadn't suffered from any shortage of good advice before consciously contacting her guide. Just about everyone who knew of her romantic plight—from her therapist to her close friends to me—had been urging her to forget Sue and move on. Still, until she felt she was hearing it directly from Jesus, she didn't dare believe that that was really where her best interests lay.

I should also mention that, prior to these events, Robin had been using the techniques of intentional manifestation in an effort to bring Sue back. She had attributed her failure to the possibility that she was not using them correctly, or often enough, or with sufficient conviction. In reality, she was not succeeding for the simple reason that she was attempting the impossible!

There are important limitations on your ability to create your life any way you want it. One of them is the right of other people to do the same. The techniques of manifestation can help you achieve the *kinds* of experiences you desire, but they won't necessarily get you some specific person or thing.

Say, for example, that you'd like to be the Pope. Well, so would a lot of other people, and it just so happens that the occupational opportunities in that particular field of endeavor are severely limited. However, while there may be little likelihood of your becoming the supreme pontiff, there's no reason why you couldn't manifest the experience of being "an influential spiritual leader" if you were sufficiently committed to achieving this goal. Similarly, the fact that we can't all marry Harrison Ford or Halle Berry doesn't mean we couldn't find partners we'd regard as "attractive, prosperous, and dynamic."

If Robin's positive thinking could have compelled Sue to return against her will, that would mean that Robin got to manifest the life she chose, while Sue did not. Fortunately, the universe doesn't play favorites this way. You can find someone to love and be loved by, but you can't make someone love you if he or she doesn't care to do so.

Guidelines for Actualizing a Soulmate Relationship

1. Stop trying to *figure out* what will make you happy, and authorize your guide to *show you* what will make you happy.

2. If you aren't aware of your guide's voice, try to read the messages your life is bringing you. For example, the things people who love you have to say may be indirect communications from your companion spirit.
3. Recognize that some things you want are possible and some impossible. Without assistance, you have no way of knowing which is which. That's why you need guidance!
4. Remember that God wills for you all the good things you will for yourself, including a soulmate relationship.

19

How to Contact Your Guide

. . . not that one's Guide is God, but one's Guide,
claiming no separate point of view from the Father's,
is that place where the Father's view shines through.

—Raj

It isn't at all difficult to receive guidance, but it's very easy to fail to recognize that it is your guide who is speaking. Remember Sarah's experience with that inner voice that shouted "No!" when she was agreeing to marry a man she didn't love? When her ego assured her that it was only inconsequential nonsense, she was quick to put it out of her mind. As a result, she subjected herself to a failed marriage she now believes she might have avoided.

Pete very nearly made the same mistake. When he received the word *incognito* in meditation, it meant nothing to him, and he was strongly tempted to dismiss it. Fortunately, he took the trouble to examine it more carefully, recognized it as the name of a place he could go to meet someone, and realized that it might be the answer he'd been seeking. Even then, if he hadn't followed through with the necessary footwork he would never have known for sure whether it was.

It should be clear by this time that not all of the voices in your mind are to be trusted. So how can you tell whether a particular train of thought or line of reasoning comes from your ego or from your guide? To begin with, there are three questions to ask yourself about what a particular voice tells you: (1) Is it true? (2) Is it loving? (3) Is it necessary?

Is It True?

Your guide is going to respond to you with the unvarnished truth, but you must remember that while we all have an inborn capacity for recognizing truth, it is only operative when the truth is our *objective*. When we are content to make snap judgments on the basis of our ego's prejudices, our false self supplies the answer *it* prefers, and then throws together a thought process designed to rationalize it.

Sarah's ego, for example, didn't encourage her to dispassionately weigh all the evidence she could gather about her second husband Phil in order to decide whether it would be a good idea to marry him. Instead, after their first night together, it decided it couldn't get along without him. From then on, she colluded with her false self to zone out on Phil's demeaning remarks, his track record in previous relationships, and all of the other clues that might have made an objective observer more inclined to apply for a restraining order than a marriage license!

Contrast this attitude of complacent self-delusion with Helene's determination never again to believe anything that wasn't true. If you truly want guidance, you must be willing to come to terms with reality, no matter how unpalatable it might be to your ego.

Is It Loving?

Another way to tell the voice of your ego from that of your guide is to ask yourself whether what it says is more consistent with the reality of love or of fear. Any inner voice that intimidates or condemns you—any train of thought that suggests that you are bad, that you deserve to suffer for what you've done, or that your behavior has been "unforgivable"—is sponsored by your ego. The same is true of any voice in your mind that suggests such things are true of another.

Your divine guide will never attempt to dominate or discourage you, or advocate needy, selfish, destructive behavior. If you are troubled by persecutory inner voices, or feel that someone or something is intruding upon your mental space or trying to impose its will upon you, these attacks are not coming from your guide, and they may well be symptoms of mental or emotional illness. The good news is that there are now some very effective treatments available for such disorders, so there is no reason to suffer in silence. Let me urge you to seek professional help without delay!

Is It Necessary?

Unlike your ego, your guide is comfortable with silence, and will not chatter on about inconsequential things just to hold your attention. Our companion spirits speak only when they have something worth saying, (e.g., "That's the man you're going to marry!"). The inner voices that drive you crazy, reciting jingles from commercials, rehashing last night's argument with your mother, cataloguing the batting averages of the players on your favorite team, or obsessing about the exact number of calories you've consumed today, are all brought to you compliments of your ego.

How to Solicit Guidance

If you are asking for guidance, your guide is responding—of that you can be absolutely certain. But, like everything else you experience, hearing guidance is a function of desire and expectation. If your desire is weak or your expectation of success low, you'll be quick to accept defeat, and to insist that you can't hear anything. If they are strong, you'll keep trying, and be willing to consider the possibility that any seemingly random thought, word, impulse, or image that arises in your mind may have been divinely inspired.

I recommend that you set aside fifteen minutes daily during which you'll relax deeply, still your ego's chatter, and listen for the voice of your inner teacher. To get a feel for the appropriate mental state, think about the way you listen to a friend when you're conversing on the phone. You ask a question, and then fall silent to listen for a reply. Your attitude might be described as one of relaxed expectancy.

Invite your guide to speak once as you begin the fifteen minutes and then wait in silence to see what thoughts, images, or other experiences arise in consciousness. Trying too hard can actually block this process. Just give your guide your undivided attention and wait to see what is forthcoming.

It's a good idea to keep a record of anything that comes to mind, so that you won't forget it, or be distracted by your fear that you will. This also helps you remain passive and receptive until you've finished meditating, since it allows you to postpone evaluating whatever you receive until later. You might try speaking your guide's words into a tape recorder, jotting notes on a pad, or even typing the entire conversation directly into a computer.

If You're Having Trouble Hearing Guidance

If your attempts to contact your guide produce no results — day after day, week after week — it's safe to conclude that there is a problem with your desire or expectation. Here are some ways to move past such blockages.

1) Review the stories in this book and remind yourself that if other perfectly ordinary people can get in touch with their guides, there's no good reason why you can't do the same.

2) Notice any fears that might make you reluctant to receive messages from your inner teacher. Do you anticipate condemnation

for your mistakes? Are you wary of being controlled? Are you afraid that hearing an inner voice might mean that you are crazy, or make others think you strange? Are you worried that you aren't going to like the advice you get, and that it might be wrong or sinful to reject it once you've heard it?

When you figure out what's holding you back, see if you can come up with a solution that doesn't involve shutting off communication with your guide. You might, for example, decide, "It's okay if I hear guidance: I just won't tell anyone I'm doing it," or "It's all right to listen to my inner teacher's advice, because I'm free to disagree."

Let me emphasize that there is no penalty for disagreeing with your inner teacher. Since guides don't have egos, they aren't capable of being offended by anything we say or do. Furthermore, each of us has an absolute moral responsibility to act on the basis of our own conscience. If what your guide is suggesting sounds wrong to you, raise your objections and see what he or she has to say in response. But don't do anything just because an inner voice tells you to. It might not even be your guide that is speaking!

3) To get the conversational ball rolling, it sometimes helps to begin sentences that you want your guide to complete: "Asking Glenn for a date would be a (good? bad?) idea."

4) Another way to get around your fears is to refuse to let them stop you. Ask yourself, "What might my guide have said if he or she *could* have gotten through to me?" Then do your best to *imagine* what the wisest, most loving answer to your question might be, and continue the dialogue as if what you imagined had actually been said.

5) Resist the temptation to dismiss what may well be guidance just because it feels as if it is only your imagination. That's exactly the way it *will* feel at first. Besides, when you invite your inner teacher to take charge of your thinking process, imagination becomes a doorway to higher consciousness that can reveal the truth, and sometimes even foretell the future. There is noth-

ing "mere" about imagination once you wrest it from your ego and invite your inner teacher to direct it!

6) It generally helps to begin your experiments with guidance by seeking advice on questions that don't matter much to you. When you inquire about issues of great personal significance, intense fear of making the wrong choice can render you too uptight to perceive, or trust your inner voice. Beginners will probably find it easier to accept an intuitive response to a question like "What should I wear to the party?" than "Should I ask Elaine to marry me?" Even within a single meditative session, it is usually best to start with subjects that arouse little anxiety, and save the more momentous issues until you've made a solid connection with your guide.

Alternate Means of Communication

Even if your ability to distinguish guidance is poorly developed, rest assured that your inner teacher is making every effort to reach you in whatever way will work. Often our guides communicate by directing our attention to meaningful coincidences. We ask for help and seem to receive no response, yet a short time later a line from a song we hear on the radio, an article we run across in a magazine, or some other seemingly random occurrence strikes us as being uniquely responsive to our concerns. Take the case of Mary, who wanted help with an important decision, but was afraid to trust her interpretation of her guidance.

Mary

A former student of mine felt a need to relocate, but didn't know where to go. Not wanting to make a mistake, she prayed for guidance. Was it only a coincidence that she began encountering the name *Santa Fe* all over the place?

Mary says that she would be driving along wondering where to move, and would look up and discover that she was crossing

Santa Fe Street. She would idly glance around in a cafe while pondering the move and notice a poster for the Santa Fe Opera Company on the wall. It began to seem as if every time she turned on her television, someone was talking about Santa Fe, and friends kept mentioning it too.

Mary told me that after several weeks of this sort of thing, she was pretty well convinced that Santa Fe was the answer she'd been seeking, but she was still afraid to trust that she was reading the signs correctly. After all, she had never been to Santa Fe, or even to New Mexico for that matter. She wasn't about to relocate there without definite knowledge that this was really divine guidance. Driving home one evening from the hospital where she'd been working as a counselor, she really laid it on the line.

"I know you're trying to get through to me," Mary told her guide, "but I can be pretty dense, and I'm afraid of making a big mistake. I'm going to need you to make the answer *really* obvious." As an afterthought she added, "And don't forget that I'm a little nearsighted. If you're planning to show me the name of the place in written form, you're going to have to write *big!*"

Just then clanging bells and flashing lights forced her to halt at a railroad crossing. A locomotive with a string of five freight cars in tow slowly huffed past the line of motorists Mary headed. Emblazoned in huge letters on the side of each car was the legend *Santa Fe*.

"All right already!" Mary laughed. "That's big enough for even *me* to see! Santa Fe it is!" She paid the city a brief visit and liked what she saw well enough to move there. Twelve years later she is still delighted with her decision.

Guidelines for Actualizing a Soulmate Relationship

1. Instead of letting habit dictate all of your decisions, allow your guide to make certain unimportant choices for you each day. "Where should I have lunch?" "Which route should I drive to work?" "Should I stop off to pick up groceries or go straight

home?" and so on. If there doesn't appear to be any harm in doing what you feel guided to do, try it out and see what happens.

2. Don't give up on guidance. You'll receive your inner teacher's messages the minute your determination to do so outweighs your fear.

3. Be alert to meaningful coincidences that may contain valuable messages from your guide.

20

Have You Found a Soulmate?

Heaven has come because it found
a home in your relationship on earth.
—A Course in Miracles

As I'm sure you can see by now, it isn't simply a matter of *finding* a soulmate, but of working out a satisfying relationship with him or her once you've gotten together. And this is likely to be challenging no matter how perfect you are for each other. If there is any illusion more destructive to your happiness than the idea that you'll infallibly recognize your true love at first sight, it is the idea that the relationship will be a stroll in the park once you do. Even a soulmate union can be wracked with strife until love entirely supplants fear.

But if soulmates fret and feud just like anybody else, how can you tell if you've found one—and, if you have, whether it is appropriate to proceed to a deeper commitment? Unfortunately, there is no simple formula that will allow you to distinguish relationship problems that can be resolved through forgiveness and deeper involvement, from those that indicate an alliance is fundamentally untenable. That's why guidance is so important!

Because our guides know what others are thinking, and are aware of factors operating behind the scenes, they are in a much better position than we are to select a course of action likely to lead to the best possible outcome. Helene's guide, for example, understood that Gideon loved her, even though he effectively concealed his feelings from her. Once you open the lines of communication with your invisible mentor, you'll no longer have to *guess* what your best move is. Until then, here are some practical suggestions that may increase your chances of making good relationship decisions.

Take It Slow!

There's usually no rush about deciding whether or not you want to spend your life with someone. To be sure, soulmates who are tuned in to their guidance sometimes receive inner confirmation of their possibilities together soon after they meet, but even they are usually well advised to take the time to check things out. Never do anything just because someone else tells you to—even if you believe that someone to be speaking on behalf of God!

Also, just because someone is right for you at the present moment doesn't mean that this is the person with whom you are destined to spend your life. Many relationships exist to teach certain lessons. Once both people have gotten what they came for, it may be time to move on.

Making a Commitment

Opportunities for long-term commitments are the exception rather than the rule. If the whole issue of a "permanent" commitment frightens you, it may also help to bear in mind that it isn't ordinarily the result of a single momentous choice, but rather the culmination of numerous small choices that have already turned out well for the most part. Each step in courtship represents a decision to take the risk of moving to a slightly more vulnerable and committed posture in order to see how it feels being there. Even making a date is a small commitment, since it obligates you to spend a few hours in another's company. Confiding personal information you wouldn't tell a stranger represents a further investment in the relationship. Introducing a new romantic interest to your family marks yet another transition, and so on.

Thus, while the process of selecting a mate often calls up imagery of the taking-the-plunge and jumping-off-the-dock variety, the transition from single person to committed one is actually a lot more like inching into the water from the beach. We move in up to our ankles and halt there for a while, deciding whether to call the unfamiliar sensation of cold water on our feet *pleasure* or *pain*. If we become comfortable where we are, we probably decide to venture in up to our knees, and then a little farther. But we are prepared to retreat back onto the shore at any moment if the situation becomes too frightening or uncomfortable.

Similarly, gradual immersion in a relationship allows you to feel out hidden obstacles and dangerous emotional currents in time to avoid them. Despite an infatuated ego's glib assurances that it's perfectly safe to dive right in, you really can't tell from the beach what lies beneath that inviting surface. The fact is, you can't hope to know in advance how taking the next step in any relationship will turn out. That's because committing at the next appropriate level—or failing to do so—inevitably changes everything.

Let's say, for example, that Jane agrees to date her current boyfriend, Mitch, exclusively. He may conclude that now that he has won Jane's heart, he doesn't need to court her any further. Indeed, he may lose interest altogether and start romancing her best friend!

On the other hand, Mitch may be so pleased and relieved to have been honored with this mark of Jane's affection that he becomes much more attentive. Now he lets down his defenses for the first time, revealing depths of sensitivity, loyalty, and tenderness she only dimly suspected him of possessing.

You won't know how a more committed relationship with anyone is going to turn out until you commit. This being the case, even soulmates must negotiate their relationships one step at a time. Perhaps you planned to be together from before your births, but that doesn't mean both of you still want what looked good to you then, or that you are prepared to do what you'd have to do to make the relationship work.

But Not Too Slow . . .

The fact that relationships always change as our emotional investment in them changes strikes some people as a good reason to freeze the process once minimally acceptable levels of intimacy and commitment have been attained. Unfortunately, a love affair that isn't growing is dying. Every time you retreat from the timely and appropriate escalation a healthy, growing relationship demands, it erodes your partner's faith in you and reduces your chances for happiness together.

In my work as a psychotherapist, I've seen many promising affairs founder on the inability of one partner to make the necessary emotional investment. Sometimes both adopt a wait-and-see attitude, each expecting the other to shoulder all of the emotional risks. But the old maxim "Nothing ventured—nothing gained" definitely applies to love. The only way to find out whether someone is worthy of your trust is to take the risk of trusting him or her—first in small things, and gradually in greater ones.

Now this doesn't mean throwing caution to the winds. But it does mean matching, and perhaps even venturing beyond, whatever level of vulnerability and commitment your partner is presently offering, so that you can see how it feels to be on increasingly intimate terms with this person. Unhappy endings become a self-fulfilling prophecy whenever you let your ego convince you to remain detached, waiting for a sense of certainty that will never come unless you *do* become more involved. Hesitate too long about investing in a relationship and you may be left with no relationship to invest in. That's what happened to Faye and Tony.

Faye and Tony

This couple met in business school and began sharing an apartment soon after. They had been living together for six years when they came to me for therapy. In the beginning, they had been very happy. So happy in fact, that by the second year, Faye had realized that she wanted Tony for her husband.

But Tony had cold feet. His parents' marriage had turned out badly, and he considered matrimony a bourgeois institution in any case. Besides, marriage would inevitably change things, wouldn't it? Why take a chance when everything was going so well for them? What difference was a piece of paper going to make? They knew how they felt about each other. That was all that mattered!

Tony's oft-expressed contempt for the institution of marriage made Faye feel embarrassed about wanting to wed, and prevented her from raising the subject very often. But that didn't make it go away. She attended her friends' weddings and couldn't help wishing that Tony cared enough about her to make a similar commitment.

At first, Faye responded to this implied criticism by trying harder to be everything Tony could possibly want in a woman. But the years passed, and nothing changed, except that Tony's eye was more likely to wander. Now whenever he looked at other women, Faye felt vulnerable. He hadn't found her worthy of being his wife. How long would it be before he met someone he would value more?

Faye was embarrassed every time friends and family would ask when she and Tony were going to tie the knot. She felt increasingly uncomfortable in her position as the live-in lover of a man who evidently didn't respect and admire her enough to want her for his wife. It was difficult for Faye to imagine their future together. Sooner or later, she felt, she would be left, and everyone would think what a shame it was that she had wasted the best years of her life on a man who didn't really love her.

Eventually, Faye's attention began to wander too. When other guys looked at her with genuine admiration, she could recall what it had once been like to feel attractive, valued, loved. Although Tony and Faye came to me saying they wanted couple's counseling, I soon discovered that she had already decided she wanted out of the relationship.

"After that first year," Faye told me, "every time Tony side-stepped a deeper commitment it was like an arrow to my heart. I'm tired of feeling like there's something wrong with me. Just because he doesn't appreciate me, that doesn't mean someone else won't. Somewhere out there, there's a man who is going to be just nuts about me. And if there isn't, then I'd rather be alone. I'm not going to go on devoting myself to someone who thinks I'm second rate!"

Tony was bewildered by the charge that he didn't love Faye. Hadn't he told her repeatedly over the years that he did?

Faye agreed that, yes, he had. But his unwillingness to claim her as his bride had spoken louder than his words. How much could he really love her, she demanded, if he felt a need to keep his options open this way?

Terrified of losing her, Tony was now more than willing to marry Faye! She had only to name the date, he assured her, and he would show up for the ceremony with rings in his pocket and a carnation in his buttonhole. But as far as Faye was concerned, it was much too late for that. Every time Tony had declined to proceed to a deeper level of commitment, she had sadly withdrawn a little more of her emotional investment from their relationship. After five years of steady erosion, there was nothing left. Faye felt only contempt for the belated proposal Tony had issued in response to her decision to terminate the relationship. She moved out shortly thereafter, leaving him brokenhearted.

Permanent Commitment
Follows a Period of Engagement

Now it's true that not every union of soulmates can, or should, include a trip to the altar. There are same-sex lovers who may not have the option of legally marrying each other. There are couples who, for a variety of practical, religious, and financial reasons, find it impossible or inadvisable to contract a legal marriage.

However, the fact that not every couple is destined for matrimony doesn't alter the fact that mutual commitment is an essential feature of a fulfilling love relationship. People can't relax while they feel that the man or woman with whom they want to spend their life is uncertain about them. During courtship this painful suspense must be tolerated, and our hopes for the future usually allow us to bear it with some degree of fortitude. But when a lover's uncertainty goes on too long, it will be read as rejection, and rejection quickly generates a whole new set of tensions that were not present in the relationship to begin with.

If you ever hope to establish a truly satisfying bond, you and your partner must keep moving in the direction of permanent commitment. But this movement appropriately occurs in stages, and it's important to realize that the ultimate stage of commitment (which for many people will be represented by marriage), is preceded by a penultimate one where both partners publicly declare their *intention* to commit permanently. This would be what marriage-bound couples would regard as a period of formal engagement. In the case of gay and lesbian couples, it might entail the announcement to their close associates of their intention to take part in some sort of commitment ceremony.

Engagement affords an opportunity for two people to find out what it *feels* like to be established partners who are planning a future together and are treated as a couple by their social circle. Like every other escalation in commitment, engagement changes the relationship. On the one hand, it affords a liberating sense of security and mutual acceptance. But it can also bring negative feelings into sharp focus. Conflicts that could be glossed over in the course of casual dating take on much greater significance when a permanent commitment is contemplated. Sometimes it is only by seeing how it feels to be engaged that one knows whether one truly wants to marry. That's how it was with my client Petra.

Petra and Russell

Petra had been seeing Russell for three years, and he felt it was high time they moved forward into marriage. But Petra couldn't decide whether she wanted Russ for her husband. She cared for him a great deal, but there were a lot of ways in which he did not seem like her ideal man. She sometimes wondered if she was staying with him only because it was comfortable and she was afraid of being alone.

"I know I shouldn't expect to love every little thing about the guy I marry—nobody's perfect. But I just don't know whether I love Russ *enough*. Am I settling for him because he's a nice guy with a good job who loves me? Would it be a terrible mistake to marry him, or a terrible mistake *not* to?"

Afraid to commit to Russell and equally afraid of losing him, Petra was finding it impossible to get in touch with either guidance, or the feelings of her soul. She kept putting Russ off, insisting that she just wasn't ready to make a decision. But she knew that to continue to do so wouldn't be fair to him. If she wasn't going to marry this man, she ought to release him to find someone else. But what if she let him go and then never found anyone else half as good?

Because Petra felt so much pressure to settle the question one way or the other, I finally suggested that she go ahead and get engaged to Russell so that she could see how a more committed relationship with him felt. If planning to marry her boyfriend left her feeling bad rather than good, I explained, she could always break off the engagement. Petra took my advice and called me two days later to tell me how things had worked out.

"I accepted Russell's ring Wednesday night when I got home from our session," she told me. "We broke open some champagne to celebrate and began calling all our friends and relatives to announce the engagement. But by Thursday morning, I knew I couldn't go through with it. Planning to marry Russ left me with the most awful feeling. It was like a grey fog had settled over me. I couldn't imagine ever having another happy day in my life!

"So less than twenty-four hours after I'd told Russell I'd marry him, I told him I wouldn't. It was pretty awful, as you can imagine, especially since we'd already announced the engagement to so many people. But, Carolyn, I feel so relieved! And I know that as painful as this process has been, it's a lot better for Russell than it would have been if I'd spent another year wavering back and forth. Now he can find someone who'll be really right for him, and so can I.

"I'm actually glad that I did it this way. If I'd just gone with my doubts in the first place and broken up with him, I know I would have spent months or years—maybe even a lifetime—wondering if I'd made a dreadful mistake. But once we were actually planning to marry, it was just so obvious that being Russell's wife wasn't what I wanted. Now I know that even if I never find anyone else, I made the right decision in not marrying him. I'll be able to move on without looking back."

When in Doubt, Proceed (Slowly)

Even in a soulmate relationship, there are likely to be doubts and misgivings every time an increased commitment is called for. But let me suggest that you risk erring on the side of love rather than fear, and go just as far as you possibly can in your relationship with every partner the universe sends into your life. When I say, "go as far as you possibly can," please understand that I mean, "as far *along your personal path* as you possibly can." When remaining with a lover would mean diverging from your path, or giving up the idea of making further progress toward your objectives, it's time to leave. While love involves giving, it never requires self-sacrifice.

However, even if progress is temporarily interrupted, you'd be well advised to try your best to get things moving again before throwing in the towel. See if you can persuade your beloved to continue on just a little farther so that you can both see what's around the next bend. If you refuse to give up until you've tried everything you reasonably can to make things work, you won't be troubled by regrets later.

Nothing Is Forever

Another thing that may help to reduce your fear of commitment to manageable proportions is to remind yourself that you can escape from even a "permanent" commitment if you feel you must. All that until-death-do-us-part talk scares off a lot of people, at the same time it encourages others to rest on their laurels. We all want our relationships to last a lifetime, but even the best of intentions don't ensure success.

Perhaps you've been thinking that a soulmate relationship would be different. If this is truly a match made in heaven, shouldn't it last forever, and shouldn't both parties experience an inner certainty that it will? Sadly, no. Not all meant-to-be relationships are meant to last a lifetime. The absolute certainty some newlyweds feel that they will be together always can be a delusion of the ego rather than a conviction of the soul.

While matrimony is a serious commitment, I believe it is one from which spouses can honorably be released. All we can vouch for on our wedding day is the present state of our feelings, our determination to do everything we possibly can to make the relationship a success, and our confidence that our partner will do the same. Realistically, none of us know what the future holds, or how we'll feel ten or twenty years from now. Why, decades in the past many of us were probably quite sure we were going to grow up to be astronauts, subsisting on a steady diet of ice cream and jelly beans!

It might be best to think of the decision to make a "permanent" commitment in the same way you'd think of a decision to accept an attractive employment contract that would require you to relocate to another part of the country. Given all the trouble and expense that would be in store for you if the job didn't work out, you'd be foolish to sign on unless you had every expectation of making a success of the venture. But you'd also be aware of the *possibility* that it might not work out, and prepared to reluctantly start over elsewhere if it didn't.

Cohabiting

If you want to find out how it will feel to share your life with someone on a day-to-day basis, it might be sensible to move in with your intended before deciding on a permanent commitment. This sort of free home trial reduces the number of unknowns, and thus, the risk of making a costly mistake.

Of course, many religions forbid cohabitation along with premarital sex. Some relationship counselors damn the practice, too, on the grounds that couples who live together out of wedlock have a higher rate of divorce than those who don't. What I think these counselors ignore is the fact that a sizable proportion of the couples who choose not to live together before matrimony probably do so because they are religious fundamentalists. Some of these people may be staying together for a lifetime, not because their marriages are unusually rewarding, but only because their faith forbids divorce.

To my mind, the risks posed by sexual intimacy before marriage are not as great as those of incompatibility afterwards. To the argument "Nobody buys the cow if he can get the milk for free," I say that if "milk" is the only reason your partner is marrying you, the relationship is doomed in any case!

How to Tell a Soulmate from an Ego Pick

Since even the truest of loves is seldom as idyllic as the producers of Disney animated features would have us believe, I don't think it's sensible to hold out for perfect mutual understanding. Indeed, given the way infatuation can create a temporary illusion of mutuality, the sense that your beloved has no faults worth mentioning can actually be a good reason to hold off on making a commitment. Here are some things to consider before you decide to sign someone up as your life's companion.

1) *Are you at ease with this person?* Bear in mind that love is secure and comfortable; it is only infatuation that is intoxicating. Of course, there are times when our ego is temporarily dazzled by the same individual who delights our soul. Just be sure that beneath that euphoric, walking-on-air feeling is a solid foundation of familiarity, liking, respect, understanding, and camaraderie. You can't go too far wrong marrying your best friend.

2) *Are you infatuated with this person to the point where you can't eat or sleep, and you are neglecting your other relationships and responsibilities?* If so, you can't seriously expect to be able to *know* whether this person is really right for you. Don't make life-changing decisions regarding unprotected sex, marriage, pregnancy, relocation, and so on until you get your feet back on the ground.

3) *Do you regard your beloved as someone who is at the same level as yourself (whatever that means to you personally)?* Or is there some feeling that one of you is the "big one," and the other, the "little one" who needs special care and attention? Love rests upon a recognition of equality. Don't confuse admiration, or a desire to nurture someone who seems helpless and dependent, with the kind of love soulmates share. It's much more satisfying to *have* a child than to marry one!

4) *Are your goals compatible?* Can you see practical ways to solve the problems you face as a couple without either one of you sacrificing something vitally important to your happiness, such as the desire to have children, pursue your calling, or live in a particular manner? While the willingness to compromise is essential to marriage, no good can come of a match where one partner must give up cherished dreams in order for the other's to be realized. A true soulmate union supports *both* partners in fulfilling their life's purposes.

5) *If your partnership brings you a lot of exciting benefits such as financial security or enhanced social status, ask yourself if you would be*

just as enthusiastic about the match without these perks. Would it make a big difference to your feelings if this gorgeous woman put on a few pounds? Would this man seem just as perfect if a glitch in the stockmarket wiped out all his holdings? Do you want this person "for better or for worse," or only "for better"?

6) *Do you feel safe being honest with this individual?* The only way to keep major secrets in a marriage is to sacrifice the intimacy that is the whole point of the arrangement. If you are worried about how your partner would react to knowing certain things about you, let me suggest that you confess and find out.

7) *What do the people who care about you think of the match?* While it's never wise to accept advice uncritically, second opinions can be very enlightening. Remember, your loved ones are concerned about your happiness, know you well, and are not blinded by infatuation. In addition, they may have an opportunity to see sides of your beloved that he or she is not showing you. Take Jessica's experience.

Jessica

At a wedding shower for my stepdaughter, Julie, I fell into conversation with her best friend, Jessica. The latter was crowing over the fact that she had known Kevin was going to be *the one* for Julie from the very first time she met him.

"How could you tell so quickly?" I asked, knowing that the bride and groom themselves had made the decision to marry gradually, over a two-year period.

"It was easy!" Jessica exclaimed. "You see, I've met a lot of the guys Julie has dated over the years. They'd generally be really nice to me as long as she was in the room, but the minute she stepped out, they just switched it off and treated me like I didn't exist. I never said anything to Julie about it, but it always kind of bothered me.

"The first time Kevin came over, it was entirely different. He seemed really interested in getting to know *me* because I was a friend of Julie's and he wanted to get to know *her*. And it was clear that he cared what kind of impression he made on me. So I said to myself, 'This one is really serious! He's thinking about marriage, not just trying to get Julie into bed!'"

8) *Do you like his or her friends?* Anthropologist Geri-Ann Galanti makes the point that most folks hang out with people very much like themselves. You may be too infatuated to see your beloved clearly, but there is no such distortion affecting your perception of his or her friends. If you think your sweetheart is all *that* and a side of fries, but consider his or her buddies pond scum, you can pretty much count on a nasty surprise when your brain chemistry returns to normal.

9) *Does your intended idolize you?* Egos idealize and even idolize those they claim to love, only to angrily devalue them a short time later when their unrealistic expectations are disappointed. A lover who recognizes your faults but is willing to try to live with them, is a much better bet than one who thinks you walk on water.

10) *Does your intended take a realistic degree of responsibility for the things that went wrong in past relationships?* If this person tends to blame everything on others, it won't be long before you become the target of his or her projections.

11) *What does your guide say about the match?* I think you can see that in the absence of guidance, neither I, nor quite a number of the people whose stories we've explored in this book, would have connected with a soulmate. Whatever else you decide to do, consult with your inner teacher!

GUIDELINES FOR ACTUALIZING A SOULMATE RELATIONSHIP

1. Proceed to greater intimacy and commitment slowly, but keep moving.
2. Solicit input from friends, relatives, counselors, and your guide, but don't let anyone else make your decision for you.

21

Don't Stop Until You Achieve the Relationship You Want!

The function of the soul is to indicate its desire, not to impose it.
The function of the mind is to choose from its alternatives.
The function of the body is to act out that choice.
When body, mind, and soul create together,
in harmony and in unity, God is made flesh.

—*Conversations with God,* Book 1

If you've done everything I've suggested in this book, it's entirely possible that you've already found a soulmate and are proceeding to explore an unconditionally loving relationship. In that case, *congratulations!* However, it's also possible that, despite the conviction that you've done all you can, no soulmate has yet appeared. What might this mean?

Are You Really Ready for Love?

Until you find the love you want, it's always worth considering the possibility that there is something further you must do to prepare for it. Each time you strip away an obstacle to love, you'll feel relieved and liberated—and usually notice some immediate improvement in your romantic affairs. But the fact that you've made progress toward your goal doesn't mean that your work is complete.

What the universe gives you in response to the prayer of your heart for a soulmate is *a conceptual map of a pathway you can follow* to the relationship of your dreams, and a guide to help you find the way. But it's up to you whether you will walk that path to its end, overcoming all obstacles that may arise along the way, so that you can collect your prize. All too many of us mentally glance at the pathway that appears, and then—because the going looks too difficult, or because the path doesn't seem to be leading in the "right" direction—simply give up and revert to our ego's strategies for finding love. Then we wonder why we never get the kind of relationship we wanted!

Think, for example, of Rick during his "dipped-in-shit" phase. The farther he went in the direction of honesty and vulnerability, the more the women he met treated him with disdain. It would have been very easy for a man in his position to conclude that honesty was the last thing women wanted, and go back to the phony act that had always made him a popular favorite. Had he done so, Rick might have gotten all the "action" a man could desire, but his soulmate would have had to look elsewhere for the honest, vulnerable, self-aware man she hoped to marry.

Setting the Stage for True Love

If you have a sincere desire to experience an unconditionally loving relationship, you can be sure that it proceeds from the will you share with God, and that your guide will do everything in her or his power to help you achieve your goal. If there is something further you need to do before finding your soulmate, your inner teacher will tell you exactly what it is. However, while each individual's path will be unique, there are some generalizations we can draw from the experiences of the couples we've discussed. There appear to be certain realizations people often achieve prior to, or in connection with, the discovery of true love, and I'll list some of them below.

However, before I do, I want to make it clear that the entrance requirements for soulmate relationships have more to do with *aspiring* to a realistic, self-reliant, unconditionally loving perspective, than with the complete mastery of it. Don't let your ego use the following list of soulmate characteristics to convince you that you won't be ready for true love until you've achieved great heights of spiritual enlightenment. That's just the same old self-improvement trap in a new disguise! What matters most is that you are actively *trying* to achieve a more enlightened perspective and are honest with yourself about the degree to which you haven't yet succeeded.

Characteristics of
Soulmate-Ready Individuals

1) *Prospective soulmates don't focus on superficial attributes, but on the way being with another person feels.* Meant-to-be lovers are not so dazzled by wealth, looks, success, or a polished social manner, that they discount the inner qualities essential to successful partnership such as kindness, generosity, loyalty, courage and humor. Being with someone really "nice" takes precedence over basking in the reflected glory of a "trophy" wife or husband.

2) *Prospective soulmates very much want an ideal life partner, but they realize they don't need one.* They are not coming from a sense of inner emptiness, and there is nothing essential to their welfare that they feel someone else must do for them, that they couldn't do for themselves if they had to. They are inner-directed and self-reliant, and this allows them to enter relationships with few demands and expectations, and to relinquish partners gracefully if things don't work out. They regard their lovers as treasured helpmates rather than romantic saviors, and look within for the power and the wisdom necessary to solve their problems and create fulfilling lives.

3) *Prospective soulmates would rather be alone than in bad relationships.* If no genuinely compatible partner is available, soulmates are capable of enjoying solitude, and deriving considerable satisfaction from their vocations, avocations, and close friendships. They make the most of the present, while remaining open to a bright future that includes a committed love relationship.

4) *Prospective soulmates are aware of having a purpose in living.* They seek partners who share their purpose, and who are in agreement with them as to the broad outlines of the kind of lives they want to live.

5) *Prospective soulmates realize that they make mistakes* and consequently have no right to expect perfection or unquestioning obedience from others. They are quick to negotiate and quick to forgive.

6) *Prospective soulmates are realistic about themselves, and what they have to offer.* Depending upon the nature of their previous illusions, this new realism may look like greater humility or increased self-esteem. People who once thought their money, looks, or sophistication ought to guarantee them romantic happiness come to see that these things count for little with individuals who relate from the level of their souls. Those who've long felt inadequate for lack of such attractions make the happy discovery that "kind hearts" truly are "more than coronets."

7) *Prospective soulmates are realistic about others.* They aren't tempted to depend upon undependable people, or expect honesty from those who clearly do not yet understand its importance. Being aware of their own egos, they know an ego-possessed person when they see one.

8) *Prospective soulmates expect the best, without being naive.* They know that there is good in everyone, and they actively look for it, although they also realize that we all have egos and are capable of behaving very badly indeed.

9) *Prospective soulmates recognize that they don't know everything,* and that much of what they think they know, is probably wrong. Thus, they approach their relationships with what has been called

the "beginner's mind," accepting that they have much to learn. When a partner violates their expectations, they are as ready to question those expectations as the other's failure to meet them. Soulmates listen and discuss, in an effort to understand their partner's perspective and communicate their own.

10) *Prospective soulmates bow to the authority of some sort of higher power, even if it is simply a moral or ethical code.* They hold themselves to high standards of behavior, and have too much self-respect to rationalize dishonest, selfish, unloving conduct. They have a stronger commitment to doing the right thing, than to getting their own way.

11) *Prospective soulmates are optimistic about life in general and their romantic futures in particular.* They trust the universe, believe in the goodness of other people, and understand that everyone deserves unconditional love—including them.

12) *Prospective soulmates pay attention to guidance (intuition).* They make a conscious effort to see the world through the eyes of love, looking past their ego's projections in order to apprehend what is really going on. They trust that they will be shown what to do when they sincerely seek the truth.

Your Readiness Isn't the Only Consideration

While you may have further obstacles to love that must be cleared before you'll be ready to create a genuinely loving relationship, it's also possible that you truly are soulmate-ready, but that the time is not yet right for you to connect with your meant-to-be love. The problem is that *your* readiness—and even that of your soulmate—are not the only variables in this particular equation. There may be a number of people who have to come into correct alignment before the relationship you want will actually manifest.

When you set your sights on a particular possible future, you pose the universe a task a little like lining up the colors on the sides of a Rubik's Cube. As with this three-dimensional puzzle, the movement of every square affects the relative positions of many others. Since the universe is not in the business of favoring the interests of one person over those of others, the timing of your relationship must be right for everyone concerned. Sometimes it takes a while to maneuver all of the players into positions where no one has to lose in order for you and your soulmate to gain.

The man who is meant for you may recognize a responsibility to remain with his present wife until she completes her education, or until their children are older. The woman of your dreams may not yet have learned enough about forgiveness to be the kind of partner you need, or may be too busy handling a medical emergency for an aging parent to have time for you right now.

We've seen a number of cases where a shift in the consciousness of one would-be soulmate resulted in an immediate encounter with his or her meant-to-be love. However, these are probably instances where everyone else involved was already in perfect alignment. As with any rendezvous, it isn't uncommon for one lover to arrive at the meeting place a little before the other. The fact that you may have to wait a while for your soulmate doesn't mean the universe has forgotten about you. You can count on your guide to arrange an introduction to someone perfect just as soon as all systems are *go*. Consider Marcia's experience with Jim.

Marcia and Jim

A twice-divorced Florida psychologist in her midforties, Marcia was eager to find a soulmate, although it had been a very long time since she'd met anyone she considered remotely interesting. Then one day she flew off to Michigan to present a workshop on intuition. As soon as Marcia arrived at the conference site, the woman working the registration desk told her that the yoga instructor had been looking for her. A little while later, she pointed

Jim out as the man she'd mentioned. As Marcia turned to look at him, she felt certain that she'd finally found her soulmate!

Jim was bronzed and fit, and Marcia thought him extraordinarily handsome. It was classic love-at-first-sight as far as she was concerned, and this breathtaking man seemed oddly taken with her as well. Both later reported an exquisite sensation of being swept up into another reality. Although they are both Caucasians, Marcia had a strong impression of the Native American warrior she intuitively felt Jim had been when he'd been her son in a past life. Jim, for his part, gazed at this petite woman and flashed back to a past life when she had been a tall, male African, and he, the man's adoring wife.

Marcia's heart soared as she gazed into Jim's eyes. Then she reflexively glanced down at his left hand to check his marital status, and it crashed back to earth with a thump! He was wearing a wedding ring.

Bitterly disappointed, the psychologist put her emotions firmly in check. She had no intention of flirting with a married man. Nevertheless, there was an instant rapport between her and Jim, and the two spent much of that evening getting acquainted. Interestingly, a member of the conference staff who saw them talking together later recalled remarking to her niece, "Do you see that couple? They're going to get married!"

When it grew late, Jim and Marcia made plans to meet and go jogging early the next morning. All perfectly platonic, of course. Yet being together felt so very natural and right that Marcia had to keep yanking herself back to reality. "He's married!" she told herself. "Hands off!"

Marcia's friend Carol was also presenting a workshop at the conference, and when they ran into each other the next day, Marcia confided her strange fascination with the yoga instructor. Carol, who is adept at handwriting analysis, suggested that they try to find out more about him.

When Marcia introduced Jim to her friend, Carol asked to look at the notebook he was carrying. Glancing over his handwriting, she remarked that he seemed to be going through a very emotional time. Jim was quick to confirm that this was so. He explained that, shortly before his departure for the conference, his wife of twenty-five years had informed him that she had decided to get a divorce. He confessed that he was experiencing a great deal of inner turmoil over the breakup.

As Marcia heard this, she felt as if the clouds had rolled away, bathing her in bright sunlight. Despite the evidence of the ring he still wore, Jim was free to explore a relationship with her. Later that afternoon she asked him why he was still wearing a ring if the marriage was over. He responded by removing his wedding band and putting it away in his duffel bag. Oddly enough, when he went to look for it later, it seemed to have disappeared into thin air. He never saw the ring again, but it was soon replaced by another. Jim and Marcia wed three months later. At this writing, they have been happily married for seventeen years.

It seems likely that the decision by Jim's wife to divorce him was the final piece of the puzzle that had to fall into place before these two soulmates could unite. Perhaps the decision to terminate the marriage was hers to make, and everyone else could do no more than wait respectfully while she made up her mind. It's certainly true that once she released Jim, he and Marcia came together with astonishing speed, meeting only a few hours after he learned that he was being put back into circulation. A lot of people field a lover on the rebound, but after all her years of waiting, it seems as if Marcia was poised to grab Jim before he'd even had time to bounce!

How Should You Proceed?

If the soulmate for whom you've been longing is not appearing, it could be because you haven't yet overcome enough of your own obstacles to love, or because she, or he, or someone else altogether, needs to do something further. How do you know whether to settle down and wait patiently, or initiate some additional changes? By consulting your inner guidance, of course!

If there are things you must do in order to clear the way for the love you want, your companion spirit will tell you what they are, as my guide directed me through the healing of my relationship with Brent. If all you have to do is wait patiently, he or she will comfort and encourage you during the interim, as Helene's guide did her. The important thing is to *ask*.

Your Quest for Love

Despite my skeptical attitude toward "fairy-tale romance," I do believe that archetypal stories can be a source of great wisdom—just as long as we don't leave them to our ego to interpret. Like the protagonists of legends, myths, and fairy tales, many of us do seem to undergo a long series of tests, trials, and initiations before we succeed in winning the hand of the "royal" partner with whom we'll be able to live "happily ever after"—or at least as contentedly as people who haven't fully transcended their egos ever do.

Of course, the dragons you and I encounter on our path to soulmate love aren't the literal, fire-breathing variety—just the fearsome illusions conjured up by our ego in its efforts to make us turn back. Nor do we have to resist sirens trying to lure us to our destruction—merely the temptation to waste our time with "enchanting" lovers who don't offer the kind of relationships we really want. And, of course, our true love isn't going to arrive disguised as a loathsome frog or a terrifying beast—although he or she may well manifest in the guise of someone who is "nice," but "not at all our type"!

But despite the dearth of giants, monsters, and evil sorcerers to be found on the contemporary singles scene, the fact remains: "The path of true love ne'er did run smooth." The obstacles that confront us in our search for a soulmate will be formidable, for all that they are nothing more than ego-generated illusions. How are you to find your way to a love that was meant to be, despite every snare and distraction your ego can conjure up to defeat you? Why not try the solution that works for people in fairy tales?

The heroes and heroines of archetypal love stories typically succeed against all odds because, instead of plowing straight ahead along the path that *appears* to lead to success, they pause and go out of their way to befriend distressed and apparently insignificant creatures their rivals have chosen to ignore. These humble companions invariably turn out to be powerful allies who possess magical powers and secret knowledge essential to the success of the protagonist's quest, and they repay their benefactor's kindness by showing him or her how to pass safely through all of the dangers and distractions that will defeat all others.

The real-life counterparts of these magical companions are, of course, our guides. Their respectful, unobtrusive manners make them seem humble and insignificant when compared with our arrogant and bombastic ego. Yet we ignore them at our peril, since they have resources and information vital to our quest for love. Could it be that the previous generations that handed on these fairy tales were unwittingly passing along the coded message that true love is ever the prize of those who heed inner guidance?

Whether you know it or not, you've waited all your life for the magical companion who is destined to show you the way past every obstacle to love. You need wait no longer. He or she is right there beside you, poised to set your feet on the path that will lead to your heart's desire. Your very own heaven-sent teacher of love is with you now, just waiting for your invitation to speak.

For They have come to gather in Their Own.
—A Course in Miracles

Author's Postscript

A number of the stories in this book were brought to my attention by readers of my previous one, *Creating Miracles: Understanding the Experience of Divine Intervention*. I'd like to invite you, too, to write me about the miracles you've experienced and would like to share with others. If you've got a personal story of love, healing, or inspiration that illustrates the activity of a higher power in your life, I'd love to hear it. Please write to me at the address below:

> Carolyn G. Miller, Ph.D.
> P. O Box 641401
> Los Angeles, CA 90064

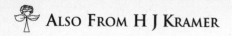 # Also From H J Kramer

DIET FOR A NEW AMERICA
by John Robbins
In this new edition of the classic that awakened the conscience of a nation, John Robbins brilliantly documents that our food choices can provide us with ways to enjoy life to the fullest, while making it possible that life itself might continue.

BLOWING ZEN
Finding an Authentic Life
by Ray Brooks
Disillusioned Londoner Ray Brooks journeys to Japan, where, through a series of serendipitous and often humorous events, he stumbles upon and begins to study the Zen flute. An inspiring read sure to satisfy; we challenge you to put it down!

THE BLUE DOLPHIN
by Robert Barnes
Boji, an exceptional bottlenose dolphin, is alive only because his pregnant mother was rescued from tuna netting by scuba divers. As he grows, many heart-stopping and poignant adventures follow as Boji finds his life purpose.

NO ORDINARY MOMENTS:
A Peaceful Warrior's Approach to Daily Life
by Dan Millman
Best-selling author Dan Millman presents a unique approach to life that turns intentions into action, challenges into strength, and experiences into wisdom.

RECLAIMING OUR HEALTH:
Exploding the Medical Myth and Embracing the Source of True Healing
by John Robbins
In his rousing and inspiring style, John Robbins, author of *Diet for a New America*, turns his attention to the national debate on health care.

Available at your local bookstore, or by calling (800) 972-6657, ext. 52. For a free book catalog, please send your name and address to: H J Kramer c/o New World Library, 14 Pamaron Way, Novato, CA 94949, or fax request to 415-884-2199.

☀ CHILDREN'S BOOKS FROM
H J KRAMER / STARSEED PRESS

SECRET OF THE PEACEFUL WARRIOR
by Dan Millman
illustrated by T. Taylor Bruce
The heartwarming tale of one boy's journey to courage and
friendship. Recipient of the Benjamin Franklin Award.

QUEST FOR THE CRYSTAL CASTLE
by Dan Millman
illustrated by T. Taylor Bruce
The inspiring story of a child's search for confidence, kindness, and the
power to overcome life's obstacles.

WHERE DOES GOD LIVE?
by Holly Bea
illustrated by Kim Howard
Beautifully illustrated by best-selling artist Kim Howard,
Where Does God Live? is a fun way to introduce children to
the concept of a loving deity.

MY SPIRITUAL ALPHABET BOOK
by Holly Bea
illustrated by Kim Howard
Four youngsters lead the way in a lively, colorful romp through the
letters of the alphabet. Lighthearted rhyming verse and joyful illustra-
tions combine to teach children the alphabet and introduce them to
the world of spirit.

THE LOVABLES IN THE KINGDOM OF SELF-ESTEEM
by Diane Loomans
illustrated by Kim Howard
A delightful frolic through the animal kingdom that introduces children to the qualities of a positive self-image. Also available in easy-to-
read board book format for younger readers.

If you are unable to find these books in your favorite bookstore, please call
800-972-6657, ext. 52, send an e-mail request to escort@nwlib.com, or
visit www.nwlib.com. For a free book catalog, please send your name and
address to H J Kramer, c/o New World Library, 14 Pamaron Way, Novato,
CA 94949, or fax request to 415-884-2199.